Adobe®
Photoshop® CS4

ILLUSTRATED

Adobe®
Photoshop® CS4

ILLUSTRATED

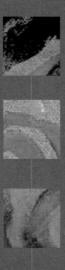

Chris Botello

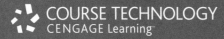

COURSE TECHNOLOGY
CENGAGE Learning

Australia • Brazil • Japan • Korea • Mexico • Singapore • Spain • United Kingdom • United States

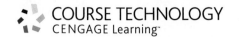
COURSE TECHNOLOGY
CENGAGE Learning™

Adobe® Photoshop® CS4—Illustrated
Chris Botello

Executive Editor: Marjorie Hunt

Senior Product Manager: Christina Kling Garrett

Associate Acquisitions Editor: Brandi Shailer

Associate Product Manager: Michelle Camisa

Editorial Assistant: Kim Klasner

Director of Marketing: Cheryl Costantini

Marketing Manager: Ryan DeGrote

Marketing Coordinator: Kristen Panciocco

Developmental Editor: Ann Fisher

Content Project Manager: Heather Furrow

Art Director: Jill Ort

Print Buyer: Fola Orekoya

Text Designer: Joseph Lee, Black Fish Design

Copyeditor: Troy Lilly

Proofreader: Harold Johnson

Indexer: Elizabeth Cunningham

QA Reviewers: John Freitas, Jeff Schwartz,
   Danielle Shaw, Ashlee Welz Smith, Susan Whalen

Cover Artist: Mark Hunt

Compositor: GEX Publishing Services

For product information and technology assistance, contact us at
Cengage Learning Customer & Sales Support, 1-800-354-9706
For permission to use material from this text or product, submit all requests online at **www.cengage.com/permissions**
Further permissions questions can be emailed to
permissionrequest@cengage.com

ISBN-13: 978-1-4239-9940-9

ISBN-10: 1-4239-9940-1

Course Technology
20 Channel Center Street
Boston, MA 02210
USA

Cengage Learning is a leading provider of customized learning solutions with office locations around the globe, including Singapore, the United Kingdom, Australia, Mexico, Brazil, and Japan. Locate your local office at:
international.cengage.com/region

Cengage Learning products are represented in Canada by Nelson Education, Ltd.

To learn more about Course Technology, visit **www.cengage.com/coursetechnology**

To learn more about Cengage Learning, visit **www.cengage.com**

Purchase any of our products at your local college store or at our preferred online store **www.ichapters.com**

Adobe product screen shot(s) reprinted with permission from Adobe Systems Incorporated

Printed in Canada
1 2 3 4 5 6 7 13 12 11 10 09

About This Book

Welcome to *Adobe® Photoshop® CS4—Illustrated*! Since the first book in the Illustrated Series was published in 1994, millions of students have used various Illustrated texts to master software skills and learn computer concepts. We are proud to bring you this new Illustrated book on Adobe Photoshop CS4, the world's best-selling digital imaging software.

Adobe Photoshop CS4—Illustrated utilizes the unique design of the Illustrated book series to provide a straightforward, topic-based, step-by-step tour of Photoshop, focusing on all the important features and concepts. Readers will gain a broad perspective of the full scope of Photoshop, building on basic concepts to investigate more advanced topics and techniques. Los Angeles-based author Chris Botello is a professional designer who works on movie posters and theatrical campaigns for the entertainment industry; Chris brings that experience to this book, focusing on essential and exciting Photoshop design skills within the context of a real-world graphics environment.

The unique design of this book, which presents each skill on two facing pages, makes it easy for novices to absorb and understand new skills, and also makes it easy for more experienced computer users to progress through the lessons quickly, with minimal reading required. We hope you enjoy exploring the features of Photoshop CS4 as you work through this book!

Author Acknowledgments

For Ann Fisher.

Chris Botello

Preface

Welcome to *Adobe® Photoshop® CS4—Illustrated*. The unique page design of the book makes it a great learning tool for both new and experienced users. Each skill is presented on two facing pages so that you don't have to turn the page to find a screen shot or finish a paragraph. See the illustration on the right to learn more about the pedagogical and design elements of a typical lesson.

This book is an ideal learning tool for a wide range of learners—the "rookies" will find the clean design easy to follow and focused with only essential information presented, and the "hot shots" will appreciate being able to move quickly through the lessons to find the information they need without reading a lot of text. The design also makes this a great reference after the course is over!

Coverage

Eight units offer thorough coverage of essential skills for working with Adobe Photoshop from both the design and production perspective, including creating and managing layer masks, creating color effects and improving images with adjustment layers, working with text and combining text and imagery, and using filters and layer styles to create eye-popping special effects.

Written by Chris Botello, a professional designer who works on movie posters and theatrical campaigns for the entertainment industry, Photoshop CS4 Illustrated offers a real-world perspective with exercises designed to develop the practical skills and techniques necessary to work effectively in a professional graphic arts environment.

Each two-page spread focuses on a single skill.

Concise text introduces the basic principles in the lesson and integrates a real-world case study.

UNIT A
Photoshop CS4

Using the Zoom Tool and the Hand Tool

When you work with Photoshop files, you will often be viewing them from different perspectives. You use the Zoom tool to enlarge and reduce the image on your screen. When the image is enlarged so much that you can't see the whole image, you can use the Hand tool to scroll around to see other areas of the image. Because the Zoom and Hand tools are used so often when working in Photoshop, it's important to learn keyboard commands to access the tools. See Table A-1 for a list of useful quick keys. Laura asks that you open a file and demonstrate your abilities with using the Zoom and Hand tools and viewing the workspace.

STEPS

1. Click File on the Application bar, click Open, navigate to the location where you store your Data Files, click PS A-1.psd, then click Open
   Figure A-3 shows the opened file in the default workspace. The name of the file appears in the document tab, which is located in the upper-left corner of the file.

   QUICK TIP
   Double-clicking the Hand tool on the Tools panel also fits the image on the screen.

2. Click View on the Application bar, then click Fit on Screen
   This command reduces the image as much as necessary to fit the entire image on your screen. The current magnification is listed in the document tab and also in the lower-left corner of the document window.

   QUICK TIP
   Note that the magnification level on the document tab changes to show the percentage at which you are viewing the image each time you click.

3. Click the Zoom tool on the Tools panel, position it over the bird's eye, then click the eye eight times to zoom in on the image
   Each time you click, the image is enlarged.

4. Click the Hand tool on the Tools panel, then click and drag the Hand tool pointer over the image to see other areas of the bird

5. Double-click, click the Zoom tool, position it directly above the eye, drag the Zoom tool pointer to create a marquee as shown in Figure A-4, then release the mouse button
   As you drag, a dotted rectangle, called a marquee, appears around the area that you drag over. When you release the Zoom tool pointer, the area inside the marquee is enlarged in the window. Dragging the Zoom tool on the image is called a marquee zoom.

6. Press and hold [Alt] (Win) or [option] (Mac), then click ten times anywhere on the image
   The image's magnification level is reduced. When you press and hold [Alt] (Win) or [option] (Mac), the Zoom tool shows a minus sign, indicating that it will reduce the view, rather than magnify it.

   QUICK TIP
   Press and hold [Ctrl] (Win) or [⌘] (Mac) then press [-] repeatedly to reduce the view. See Table A-1 for other useful quick keys.

7. Press and hold [Ctrl] (Win) or [⌘] (Mac) then press [+] repeatedly to enlarge the view

8. Click View on the Application bar, then click Fit on Screen

---

Accessing the Zoom and Hand tools

When you're working with various tools, you will find yourself having to continuously switch to the Zoom tool to enlarge your view or to the Hand tool to change your view. This will slow you down. Take time to practice and master the quick keys that allow you to temporarily switch to the Zoom or Hand tool while remaining in the current tool. Press and hold [Spacebar] to access the Hand tool.

Press and hold [Spacebar] [Ctrl] (Win) or [Spacebar] [⌘] (Mac) to access the Zoom Plus tool. Press and hold [Spacebar] [Alt] (Win) or [Spacebar] [option] (Mac) to access the Zoom Minus tool. When you release the quick keys, the current tool is active again. These three keyboard commands will help you enormously in speeding up your workflow.

Photoshop CS4 6   Getting Started with Photoshop CS4

Clues to Use boxes provide concise information that either expands on the major lesson skill or describe an independent task that in some way relates to the major lesson skill.

Every lesson features large, full-color representations of what the screen should look like as students complete the numbered steps.

FIGURE A-3: Viewing the document in the Essentials workspace

Document tab

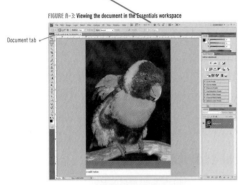

FIGURE A-4: Creating a marquee with the Zoom tool

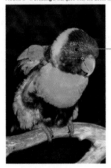

This area will be magnified

TABLE A-1: Useful quick keys

command	Windows	Macintosh
Open	[Ctrl][O]	⌘ [O]
Fit on Screen	[Ctrl][0] (zero)	⌘ [0] (zero)
Fit on Screen	Double-click Hand tool	Double-click Hand tool
Zoom In	[Ctrl][+]	⌘ [+]
Zoom Out	[Ctrl][-]	⌘ [-]
Access Zoom Plus tool	[Spacebar][Ctrl]	[Spacebar] ⌘
Access Zoom Minus tool	[Spacebar][Alt]	[Spacebar][option]
Access Hand tool	[Spacebar]	[Spacebar]

Getting Started with Photoshop CS4

Tables are quickly accessible summaries of key terms, tool options, or keyboard alternatives connected with the lesson material.

Assignments

The lessons use MegaPixel, a graphic arts design agency, as the case study. The assignments on the light purple pages at the end of each unit increase in difficulty. Additional case studies provide a variety of interesting and relevant exercises for students to practice skills.

Assignments include:

- **Concepts Reviews** consist of multiple choice, matching, and screen identification questions.

- **Skills Reviews** provide additional hands-on, step-by-step reinforcement.

- **Independent Challenges** are case projects requiring critical thinking and application of the unit skills. The Independent Challenges increase in difficulty, with the first one in each unit being the easiest. Independent Challenges 2 and 3 become increasingly open-ended, requiring more independent problem solving.

- **Real Life Independent Challenges** are practical exercises to help students with their everyday lives by focusing on important and useful essential skills, including creating photo montages for scrapbooks and photo albums, retouching and color-correcting family photos, applying layer styles and getting Photoshop Help online.

- **Advanced Challenge Exercises** set within the Independent Challenges provide optional steps for more advanced students.

- **Visual Workshops** are practical, self-graded capstone projects that require independent problem solving.

Other Illustrated Series Titles

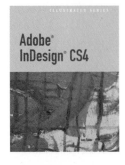

ADOBE® INDESIGN® CS4—ILLUSTRATED
Ann Fisher (1423999398)

Eight units provide essential training on using Adobe InDesign CS4 for designing simple layouts, combining text, graphics, and color, as well as multi-page documents, layered documents, tables, and InDesign libraries.

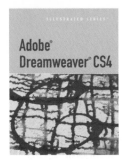

ADOBE® DREAMWEAVER® CS4—ILLUSTRATED
Sherry Bishop (1439035792)

Nine units provide essential training on using Dreamweaver CS4 to create Web sites. Coverage includes creating a Web site, developing Web pages, formatting text, using and managing images, creating links and navigation bars, using CSS to layout pages, and collecting data with forms.

Praise for the Illustrated Dreamweaver book:

"I use the Dreamweaver Illustrated Series textbook by Sherry Bishop. I have used this text for 6 years now. My students love this textbook. They find it easy to follow and the illustrations make the steps easy for the visual learners. I have never had a complaint from a student on the Dreamweaver textbook, they only rave about it. This makes my job so much easier."—Michael Cokkinos, Fashion Institute of Technology, New York, New York

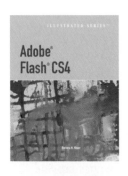

ADOBE® FLASH® CS4—ILLUSTRATED
Barbara Waxer (1439039658)

Eight units provide essential training on using Adobe Flash CS4 including creating graphics and text, using the Timeline, creating animation, creating buttons and using media, adding interactivity, and integrating with other programs.

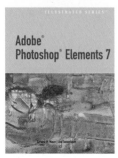

ADOBE® PHOTOSHOP® ELEMENTS 7—ILLUSTRATED
Barbara Waxer/Lisa Tannenbaum (142399941X)

Eight units cover the basics of using Photoshop Elements to work with digital photos including managing and editing photos, adjusting contrast and color, using brushes and retouching tools, creating special effects, and sharing photos.

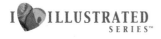

For more information on the Illustrated Series, please click on:
www.cengage.com/ct/illustrated

Instructor Resources

The Instructor Resources CD is Course Technology's way of putting the resources and information needed to teach and learn effectively into your hands. With an integrated array of teaching and learning tools that offer you and your students a broad range of technology-based instructional options, we believe this CD represents the highest quality and most cutting edge resources available to instructors today. Many of these resources are available at *www.cengage.com/coursetechnology*. The resources available with this book are:

• **Instructor's Manual**—Available as an electronic file, the Instructor's Manual includes detailed lecture topics with teaching tips for each unit.

• **Sample Syllabus**—Prepare and customize your course easily using this sample course outline.

• **PowerPoint Presentations**—Each unit has a corresponding PowerPoint presentation that you can use in lecture, distribute to your students, or customize to suit your course.

• **Figure Files**—The figures in the text are provided on the Instructor Resources CD to help you illustrate key topics or concepts. You can create traditional overhead transparencies by printing the figure files. Or you can create electronic slide shows by using the figures in a presentation program such as PowerPoint.

• **Solutions to Exercises**—Solutions to Exercises contains files students are asked to create or modify in the lessons and end-of-unit material. Also provided in this section is a document outlining the solutions for the end-of-unit Concepts Review, Skills Review, and Independent Challenges.

• **Data Files for Students**—To complete the units in this book, your students will need Data Files. You can post the Data Files on a file server for students to copy. The Data Files available on the Instructor Resources CD are also included on a CD located at the front of the textbook.

Instruct students to use the Data Files List included on the CD found at the front of the book and the Instructor Resources CD. This list gives instructions on copying and organizing files.

• **ExamView**—ExamView is a powerful testing software package that allows you to create and administer printed, computer (LAN-based), and Internet exams. ExamView includes hundreds of questions that correspond to the topics covered in this text, enabling students to generate detailed study guides that include page references for further review. The computer-based and Internet testing components allow students to take exams at their computers, and also saves you time by grading each exam automatically.

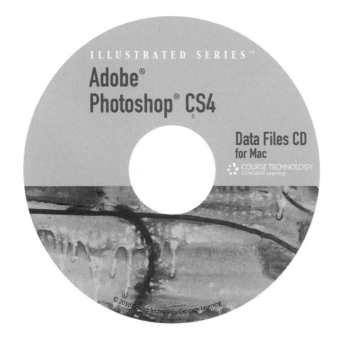

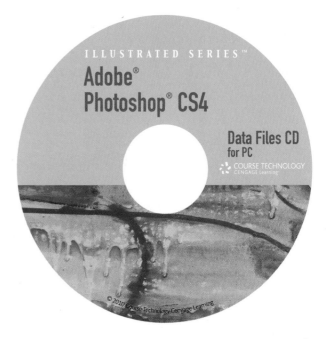

Brief Contents

Contents

PHOTOSHOP CS4   **Unit C: Working with Layers**   **57**

Read This Before You Begin

This book assumes the following:

1. The software has been registered properly. If the product is not registered, students must respond to Registration and dialog boxes each time they start the software.
2. Default tools in the Tools panel might differ, but tool options and other settings do not carry over to the EOU or between units.
3. Students know how to create a folder using a file management utility.
4. After introduction and reinforcement in initial units, the student will be able to respond to the dialog boxes that open when saving a file. Later units do not provide step-by-step guidance.
5. Panels, windows, and dialog boxes have default settings when opened. Exceptions may occur when students open these elements repeatedly in a lesson or in the unit.
6. Students will be instructed in the early units on how to update missing links. Later units do not provide step-by-step guidance.
7. The few exercises that do contain live type were created using commonly available fonts. Nevertheless, it is possible, that students may run into a missing font issue when opening a data file. In that case, students should use an available font that is similar to the size and weight of the type shown in the lesson.

Frequently Asked Questions

What are the Minimum System Requirements (Windows)?

- 2GHz or faster processor with 1GB RAM
- Microsoft Windows XP with Service Pack 2 or 3, or Windows Vista
- 1.5GB of available hard disk space
- Color monitor with 16-bit color video card
- CD-ROM
- Adobe Photoshop CS4

What are Data Files and where are they located?

The Data Files for this text are mostly Photoshop files that you will use to complete the steps in the lessons and end-of-unit material. The Data Files for this text are located on a CD included at the front of this book. Insert the CD into a CD-ROM drive to access the files. Your instructor may have you copy them to a network or removable drive.

What software was used to write and test this book?

This book was written and tested with Adobe Photoshop CS4 using a typical installation of Microsoft Windows Vista Ultimate with Aero turned off.

Do I need to be connected to the Internet to complete the steps and exercises in this book?

The exercises in this text do not require that your computer be connected to the internet. However, you would need to be connected to the internet to access Adobe's online Photoshop Help utility.

What do I do if my screen is different from the figures shown in this book?

This book was written and tested on computers with monitors set at a resolution of 1280 × 1024. If your screen shows more or less information than the figures in the book, your monitor is probably set at a higher or lower resolution. If you don't see something on your screen, you might have to scroll down or up to see the object identified in the figures.

Getting Started with Photoshop CS4

Adobe Photoshop CS4 is the latest version of the revolutionary, best-selling, photo editing software from Adobe Systems Incorporated. Photoshop offers a set of powerful tools and easy-to-use panels that let you perform all kinds of image editing, from simple to complex. In this unit, you will learn essential skills for viewing and navigating a document and investigate the basic building blocks of a Photoshop image. MegaPixel is a graphic arts service bureau and design agency. Laura Jacobs, the owner of MegaPixel, has hired you as a production artist. Your job will involve using Photoshop CS4 to address a variety of image-processing issues to produce high-quality Photoshop files.

OBJECTIVES

Define photo editing software

Start Photoshop and view the workspace

Use the Zoom tool and the Hand tool

Save a document and understand file formats

Understand and change resolution

Change image size

Create a new document

Transform the canvas

Crop an image

Crop an image to a specific size

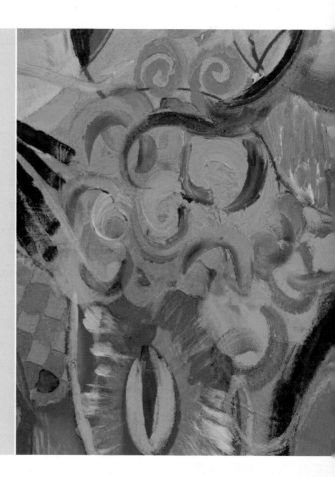

Defining Photo Editing Software

Photoshop CS4 is photo editing software. In a nutshell, Photoshop offers you a variety of tools, menu commands, and panels that allow you to edit and manipulate **digital images**—images that you get from a digital camera, from scanning a photograph or a slide, or that you create from scratch. Photoshop CS4 allows you to edit images in a variety of ways in order to enhance them or to process them for different types of uses, such as for print or for the Web. 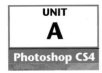 Laura Jacobs invites you to her office for an orientation meeting on your first day at MegaPixel. The conversation turns to Photoshop, and you share with her some of your experiences with the many uses of the application.

DETAILS

The following are just some of the tasks you can use Photoshop CS4 to accomplish:

- **Acquire images from a variety of devices**

  Transfer images from CDs, DVDs, digital cameras, and scanners into Photoshop. Download images from the Web and open them in Photoshop. With some digital cameras, you can use Photoshop to preview images from your camera before you open them in Photoshop.

- **Apply basic processing procedures**

  Crop an image to get rid of unwanted elements or to focus more dramatically on your subject. Rotate an image if it is upside down, on its side, or crooked. Resize an image so that it prints to fit the frame you just bought. All of these are essential and practical procedures that Photoshop can do quickly and efficiently.

- **Improve the color and quality of images**

  Photoshop has many sophisticated color tools that allow you to enhance the appearance of photographs. You can brighten images that are too dark, or darken images that are overexposed. Turn an otherwise plain image into something striking with a quick increase in contrast. Make the color more vivid or remove it entirely to create a dramatic black-and-white image.

- **Fix image flaws**

  Photoshop's retouching tools and production filters offer you many options for fixing flaws in an image such as dust and scratches, graininess, and red eye. You can also retouch photos of your family and friends: Best of all, retouch and restore old family photos and give them as gifts to be treasured. Figure A-1 shows some sample images that have been fixed.

- **Add special effects**

  If you can think of it, you can do it in Photoshop. Turn a brand-new photo into an old-looking photo or take a typical black-and-white photo and make it look hand-tinted. Add grain effects or blur effects to give an ordinary photo a custom look. Distort photos: Give your friends big heads on little bodies, or make your sister appear to be a giant 40-foot woman crashing her way down Fifth Avenue. Photoshop makes your imagination a reality.

- **Batch-process image files**

  Photoshop is also a production workhorse. For example, Photoshop can automatically process a batch of files for one type of output, such as professional printing, and then reprocess the same batch of files by reducing their physical size and file size, and changing their format for use on the Web. And that's literally with the click of one button.

- **Output to various devices**

  You can use Photoshop to create graphics for slide shows, video presentations, and electronic billboards. Photoshop is used every day to create elements for on-screen animation projects. Photoshop comes complete with software you can use to save images for your cell phone or your iPod. Photoshop can even process a bunch of different sized images into one contact sheet.

FIGURE A-1: Various effects with an old photo

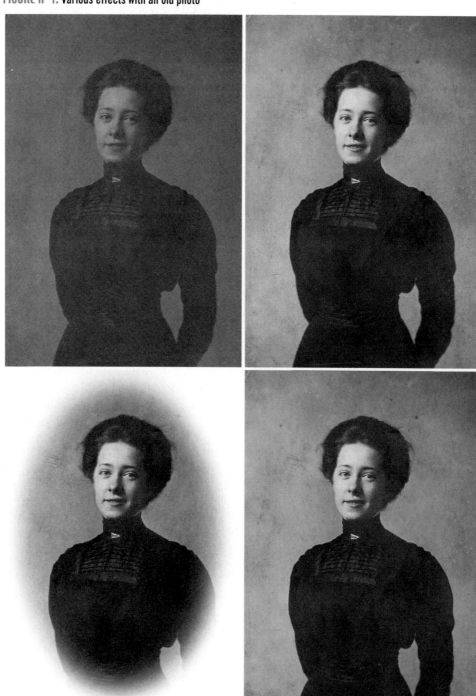

Understanding graphics programs

The term **graphics program** can refer to a wide range of software applications. Generally speaking, though, graphics programs fall into three basic categories: bitmap, vector, and animation. You can think of **bitmap graphics** (also called **raster graphics**) as very sophisticated mosaics. Instead of using colored tiles, bitmap graphics use **pixels**—colored squares that are so small that your eye perceives only the whole image, not the pixels themselves. All digital photographs are bitmap graphics, and all Photoshop files are bitmap graphics. **Vector graphics** are often created on a computer, not

through scanning or downloading. Many times, vector-based programs are called **draw programs**, because vector graphics are created by drawing lines, creating objects, and filling them with color. Adobe Illustrator CS4 is a vector-based program. Finally, **animation programs**, such as Adobe Flash, use timeline structures to create sequences of graphics—both bitmap and vector graphics—then create the illusion of motion and animation by presenting that sequence of images so quickly that your eye perceives movement.

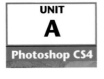

Starting Photoshop and Viewing the Workspace

You start Photoshop by launching the program or by opening a Photoshop file that is already created. Once in Photoshop, before you open or create a new document, the **workspace** becomes available. The workspace consists of the Application bar at the top of the screen, the Tools panel on the left of the screen, and the dock of panels on the right of the screen. The Application bar contains the Application icon, the Photoshop menus, some basic tools like the Zoom tool and the Hand tool, and the workspace switcher, which allows you to choose from a list of custom workspaces. You can rearrange the elements of the work-space to your liking to create and save your own customized workspace. ▰▰▰▰ Laura has shown you your office and new computer. You start Photoshop and familiarize yourself with the workspace.

STEPS

QUICK TIP

The Application bar may appear as two rows, depending on your monitor resolution and if you are using a Macintosh.

1. Click the Start button ⊕ on the taskbar, point to All Programs, click Adobe Design Standard CS4 (or the name of your specific Adobe Creative Suite package) if necessary, then click Adobe Photoshop CS4 (Win) or Open the Finder, double-click Applications, double-click Adobe Photoshop CS4, then double-click Adobe Photoshop CS4 (Mac)

   The Photoshop window opens, as shown in Figure A-2, displaying the Essentials workspace. Essentials is one of many preset workspaces that comes with Photoshop. Different workspaces are designed for different tasks. For example, the Painting workspace opens a number of color panels and the Brushes panel, all of which are very useful when painting.

QUICK TIP

You can click the Collapse to Icons button to view panels as icons.

2. Note the Tools panel on the left, then click the double arrows at the top of the Tools panel repeatedly to toggle between a single and double row of tools

3. In the panels dock on the right, click the tabs of each panel to show Each panel

   These are the panels that are displayed when the Essentials workspace is chosen.

QUICK TIP

Use the Window menu to access all of the panels in Photoshop.

4. Click Window on the Application bar, then click Character

   The Character panel opens. Note that by default it is grouped with the Paragraph panel.

5. Drag the Character panel name tab to the center of the workspace

   The Character panel is separated from the Paragraph panel.

6. Drag the Paragraph panel name tab over the Character panel until you see a light blue frame around the Character panel, then release the mouse button

   The panels are grouped once again.

QUICK TIP

Double-clicking the name tab of an open panel minimizes the panel.

7. Double-click the name tab of any visible panels in the panels dock

FIGURE A-2: The Essentials workspace

Application bar
Tools panel

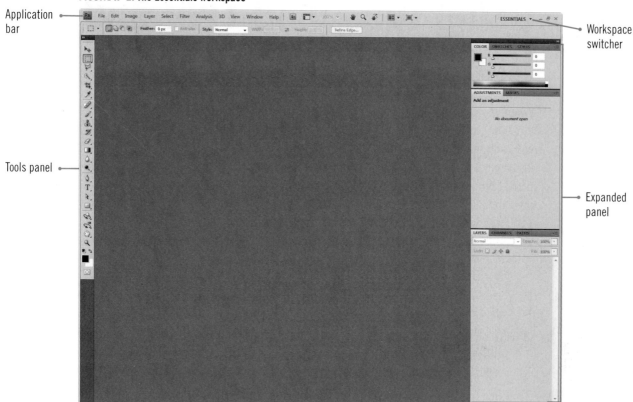

Workspace switcher
Expanded panel

Getting help in Photoshop CS4

Whenever you have a question about what you're doing in Photoshop or want to learn more about a tool or a feature, remember that you always have the Help menu close at hand. Installing Photoshop on your computer automatically gives you access to Adobe's online help site.

To access Photoshop Help, click Help on the Application bar, and then click Photoshop Help. The Photoshop Help and Support Web site opens.

You can access Photoshop help by clicking the Photoshop help (web) link on the right side of the window. This opens the Adobe Photoshop CS4 help Web site, where you have a few choices for finding information.

You can browse through the categories of help topics on the left or enter specific information in the Search text box at the top of the Web page. For example, if you want to learn more about layer styles, type "layer styles" in the Search text box, then press [Enter] (Win) or [return] (Mac).

Managing the workspace

Think of the Photoshop workspace just as you would your own home or apartment: you want to have things how you like them and where you like them. For example, click the double arrows above the Tools panel to display the tools in one or two rows. Your biggest consideration with the workspace is always maximizing the room available to view the image you are working on.

For this reason, managing the panels on the right of the window is important, because open panels can take up a lot of space in the document window. Condensing panels by grouping them with other panels is a smart choice for maximizing working space. Minimizing panels is the best choice for keeping essential panels open but out of the way.

Using the Zoom Tool and the Hand Tool

When you work with Photoshop files, you will often be viewing them from different perspectives. You use the Zoom tool to enlarge and reduce the image on your screen. When the image is enlarged so much that you can't see the whole image, you can use the Hand tool to scroll around to see other areas of the image. Because the Zoom and Hand tools are used so often when working in Photoshop, it's important to learn keyboard commands to access the tools. See Table A-1 for a list of useful quick keys. Laura asks that you open a file and demonstrate your abilities with using the Zoom and Hand tools and viewing the workspace.

STEPS

1. **Click File on the Application bar, click Open, navigate to the location where you store your Data Files, click PS A-1.psd, then click Open**

   Figure A-3 shows the opened file in the default workspace. The name of the file appears in the document tab, which is located in the upper-left corner of the file.

> **QUICK TIP**
> Double-clicking the Hand tool on the Tools panel also fits the image on the screen.

2. **Click View on the Application bar, then click Fit on Screen**

   This command reduces the image as much as necessary to fit the entire image on your screen. The current magnification is listed in the document tab and also in the lower-left corner of the document window.

> **QUICK TIP**
> Note that the magnification level on the document tab changes to show the percentage at which you are viewing the image each time you click.

3. **Click the Zoom tool 🔍 on the Tools panel, position it over the bird's eye, then click the eye eight times to zoom in on the image**

   Each time you click, the image is enlarged.

4. **Click the Hand tool 🖐 on the Tools panel, then click and drag the Hand tool pointer over the image to see other areas of the bird**

5. **Double-click 🖐, click the Zoom tool 🔍, position it directly above the eye, drag the Zoom tool pointer to create a marquee as shown in Figure A-4, then release the mouse button**

   As you drag, a dotted rectangle, called a **marquee**, appears around the area that you drag over. When you release the Zoom tool pointer, the area inside the marquee is enlarged in the window. Dragging the Zoom tool on the image is called a **marquee zoom**.

6. **Press and hold [Alt] (Win) or [option] (Mac), then click ten times anywhere on the image**

   The image's magnification level is reduced. When you press and hold [Alt] (Win) or [option] (Mac), the Zoom tool shows a minus sign, indicating that it will reduce the view, rather than magnify it.

> **QUICK TIP**
> Press and hold [Ctrl] (Win) or ⌘ (Mac) then press [-] repeatedly to reduce the view. See Table A-1 for other useful quick keys.

7. **Press and hold [Ctrl] (Win) or ⌘ (Mac) then press [+] repeatedly to enlarge the view**

8. **Click View on the Application bar, then click Fit on Screen**

Accessing the Zoom and Hand tools

When you're working with various tools, you will find yourself having to continuously switch to the Zoom tool to enlarge your view or to the Hand tool to change your view. This will slow you down. Take time to practice and master the quick keys that allow you to temporarily switch to the Zoom or Hand tool while remaining in the current tool. Press and hold [Spacebar] to access the Hand tool.

Press and hold [Spacebar] [Ctrl] (Win) or [Spacebar] ⌘ (Mac) to access the Zoom Plus tool. Press and hold [Spacebar] [Alt] (Win) or [Spacebar] [option] (Mac) to access the Zoom Minus tool. When you release the quick keys, the current tool is active again. These three keyboard commands will help you enormously in speeding up your workflow.

FIGURE A-3: Viewing the document in the Essentials workspace

Document tab

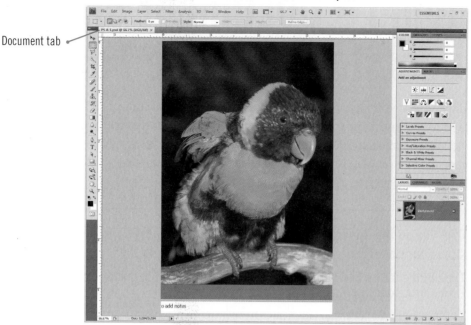

FIGURE A-4: Creating a marquee with the Zoom tool

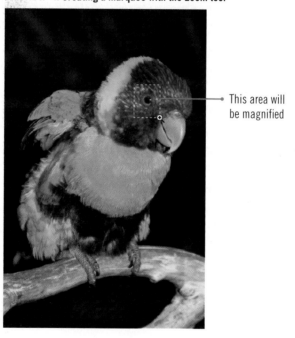

This area will
be magnified

TABLE A-1: Useful quick keys

command	Windows	Macintosh
Open	[Ctrl][O]	⌘ [O]
Fit on Screen	[Ctrl][0] (zero)	⌘ [0] (zero)
Fit on Screen	Double-click Hand tool	Double-click Hand tool
Zoom In	[Ctrl][+]	⌘ [+]
Zoom Out	[Ctrl][-]	⌘ [-]
Access Zoom Plus tool	[Spacebar][Ctrl]	[Spacebar] ⌘
Access Zoom Minus tool	[Spacebar][Alt]	[Spacebar][option]
Access Hand tool	[Spacebar]	[Spacebar]

Saving a Document and Understanding File Formats

File formats are specific types of computer code that you use to save an image for various types of output or use with other applications. Table A-2 shows a list of common file formats you can use with Photoshop. PSD stands for Photoshop Document and is the basic format for saving a Photoshop file. All other Adobe programs can open and/or place a file saved as a PSD. You refresh your knowledge of file formats by saving the bird image as a PSD, a TIFF, and a JPEG.

STEPS

1. **Click** File **on the Application bar, click** Save As, **then navigate to the location where you store your Data Files**

2. **Type** Birdie **in the File name text box, click the** Format list arrow, **click** Photoshop (*.PSD, *PDD), **if necessary, then click** Save

   The filename in the document tab changes to Birdie.psd.

3. **Click** File **on the Application bar, click** Save As, **click the** Format list arrow, **click** TIFF (*.TIF, *.TIFF), **then compare your dialog box to Figure A-5**

4. **Click** Save, **then click** OK **in the TIFF Options dialog box**

   TIFF is an acronym for Tagged Image File Format. TIFF is a standard file format for placing digital images for print in page layout programs, such QuarkXPress or Adobe InDesign.

5. **Click** File **on the Application bar, click** Save As, **click the** Format list arrow, **click** JPEG (*.JPG, *.JPEG, *.JPE), **then click** Save

   The JPEG Options dialog box opens, as shown in Figure A-6. The JPEG file format is a lossy compression format often used for images on the World Wide Web and for images that will be e-mailed. Because it compresses a file by removing data, the JPEG format always reduces an image's file size.

6. **Drag the** Quality slider **to 6**

   The file size is reduced to approximately 176.6K.

7. **Click** OK, **click** File **on the Application bar, then click** Close

TABLE A-2: Standard file formats for Photoshop files

file format	extension	use
Bitmap	.bmp	Bitmap images, popular with Windows and OS/2 operating systems
CompuServe GIF	.gif	Web graphics
Photoshop EPS	.eps	Photoshop graphics with live type or shape layers
Photoshop PSD	.psd	Basic format for all Photoshop documents
JPEG	.jpg, .jpeg	Web graphics, images to be e-mailed
PICT	.pct, .pict	Graphics to be used in presentation programs, such as PowerPoint
Portable Network Graphics	.png	High-quality Web graphics
Tagged Image Format	.tif, .tiff	Graphics to be used for print in page layout programs

FIGURE A-5: Save As dialog box

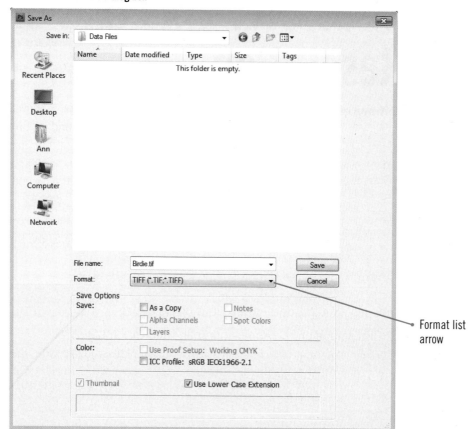

Format list arrow

FIGURE A-6: JPEG Options dialog box

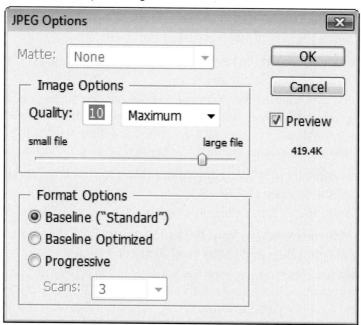

Choosing the right file format

In the real world, working with file formats is seldom challenging. You'll save the vast majority of your files as basic PSD documents, and if you're saving a file at work or for a client, usually you'll be told which format to choose. The key to choosing a file format is understanding what the file will be used for. For Web graphics, you'll usually choose JPEG. For PowerPoint graphics, you'll usually choose PICT. With a little bit of experience, you will soon be comfortable knowing which file format to choose for a given output or to interface with another software package.

Understanding and Changing Resolution

A **bitmap graphic** is a graphic composed of pixels. The word **pixel** is derived from the words picture and element—pixel. You can think of a bitmap image as being a grid of pixels—thousands of them. All Photoshop files are bitmap graphics. **Resolution** is a measurement: the number of pixels per inch (ppi). For example, if you had a 1" × 1" Photoshop file with a resolution of 100 pixels per inch, that file would contain a total of 10,000 pixels (100 pixels wide × 100 pixels high = 10,000 pixels). In this lesson, you'll investigate how to change resolution in the Image Size dialog box. 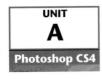 Jon Schenk, a lead art director at MegaPixel, asks that you to use the Image Size dialog box to change the resolution of an image. He asks that you change the resolution twice, first with no loss of image data, and then with a loss of data so that you can show him the difference.

STEPS

1. **Open PS A-2.psd, then save it as** Birdie Resize

2. **Click** Image **on the Application bar, then click** Image Size

   The Image Size dialog box open. The Document Size section specifies that this is a 2" × 2" file with a resolution of 300 ppi—thus making this a high-resolution file. The Pixel Dimensions section specifies that the full width of the file is 600 pixels (300 ppi × 2"), and the height is 600 pixels. Therefore, this image is composed of exactly 360,000 pixels.

3. **Click the** Resample Image check box **to remove the check mark**

   Resampling means changing the total pixel count of an image. The Resample Image check box is perhaps the most important option in this dialog box. When the Resample Image check box is not checked, the total number of pixels in the image must remain the same. In other words, no matter how you resize the image or change the resolution, no pixels can be added or discarded.

4. **Double-click 300 in the Resolution text box, type 100, press [Tab], then note the changes in the Width and Height values**

   As shown in Figure A-7, the width and height of the file changes to 6". Because the pixel dimension of 600 pixels cannot change, when the number of pixels per inch is reduced to 100, the file must enlarge to six inches wide and six inches tall to accommodate all the pixels. In other words, no pixels were added or discarded with the change in resolution—they were simply redistributed.

5. **Press and hold [Alt] (Win) or [option] (Mac) so that the Cancel button changes to the Reset button, then click** Reset

   The Image Size dialog box returns to its original values and the Resample Image check box is checked.

6. **Change the resolution from 300 to 150, press [Tab], then note the changes to the Width and Height values and to the Pixel Dimension values**

   As shown in Figure A-8, the resolution is reduced to 150 ppi, but the width and height remain at 2". The Pixel Dimensions show that the full width of the file is 300 pixels (150 ppi × 2") and the full height is 300 pixels. This means that, if you click OK, the total number of pixels will be 90,000. 75% of the original 360,000 pixels will be discarded because of the reduction in resolution from 300 to 150 ppi.

7. **Click** OK

   Though the image doesn't look much different on your screen, 75% of its original data has been discarded.

8. **Save your work, then close Birdie Resize.psd**

FIGURE A-7: Decreasing resolution without resampling

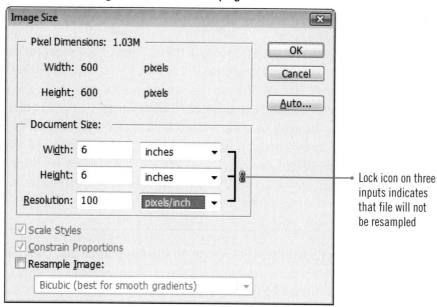

Lock icon on three inputs indicates that file will not be resampled

FIGURE A-8: Decreasing resolution with resampling

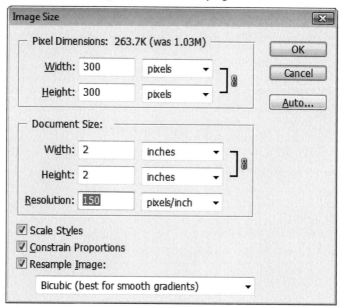

Understanding the difference between image size and file size

Don't confuse the terms image size and file size. Image size refers to the physical dimensions of the image—its width and height. So if you say an image is 8" × 10", you are referring to its image size. File size refers to how big the file is in computer memory—how much storage space it takes up on your computer. If an image is 42 MB (megabytes), that is its file size. Remember that every pixel in an image increases the file size of the image. Therefore, resolution and image size both affect file size. The greater the resolution—the more pixels per inch—the greater the file size. The greater the image size—the more inches of pixels—the greater the file size. If you were printing an 8" × 10" color poster at 300 ppi, your file size would be somewhere close to 27 MB, and the image would be composed of more than 7 million pixels!

Changing Image Size

Image size refers to the dimensions of the Photoshop file. Image size is not dependent on resolution; in other words, you could create two 3" × 5" inch files, one with a resolution of 72 ppi and the other with a resolution of 300 ppi. The two files would have the same image size but different resolutions. Image size is, however, related to resolution: All bitmap images, regardless of their physical dimensions, have a resolution. Changing the width and/or height of an image will affect its resolution. Also, because resolution is so closely associated with image quality, resizing an image may have a negative effect on its appearance. Jon Schenk gives you a 2" × 2" file from his client. The file needs to be printed at 4" × 4" for a glossy magazine then saved at the same size for the client's Web site. You create two files at two different resolutions for the two different types of use.

STEPS

1. **Open PS A-3.psd, click Image on the Application bar, then click Image Size**

   The Document Size section specifies that this is a 2" × 2" file with a resolution of 300 ppi. The Pixel Dimensions section specifies that the full width of the file is 600 pixels (300 ppi × 2") and the height is 600 pixels. Thus, this image is composed of exactly 360,000 pixels.

2. **Verify that the Resample Image check box is checked**

   This file is 2" × 2" and you need it to be 4" × 4".

3. **Change the Width value to 4, then compare your dialog box to Figure A-9**

   In order to be used in a color magazine at the specified size of 4" x 4", the file must be 300 ppi at that size. Photoshop is able to scale the image to that size and resolution. However, note the pixel dimensions. Because we've doubled the size of the original, the new size now must contain 1,440,000 pixels to maintain a resolution of 300 pixels per inch. The supplied image was scanned at 360,000 total pixels. Where did all the new pixels come from? If you click OK, Photoshop will create them from the existing pixels in a process called **interpolation**.

4. **Click OK, then evaluate the enlargement in terms of image quality**

> **QUICK TIP**
> When inspecting an image for quality, you should view it at 100% or larger.

5. **Double-click the Zoom tool 🔍 to view the image at 100%**

   The image still looks good overall. However, for quality print reproduction, this image is unacceptable because it is composed of 75% interpolated data.

6. **Save the file with the name Birdie Magazine as a Photoshop document, close it, then open PS A-3.psd again**

7. **Open the Image Size dialog box, and note that the Resample Image check box is checked**

   Now you will resize the file to be used on the client's Web site.

8. **Change the Width and Height values to 4, change the Resolution to 72, then compare your dialog box to Figure A-10**

   As shown in the Pixel Dimensions section, the file size will be reduced from 1.03MB to 243K. Even though the image was doubled in size, the reduction in resolution from 300 ppi to 72 ppi resulted in the need for fewer than 25% of the number of original pixels.

> **QUICK TIP**
> Reducing an image's size or resolution does not involve the creation of interpolated data and is therefore acceptable in terms of image quality.

9. **Click OK, then evaluate the enlargement in terms of image quality**

   Viewed at 100%, the image looks great on screen, which is our goal, given that it will be used on a Web site. Even though Photoshop has discarded more than 75% of the original number of pixels, the reduced image contains only original data and no interpolated data.

10. **Save the file as a .jpg file with a quality setting of 10 named Birdie Web Graphic, then close it**

FIGURE A-9: Increasing image size and resampling pixels

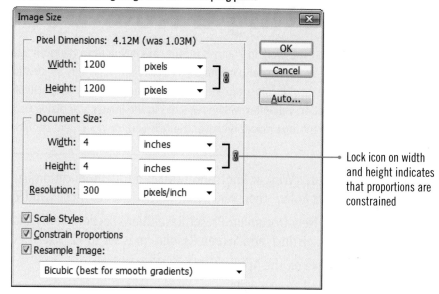

Lock icon on width and height indicates that proportions are constrained

FIGURE A-10: Decreasing image size and resampling pixels

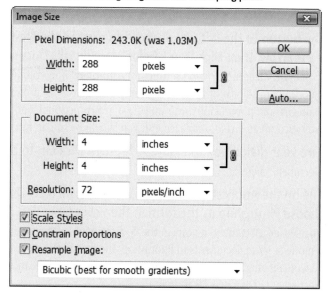

What is "high-res" exactly?

Pixels must be small to create the representation of a photographic image—you want to see the image, not the pixels. 300 ppi is considered a high resolution for any file that will be professionally printed. For a home desktop printer, 150 ppi is generally enough resolution for a good-looking print. For the Web and other "on-screen" graphics, the standard resolution is low—just 72 ppi.

"High-res" is a shortened form of "high-resolution", and generally speaking, a "high-res" file pertains only to the world of printing. So when you think of "high-res," think of images—color or black-and-white—printing at a high quality, like in a magazine or a poster. This type of reproduction requires the industry standard of 300 pixels per inch.

Creating a New Document

Usually when you work in Photoshop, the image you're working on was either scanned or captured by a digital camera. You can also create pixels from scratch, simply by creating a new document in Photoshop. You create a new document in the New dialog box, where you specify its width, height, and its resolution. The information you enter will be reflected in the Image Size dialog box. ■■■■■ Jon asks you to create a new document for a magazine cover. He tells you the document should be 8.125" × 11.25".

1. Click **Edit** (Win) or **Photoshop** (Mac) on the Application bar, point to **Preferences**, click **Units & Rulers**, then verify that Rulers is set to inches and Type is set to points

2. In the New Document Preset Resolutions section, verify that Print Resolution is set to 300 pixels/inch and Screen Resolution is set to 72 pixels/inch, then click **OK**

3. Click **File** on the Application bar, then click **New**
   The New dialog box opens.

4. Click the **list arrow** next to Width, then click **inches**

5. Change the Width value to **8.125**, change the Height value to **11.25**, then change the resolution to **300**
   You set the resolution to 300 ppi because you know in advance that the file will be used on a magazine cover.

6. Click the **Color Mode list arrow**, then click **CMYK Color**
   CMYK Color is the mode used for images that will be printed using traditional methods.

7. Click the button to the left of Advanced to expand the New dialog box, click the **Color Profile list arrow**, then click **Don't Color Manage this Document**
   A **color profile** is a group of preset settings for controlling how color will appear on your monitor and in a printed document. Color profiles are used almost exclusively in professional settings such as ad agencies, service bureaus, and photography houses. For your own personal work, or if you're working for a business that hasn't incorporated color management, you should be sure to turn off the default color profiles.

8. Compare your dialog box to Figure A-11, then click **OK** to close the New dialog box
   A new document opens.

9. Click **File** on the Application bar, click **Save As**, type **New Document** in the File name text box, choose Photoshop as the format, then click **Save**
   The filename New Document appears in the document tab in the upper-left corner of the document. When you open one or more documents in Photoshop, the documents are docked together as tabbed documents. Click a document tab to activate that document in the window or rearrange the order of documents by dragging a document tab to a new location in the dock.

Using the Revert command

The Revert command on the File menu is one of your best methods for undoing lots of moves. When you choose the Revert command, the file is reverted to the same status it was at when you last saved. This can be an enormous help if you've made more changes than you cannot undo with the Undo command. Simply click File on the Application bar, click Revert, and you're back to where you were when you last saved. This is another reason to remember to save often when you work, preferably every ten minutes.

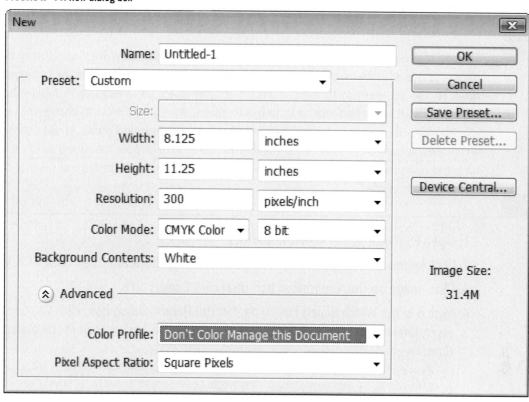

Photoshop CS4

Introducing color models and color modes

A **color model** defines the colors we see and work with in digital images. RGB (red, green, blue), CMYK (cyan, magenta, yellow, black), and HSB (hue, saturation, brightness) are all color models, and each uses a different method for describing color.

In Photoshop, a document's **color mode** is listed on the Image menu. The color mode determines which color model is being used to display and print the image you are working on. In most cases, you will be working in RGB Color for color images and Grayscale for black-and-white images.

RGB Color is the standard color mode for working with color images. Choosing a color mode has an impact on which tools and file formats are available. All of Photoshop's tools and features are

available to files in the RGB Color mode. Many of them are not available to files in the CMYK Color mode. That's one of many reasons why it's best to do all of your color work in RGB, not CMYK.

All files that are printed traditionally must at some point be CMYK files, so therefore it is likely that you will eventually switch to CMYK Color mode. However, most designers do all their color work in RGB Color then save a CMYK Color copy for printing. In other words, they use CMYK Color as part of the saving and output procedure, not part of the Photoshop design work itself. To change the color mode, click Image on the Application bar, point to Mode, then click one of the color modes on the menu.

Transforming the Canvas

The bed of pixels that make up an image is referred to as the **canvas**. When you open an image, usually the image uses all of the pixels available on the canvas. However, the canvas can be enlarged to add more pixels to the file—perhaps to make room for another image to overlap or sit beside the original. In Photoshop, the term **transform** refers to specific operations that you make to change the location of pixels. Transformations include scaling, rotating, skewing, and distorting pixels. In this lesson, you'll learn techniques for transforming the canvas. ▓▓▓▓▓ Jon asks you to increase the canvas size in an existing document to make room to place a second image over the first. You open the file and see that the image will also need to be rotated.

STEPS

1. **Open PS A-4.psd then save it as** Parrots

2. **Click** Image **on the Application bar, point to** Image Rotation, **then click** 90° CW

3. **Click** Image **on the Application bar, then click** Canvas Size

4. **Type** 6 **in the Width dialog box, type** 8 **in the Height dialog box, click the** Canvas extension color list arrow, **click** White, **then note the Anchor icon in the dialog box**

   The Anchor is used to determine where new pixels will be placed relative to the location of the existing canvas. By default, when you open the dialog box, the existing canvas is represented by the square in the middle of the grid. If you were to add pixels, they would be evenly distributed on all sides of the existing canvas.

5. **Click the** lower-left square in the grid

   Clicking the lower-left square of the Anchor indicates that the new pixels will be positioned above and to the right of the existing canvas.

6. **Click** OK, **then compare your canvas to Figure A-12**

   The canvas is enlarged to the new dimensions. White pixels are added above and to the right of the original canvas.

7. **Open PS A-5.psd, click** Image **on the Application bar, point to** Image Rotation, **then click** Flip Canvas Horizontal

8. **Click** Select **on the Application bar, click** All, **click** Edit **on the Application bar, click** Copy, **then close the file without saving changes**

9. **Click** Edit **on the Application bar, then click** Paste

   The image you copied is pasted.

QUICK TIP
For precise moves, use the arrow keys to move the image one pixel at a time. Press and hold [Shift] while pressing the arrow keys to move the image in ten-pixel increments.

▶ 10. **Click the** Move tool ▸⊕, **drag the little parrot image to the position shown in Figure A-13, save your work, then close the Parrots file**

"Res-ing up" when you have no choice

Inevitably, there will come a time when you have no other choice but to increase the resolution or the image size of a file and live with the results. In the working world, this often happens when a client delivers an original file at one size and wants you to use it at a much larger size. In that case, you'll want to be smart about how you increase the size or resolution of the image. Remember that Photoshop is running complex algorithms to create that new data.

Don't make it more complicated by enlarging by odd numbers. For example, if you have a 3" square image that needs to print as a 5.75" square, double the image size to a 6" square. It's much easier for Photoshop to interpolate data with a simple doubling of the existing image size; this will result in a higher quality interpolation and a better result for your enlarged image.

FIGURE A-12: Viewing new pixels added to the canvas

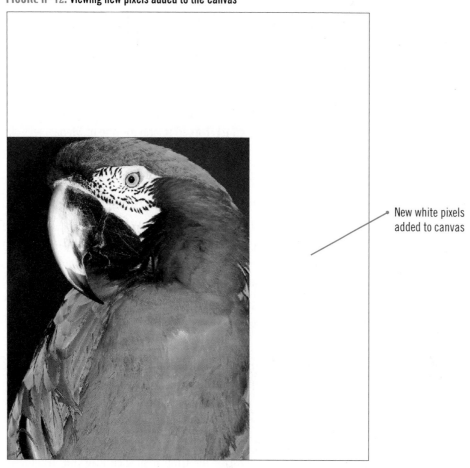

New white pixels
added to canvas

FIGURE A-13: Positioning a second image over the new pixels

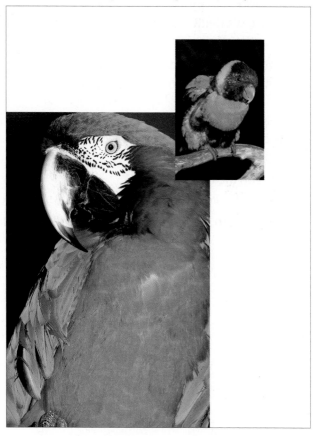

Cropping an Image

Cropping an image is a basic task in which you define an area of an image that you want to keep and then discard the remainder of the image. Photoshop's Crop tool makes it easy to execute a simple crop and also provides you with options for previewing the crop before you execute it. Cropping an image can often be an artistic choice: an interesting crop can turn a basic boring image into something eye-catching and intriguing. ▓▓▓▓ You are asked to crop an image for one of MegaPixel's clients, the United States office of the Estonia Travel and Tourism Board. They will use the cropped image as an e-mail postcard.

STEPS

1. **Open PS A-6.psd, then save it as Estonia House**

2. **Click Window on the Application bar, then click Info**

   The Info panel opens. The Info panel provides lots of different types of information about a Photoshop document, everything from image size and file size to color information for every pixel on the canvas. The Info panel may help you determine the size of an image as you apply the Crop tool.

3. **Click the Info panel list arrow, then click Panel Options**

   The Info Panel Options dialog box lets you choose what type of information you want to view about your document. By default, the Info panel does not display the document size or document dimensions.

   > **QUICK TIP**
   > Viewing document dimensions in the Info panel is faster than relying on the Image Size dialog box.

4. **Click the Document Size and the Document Dimensions check boxes to select them, if they are not already checked, then click OK**

   The Document Size (Doc) refers to the size of the file in megabytes. The document dimensions refer to the physical dimensions of the file. They are listed below the Doc size at the bottom of the Info panel.

   > **QUICK TIP**
   > Double-clicking a tool selects the tool and changes the settings in the Options bar to those that are specific for that tool.

5. **Double-click the Crop tool 🔲 on the Tools panel**

   The Options bar lists options for the Crop tool, such as width, height, and resolution information for the crop.

6. **Verify that the Width, Height, and Resolution text boxes on the Options bar are empty or click Clear to clear them**

   If you do not clear the Options bar, you may end up using the values that were last used with the Crop tool.

7. **Using Figure A-14 as a guide, drag the Crop tool pointer around the house so that only the house remains and the two other buildings are discarded, then release the Crop tool pointer**

   As you drag, a dotted line, called a **crop marquee**, is created. The area inside the crop marquee is what will remain after the crop is executed. You can continue to adjust the marquee by dragging the selection handles of the crop marquee to resize it.

   > **QUICK TIP**
   > You can also press [Enter] (Win) or [return] (Mac) to execute a crop. To remove a crop marquee from the canvas, click the Move tool or the Crop tool, then click Don't Crop or press [Esc].

8. **Double-click inside the crop marquee**

   The image is cropped. All pixels that were outside of the crop marquee are discarded.

9. **Compare your result to Figure A-15, save your work, then close the file**

FIGURE A-14: **Creating a crop marquee**

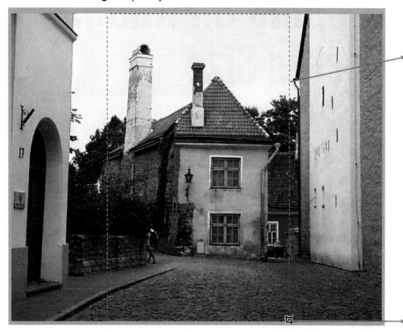

• Crop marquee

• Crop tool

FIGURE A-15: **The cropped image**

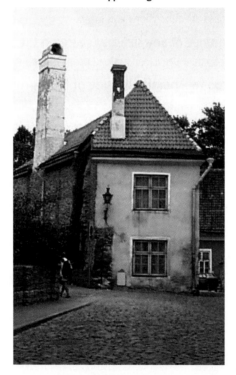

Setting opacity for the Crop tool

Opacity refers to how opaque something is. It is a term you will see used for a number of different Photoshop elements. When using the Crop tool, you can change the shield color and opacity of the area outside the crop using the Shield Color and Opacity settings on the Options bar. Black is the default shield color on the Options bar. For example, if you set the opacity to 100%, everything outside of the crop marquee becomes 100% black. You can click the Color box to open the Color Picker and choose a new shield color. This is a great option for previewing the image as it would look if cropped, especially if you hide the crop marquee. The more you reduce the opacity, the more the pixels outside of the marquee will be visible, which is useful for seeing where your crop lines are falling in the image and what would be discarded if you execute the crop. As a preview before cropping, many designers set the opacity to 50% while they're experimenting and then, when they think they've found a crop that they like, they increase the opacity to 100%. If you prefer to crop without using color or opacity, click the Shield Color check box to remove the check mark.

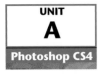

Cropping an Image to a Specific Size

The Crop tool has a number of options attached to it that enable the tool to execute more than just a simple crop. After you create a crop marquee, the Crop tool pointer becomes an arrow pointer when inside the marquee. Using the arrow, you can move the marquee to crop a different area of the image. When the Crop tool pointer is outside of the crop marquee, it becomes a rotate pointer that allows you to rotate the crop marquee. You can also input specific width and height dimensions to create a crop marquee at a specific size. A client of MegaPixel has provided you with an image they would like cropped vertically to 2.25" × 4". You crop the image and then rotate the crop marquee in order to improve the appearance of the image.

STEPS

1. **Open PS A-7.psd, then save it as Hotel Postcard**

2. **Click the Crop tool , type 2.25 in the Width text box on the Options bar, then type 4 in the Height text box**
    When you input specific size values for the width and height of the crop, any size crop you create will result in a file with the physical dimensions you input.

3. **Drag a crop marquee of any size anywhere on the canvas**
    As you drag, the crop marquee is constrained proportionally to the values you input.

4. **Position the Crop tool pointer outside of the marquee**
    The pointer changes to a rotate pointer.

> **QUICK TIP**
> You can hide the marquee if you find it distracting by clicking [Ctrl][H] (Win) or ⌘ [H] (Mac).

5. **Using Figure A-16 as a guide, drag the rotate pointer to rotate the marquee, then size and position it as shown, being sure that the crop marquee remains within the borders of the canvas**
    Note that the bottom of the marquee is parallel to the step that the girl is standing on.

6. **Execute the crop, then compare your result to Figure A-17**

7. **Note in the Info panel that the resulting image size is 2.25" × 4"**

8. **Save the document, then close the file**

9. **Click File (Win) or Photoshop (Mac) on the Application bar, then click Exit (Win) or Quit (Mac)**

Cropping, resolution, and image size

When you select the Crop tool, you can enter a specific width and height to crop an image to. You can also enter a specific resolution using the Resolution text box on the Options bar. It may occur to you that the options for the Crop tool make it function much like the Image Size dialog box. Think about it: In the Image Size dialog box, you modify width, height, resolution, or all three. The same is true for the Crop tool. That being said, it's important that you don't mistakenly resample an image by using the Crop tool. The key to making sure this doesn't happen is to understand that if you input a new height or width value in the Options bar but leave the Resolution text box empty, the resolution cannot change. It's like turning off the Resample Image option in the Image Size dialog box. No matter where you crop or what size crop marquee you create, new pixels cannot be added or deleted, only redistributed. Make no mistake, the Crop tool is not intended to be used as a practical alternative to the Image Size dialog box. However, the Crop tool options are most practical when you have a target size and resolution that you want as a result. For example, it's often the case that you will be given high-res files and asked to crop them to a specific size for a use on a Web site. In that case, you could simply enter the specific width and height, enter a resolution of 72 ppi, and crop the image. Your result would be cropped to that size and resolution in one step.

FIGURE A-16: Rotating the crop marquee

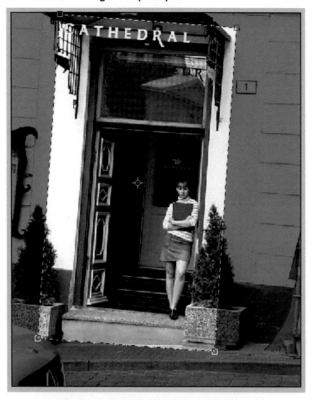

FIGURE A-17: The cropped, rotated, and resized image

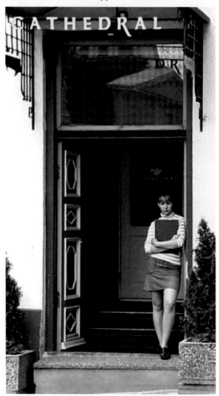

Moving the crop marquee

Sometimes you'll have a crop marquee drawn at a specific size, and you'll want to move it around the canvas to see different crops. Simply position your cursor anywhere over the inside of the marquee, then click and drag to move the marquee. To make very small and precise movements, use the arrow keys.

Practice

▼ CONCEPTS REVIEW

Label each element shown in Figure A-18

FIGURE A-18

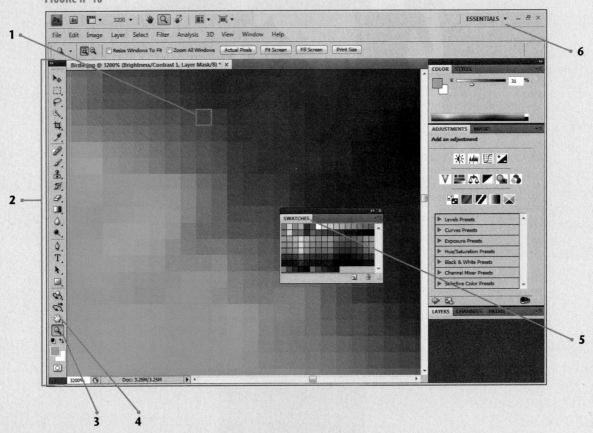

1. Which item points to the Tools panel?
2. Which item points to the workspace switcher?
3. Which item points to the Hand tool?
4. Which item points to the Zoom tool?
5. Which item points to a pixel?
6. Which item points to a panel?

Match each term with the statement that best describes it.

7. **Pixel**
8. **Resolution**
9. **Image Size**
10. **File Size**
11. **Canvas**
12. **Application bar**
13. **JPEG**
14. **Cropping**

a. The bed of pixels in a Photoshop file
b. The physical dimensions of an image
c. Removing unwanted areas of an image
d. File format often used for Web graphics
e. Picture element
f. The amount of memory a file takes up
g. Part of the workspace that contains menu items
h. The number of pixels per inch

Select the best answer from the list of choices.

15. **What is the name of the tool that you use to enlarge and reduce the view of a document?**
    - **a.** Hand
    - **b.** Window
    - **c.** Zoom
    - **d.** Control

16. **Which dialog box do you use to change the resolution of a file?**
    - **a.** Image Size dialog box
    - **b.** Canvas Size dialog box
    - **c.** New dialog box
    - **d.** Both a & b but not c

17. **Which of the following can you not specify in the New dialog box?**
    - **a.** Resolution
    - **b.** Units & Rulers
    - **c.** Width & Height
    - **d.** Color Mode

18. **Which of the following can you use to change the size of an image?**
    - **a.** Canvas Size dialog box
    - **b.** Crop tool
    - **c.** New dialog box
    - **d.** Both a & b but not c

19. **Which of the following occurs every time you enlarge an image?**
    - **a.** New pixels are added based on existing pixels
    - **b.** Increase in file size
    - **c.** Reduction in quality
    - **d.** All of the above

20. **When you enlarge an image and Photoshop creates pixels from existing pixels, what is that process called?**
    - **a.** Interpretation
    - **b.** Intertranslation
    - **c.** Interrelation
    - **d.** Interpolation

▼ SKILLS REVIEW

1. **Define photo editing software.**
    - **a.** List four tasks that you can accomplish with Photoshop CS4.
    - **b.** If you were publishing a monthly magazine, what role would Photoshop play in the production of that magazine?
    - **c.** If you have a box full of family photos, what could you use Photoshop to do with them?
    - **d.** If you have an old photo that is torn and faded, what help would Photoshop be for that situation?

2. **Start Photoshop and view the workspace.**
    - **a.** Click the Start button on the taskbar, point to All Programs, click Adobe Design Standard CS4 (or the name of your specific Adobe Creative Suite package) if necessary, then click Adobe Photoshop CS4 (Win) or open the Finder, double-click Applications, double-click Adobe Photoshop CS4, then double-click Adobe Photoshop (Mac).
    - **b.** Identify the Application bar.
    - **c.** Toggle the Tools panel between being a single and double row of tools.
    - **d.** On the panels dock on the right, click the tabs of each panel to show each panel.
    - **e.** Click Window on the Application bar, point to Workspace, then click Painting.
    - **f.** Click Window on the Application bar, point to Workspace, then click Essentials.
    - **g.** Click Window on the Application bar, then click Character.
    - **h.** Drag the Character panel to the center of the workspace, separating it from the Paragraph panel.
    - **i.** Drag the Paragraph panel back over the Character panel name tab to group the two panels together.
    - **j.** Double-click the name tab of any visible panels in the panels dock to minimize them.

3. **Use the Zoom tool and the Hand tool.**
    - **a.** Click File on the Application bar, click Open, navigate to the location where you store your Data Files, click PS A-8.psd, then click Open.
    - **b.** Click View on the Application bar, then click Fit on Screen.
    - **c.** Click the Zoom tool on the Tools panel, position it over the black steeple in the middle ground, then click five times to zoom in on the image.
    - **d.** Click the Hand tool on the Tools panel, then drag the Hand tool pointer over the image to see other areas of the image.
    - **e.** Double-click the Hand tool.

    f. Click the Zoom tool, then click and drag a marquee around the same steeple.

    g. Press and hold [Alt] (Win) or [option] (Mac), then click four times anywhere on the image.

    h. Press and hold [Ctrl] (Win) or ⌘ (Mac), then press [+] repeatedly to enlarge the view.

    i. Click View on the Application bar, then click Fit on Screen.

4. Save a document and understand file formats.

    a. Click File on the Application bar, click Save As, then navigate to the location where you store your Data Files.

    b. Type **Tallinn** in the File name text box, click the Format list arrow to see all the file formats available, click Photoshop (*.PSD, *PDD) then click Save.

    c. Click File on the Application bar, click Save As, click the Format list arrow, then click TIFF (*.TIF, *.TIFF).

    d. Click Save, accept the defaults in the TIFF Options dialog box, then click Save again.

    e. Click File on the Application bar, click Save As, click the Format list arrow, click JPEG (*.JPG, *.JPEG, *.JPE), then click Save.

    f. Drag the quality slider so that the file size is less 200K but greater than 100K.

    g. Click OK, then close Tallinn.jpg.

5. Understand and change resolution.

    a. Open PS A-9.psd, then save it as **Eagle Resize**.

    b. Click Image on the Application bar, then click Image Size.

    c. Click the Resample Image check box to remove the check mark.

    d. Change the value in the Resolution text box to 100, press [Tab], then note the changes in the Width and Height values.

    e. Press and hold [Alt] (Win) or [option] (Mac) so that the Cancel button changes to the Reset button, then click the Reset button.

    f. Change the resolution from 300 to 150, press [Tab], then note the changes to the Width and Height values and to the Pixel Dimensions.

    g. Click OK.

    h. Click File on the Application bar, then click Revert.

6. Change image size.

    a. Click Image on the Application bar, then click Image Size.

    b. Note that the Resample Image check box is checked by default.

    c. Change the Width value to **8**.

    d. Click OK, then evaluate the enlargement in terms of image quality.

    e. Revert the file, open the Image Size dialog box, and note that the Resample Image check box is checked.

    f. Change the Width value to **8**, then change the resolution to **72**.

    g. Click OK, then evaluate the enlargement in terms of image quality.

    h. Save changes, then close the file.

7. Create a new document.

    a. Click Edit (Win) or Photoshop (Mac) on the Application bar, point to Preferences, then click Units & Rulers.

    b. Verify that Rulers is set to inches and Type is set to points.

    c. In the New Document Preset Resolutions section, verify that Print Resolution is set to 300 ppi and Screen Resolution is set to 72 ppi.

    d. Click OK, click File on the Application bar, then click New.

    e. Click the list arrow next to Width, then click inches.

    f. Change the Width value to **5**, change the Height value to **7**, then change the resolution to **300**.

    g. Click the Color Mode list arrow, then click CMYK Color.

    h. Click the Advanced button to expand the New dialog box, click the Color Profile list arrow, then choose Don't Color Manage this Document.

    i. Click OK.

    j. Save the file as **Skills New**, then close the file.

8. **Transform the canvas.**
   a. Open PS A-10.psd, then save it as **Make Room For Title**.
   b. Click Image on the Application bar, point to Image Rotation, then click Flip Canvas Horizontal.
   c. Click Image on the Application bar, then click Canvas Size.
   d. Type **4** in the Height text box.
   e. Click the lower-center square in the Anchor, then click OK.
   f. Save your work, then close Make Room For Title.psd.

9. **Crop an image.**
   a. Open PS A-11.psd, then save it as **Email Postcard**.
   b. Click Window on the Application bar, then click Info.
   c. Click the Info panel list arrow, then click Panel Options.
   d. In the Status Information section, verify that both the Document Sizes and Document Dimensions check boxes are checked, then click OK.
   e. Double-click the Crop tool on the Tools panel.
   f. Verify that the Width, Height, and Resolution text boxes in the Options bar are empty or click Clear to clear them.
   g. Drag the Crop tool anywhere on the canvas to create a crop marquee and note the width and height values on the Info panel as you drag.
   h. Drag the resizing handles to define an area similar to that shown in Figure A-19.
   i. Click the Crop tool, then click Crop.
   j. Save your work, then close Email Postcard.psd.

FIGURE A-19

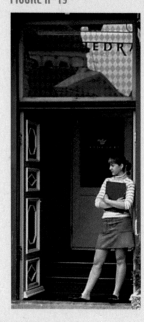

10. **Crop an image to a specific size.**
    a. Open PS A-12.psd, then save it as **San Francisco**.
    b. Click the Crop tool on the Tools panel.
    c. Click the Clear button on the Options bar.
    d. On the Options bar, type **6** in the Width field.
    e. Click and drag a marquee to the full size of the canvas.
    f. Float your cursor outside of the marquee to see the rotate pointer, then rotate the marquee so that the skyline is parallel to the bottom of the marquee.
    g. Drag the resizing handles of the marquee so that all four are on the canvas.
    h. Execute the crop, then compare your result to Figure A-20.
    i. Save changes, then close San Francisco.psd.
    j. Click File on the Application bar, then click Exit (Win) or Quit (Mac).

FIGURE A-20

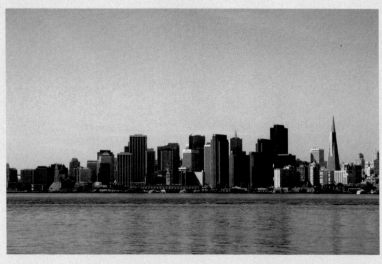

Photoshop CS4

▼ INDEPENDENT CHALLENGE 1

Your first client, the Estonia Travel and Tourism Board, has sent you three files that they want to put on their Web site to promote all the construction, development, and restoration going on in the city. Each image needs to be a 3" square with a file size less than 100 K each.

a. Open PS A-13.psd.

b. Check the Image Size dialog box to verify that the image is larger than 3" × 3" and has a resolution higher than 72 ppi.

c. Click Image on the Application bar, point to Mode, then click RGB Color.

d. Click the Crop tool, then click Clear on the Options bar.

e. Type **3** in the Width and Height text boxes.

f. Type **72** in the Resolution text box.

g. Crop the image in a way that you think is aesthetically pleasing.

h. Open the Image Size dialog box to verify the settings.

i. Open PS A-14.psd.

j. Using the same settings, crop PS A-14.psd in a way that the size and position within the frame of the subject's head and body are consistent with the cropped PS A-13.psd.

k. Open PS A-15.psd, then crop it in a way that is consistent with the two previous crops you executed.

l. Position the three documents side by side, then compare your screen to Figure A-21. (*Hint*: The sample in the figure shows the three heads on the same horizontal line and the subject's boot in the left photo is on the same baseline as his knee in the right photo.)

m. If you don't like the relationships between any of the three photos, revert the files and then recrop.

n. Save PS A-13.psd as a JPEG named **Web Graphic 1**, then choose a compression setting that will compress the file to under 100 K.

o. Save PS A-14.psd as a JPEG named **Web Graphic 2**.

p. Save PS A-15.psd as a JPEG named **Web Graphic 3**.

Advanced Challenge Exercise

- Verify that the Web Graphic 3 file is active in the document window.
- Click Image on the Application bar, point to Mode, then click CMYK Color.
- Click Image on the Application bar, point to Mode, then click Grayscale.
- Click Discard (Win) or OK (Mac) in the dialog box that follows.

q. Close the three files, then exit Photoshop.

FIGURE A-21

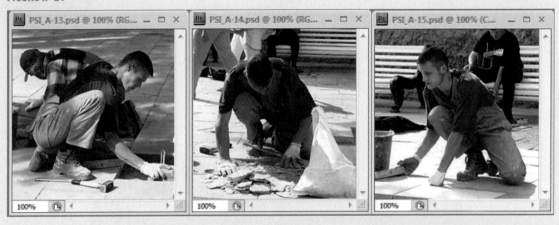

▼ INDEPENDENT CHALLENGE 2

The Estonia Travel and Tourism Board provides you with three images. They ask you to create one file with all three images displayed vertically. They ask that you leave 1/8" space between each image, and the space between should be black. You open the three Photoshop files. Each one is in RGB Color mode and has been cropped to 3" × 3" at 72 pixels per inch.

   a. Open PS A-16.psd, PS A-17.psd, and PS A-18.psd.

   b. Save PS A-16.psd as **Triptych**.

   c. Open the Canvas Size dialog box.

   d. Change the dimension of the canvas to accommodate the client's specifications.

   e. Triptych will be the topmost of the three images, so click the appropriate box in the Anchor to accommodate the other two images.

   f. Specify that the new pixels will be black, then click OK.

   g. In PS A-18.psd, select all, copy, then close the file.

   h. Paste into the Triptych file.

   i. Click the Move tool, then use the arrow keys to move the image down to the bottom of the file.

   j. Zoom in to be sure that the pasted image is at the very bottom of the file and no black pixels are showing beneath it.

   k. Fit on screen.

   l. Copy and paste PS A-17.psd into the file, then close PS A-17.

   m. Save your work.

   n. Save the Triptych file as a JPEG and choose a compression setting that will output the file at less than 200 K.

   o. Compare your result to Figure A-22, close Triptych.jpg, then exit Photoshop.

FIGURE A-22

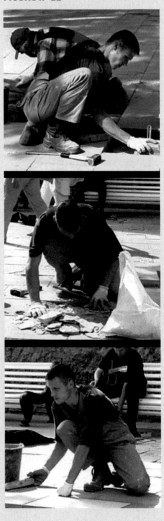

▼ INDEPENDENT CHALLENGE 3

The city zoo is planning on creating a series of animal bookmarks that they will sell in their gift shop. They want you to create a preliminary design for the first bookmark. The width must be between 1" and 2.5" and the height must be between 6" and 7.5" They want the bookmark to be "interesting and unexpected." Since there's a range of acceptable sizes, you decide to first experiment with the Crop tool to find an interesting crop, then change the physical size after you crop. Because this is just a preliminary design, you're not worried about resolution or quality issues that might occur with resizing the file after you crop.

a. Open PS A-19.psd then save it as **Bookmark**.
b. Click the Crop tool, then click Clear on the Options bar.
c. Create a crop marquee of any size anywhere on the canvas.
d. Drag the Opacity slider on the Options bar to 100%.
e. Experiment with different crops of different sizes.

Advanced Challenge Exercise

■ Verify that you have an active crop marquee.
■ Click the Color box to the right of the Shield Color check box on the Options bar.
■ Click in the red area of the Color Picker, then click OK.
■ Drag the Opacity slider to 75%.

f. Decide on a crop that you feel is "interesting and unexpected", then execute the crop. (*Hint*: Remember that you can rotate the crop marquee, which could produce interesting results.)
g. Open the Image Size dialog box, then verify that the Resample Image check box is checked.
h. Change the height value to 6", note the new width, then click OK.
i. Compare your result to the sample shown in Figure A-23, save your work, then exit Photoshop.

FIGURE A-23

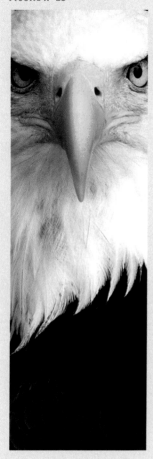

▼ REAL LIFE INDEPENDENT CHALLENGE

You have a digital camera, and you've just captured a great picture of your sister and her young daughter. You want to e-mail it to your aunt and uncle who live on the opposite coast—just so they can see it. You know they don't have a high-speed Internet line, but you want it large enough for them to enjoy, and you want the image quality to be there, too. You decide to make the image 5" wide on its longest side and the resolution 150 ppi. Your goal is to get the image at that resolution and the size to be under 750 K when saved.

a. Open PS A-20.psd, then save it as **Mother's Love**.

b. Look at the image size and resolution of the file.

c. Click the Crop tool, then click Clear on the Options bar.

d. Crop the image (without changing the resolution) in a way that you think is aesthetically pleasing.

e. Open the Image Size dialog box to see the physical size you cropped the image to.

f. Change the width or the height—whichever is largest—to 5 inches.

g. Reduce the resolution to 150 ppi.

h. Check the before-and-after file size at the top of the dialog box to verify that the file size is being reduced, not enlarged.

i. Click OK, then compare your screen to Figure A-24 and Figure A-25. (*Hint*: The figures show two sample crops—the first is more of a standard crop. In the second, the very tight crop conveys a sense of the closeness of the mother and daughter.)

j. Save your file as a JPEG and choose a quality setting that produces a file size that's less than 750 K.

k. Close Mother's Love.psd, then exit Photoshop.

FIGURE A-24

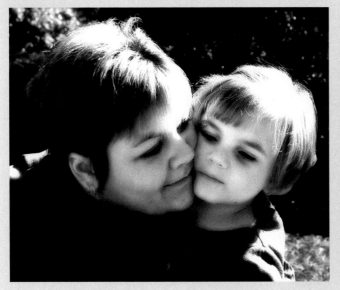

FIGURE A-25

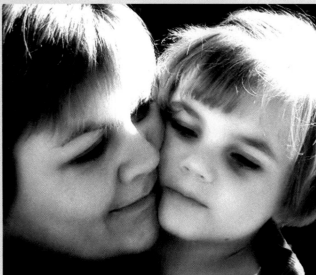

Open PS A-21.psd, then save it as **Visual Solution**. Crop the image so that it resembles the one shown in Figure A-26.

FIGURE A-26

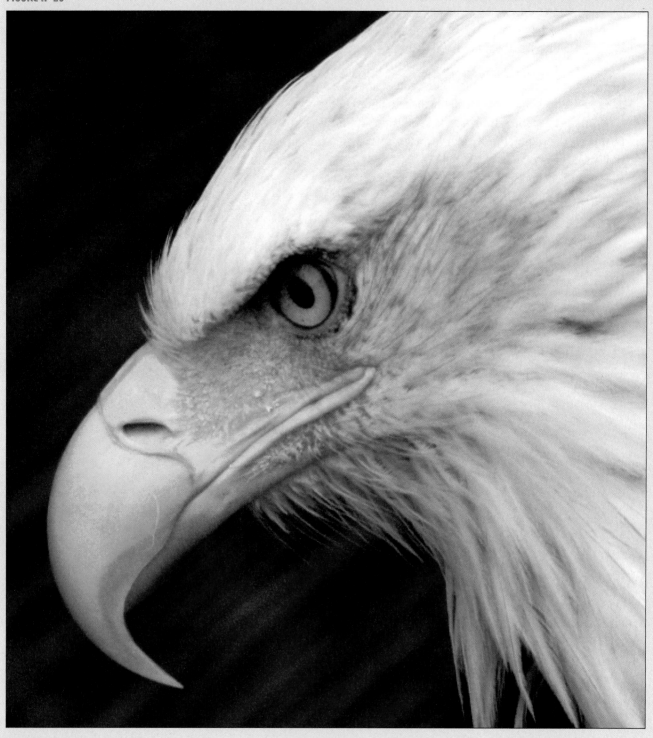

Selecting Pixels

In order to modify specific pixels, you first need to select them. Making selections is one of the most fundamental procedures you'll do in Photoshop. The Tools panel houses three types of selection tools: The Marquee tools, the Lasso tools, and the Magic Wand tool. Making selections is just one component of working with selections. In this unit, you'll learn how to define a selection edge—with a feather, for example—how to save a selection, how to preview a selection in Quick Mask, and how to refine a selection's edge. You'll also gain an understanding of issues involved with moving pixels to a new location on the canvas. At MegaPixel, Laura has prepared a number of projects for you that will test your abilities with making selections, previewing them, saving them, and refining selection edges.

OBJECTIVES

Use the Marquee tools

Use the Lasso tools

Use the Magic Wand tool

Save and load selections

Work with and save alpha channels

Understand anti-aliased edges

Work with a feathered edge

Refine selection edges

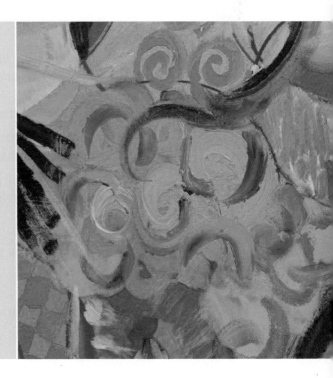

Using the Marquee Tools

The Marquee tools are the most basic tools available for making selections in Photoshop. The Rectangular Marquee tool is used for making rectangular or square selections and the Elliptical Marquee tool is used for making oval or circular selections. You can add pixels to an existing selection and remove pixels from a selection using simple quick keys. If you are not happy with a selection, you can deselect and start over. [image] Laura has given you a Photoshop file which is a puzzle that the company uses to test new employees' understanding of basic selections. You use the Rectangular Marquee tool and the Elliptical Marquee tool to select the first four pieces of the puzzle.

STEPS

QUICK TIP
The black triangle on some tool icons indicates that there are more tools hidden beneath the current tool.

QUICK TIP
If you need to start over, deselect by pressing [Ctrl][D] (Win) or ⌘ [D] (Mac) or click Select on the Application bar, then click Deselect.

QUICK TIP
To switch quickly between the marquee tools and the Move tool, press [M] to select the current marquee tool and [V] to select the Move tool.

Note: Before starting these steps: Verify that only the Tools panel is open. Press [D] so that the foreground and background colors on the Tools panel are black over white. Use all the zooming and scrolling techniques you learned in Unit A.

1. **Open PS B-1.psd, save it as Selections Puzzle, zoom in on the #1 piece, then click the Rectangular Marquee tool** [icon]

2. **Position the center of the crosshair on the upper-left corner of the puzzle piece, drag downward until the center of the crosshair is on the lower-right corner, then release the mouse pointer**

3. **Fit on screen, click the Move tool** [icon]**, drag the piece to the correct position on the hot air balloon image, as shown in Figure B-1, then deselect**
   You will be positioning puzzle pieces 2, 3, and 4 for the remainder of this lesson. Each time you select a puzzle piece, zoom in on the piece, select it, zoom out, move it to the correct position on the hot air balloon, then deselect.

4. **Click the Rectangular Marquee tool** [icon]**, select the top square in the #2 piece, press and hold [Shift], position the crosshair over the lower-right corner, drag a second marquee that overlaps the first, then release the mouse pointer**
   The entire piece is selected. Pressing and holding [Shift] when making a selection adds pixels to the existing selection.

5. **Select the outer square in the #3 piece, press and hold [Alt] (Win) or [option] (Mac), then select the white inner rectangle**
   The white inner rectangle is removed from the selection. Pressing and holding [Alt] (Win) or [option] (Mac) when making a selection removes pixels from the existing selection.

6. **Press and hold the Rectangular Marquee tool** [icon]**, click the Elliptical Marquee tool** [icon]**, then position the crosshair icon over the white pixel at the center of the #4 piece**

7. **Press and hold [Alt][Shift] (Win) or [option][Shift] (Mac), then drag to the edge of the circle to complete the selection**
   Pressing and holding [Alt] (Win) or [option] (Mac) when no pixels are selected creates a marquee selection that starts in the center and grows outward. Pressing and holding [Shift] while dragging a marquee tool constrains the marquee selection to a perfect circle or square. Don't worry if you have a slight white halo at the edge of your selection.

8. **Press [Ctrl][H] (Win) or ⌘[H] (Mac) to hide the marquee, then move the piece into position so that your canvas resembles Figure B-2**

9. **Deselect, then save your work**

FIGURE B-1: Positioning the first piece

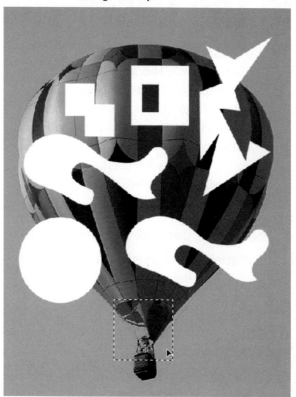

FIGURE B-2: Positioning the circle piece

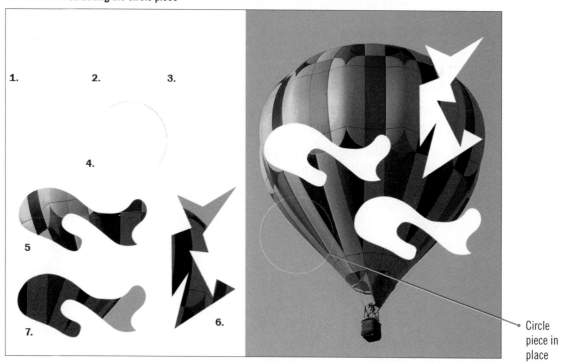

Circle piece in place

The Shift key: Doing double duty

As you've seen in this lesson, the Shift key does two important things: it adds to an existing selection, and it constrains a selection to a perfect shape. What if you wanted to do both—to select two perfect squares? You would press and hold [Shift] while selecting the first square to make a square marquee. To select the second square, you would need to press [Shift] to add to the first selection. So how would you use the Shift key to add to the first square *and* constrain the shape of the second selection as a square? Release the Shift key while dragging, then press it again and it will constrain the selection.

Using the Lasso Tools

There are three types of Lasso tools in Photoshop: Lasso, Polygonal, and Magnetic. Lasso tools are also used for making free-form selections: Simply click and drag anywhere on the canvas to create a section of pixels. When selecting a complex shape with the Lasso tool, you will usually find it easier to make small selections then add to them with the Shift key. The Polygonal Lasso tool functions like the Lasso tool, but it does so with straight lines. This makes the tool very effective for making quick selections or selecting areas of the canvas that are geometric in shape, as the tool's name implies. ▨▨▨▨ Laura instructs you to move on to select the free-form pieces of the puzzle. You use the Lasso tool to select an organically shaped object and the Polygonal Lasso tool to select a multi-lateral object.

STEPS

1. Zoom in on the #5 piece, then click the Lasso tool ⌁.

2. Click and drag to select just an interior section of the piece, as shown in Figure B-3
   Your selection may differ from the figure.

3. Press [Shift] while using the Lasso tool to keep adding to the selection until the entire shape is selected

4. If necessary, press [Alt] (Win) or [option] (Mac) while using the Lasso tool to remove unwanted selected areas you might create outside of the shape

5. Move the piece into place in the puzzle, as shown in Figure B-4
   Don't worry if the selection isn't perfect. This is just for practice with the Lasso tool; you will learn more precise methods for selecting these types of shapes.

6. Zoom in on the #6 piece, click the Polygonal Lasso tool ⌁, then press [Caps Lock] so that the Lasso Tool icon is a precise crosshair

7. Position the crosshair at the tip of the upper-right point of the shape, click, release the mouse button, then move the mouse pointer to the next corner on the shape and click

8. Using the same method, move the mouse pointer around the shape, clicking on the next 12 corners of the shape

9. Float over the original point you clicked so that the Polygonal Lasso tool icon appears with a small "o" beside it, then click to close the selection

10. Move the piece into place in the puzzle, deselect, then compare your result to Figure B-5

FIGURE B-3: Selecting the interior of the object

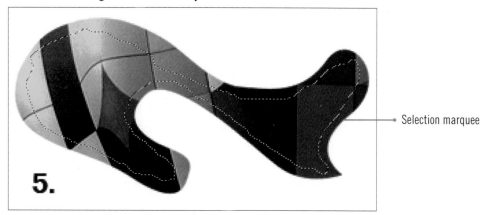

Selection marquee

FIGURE B-4: Positioning piece #5

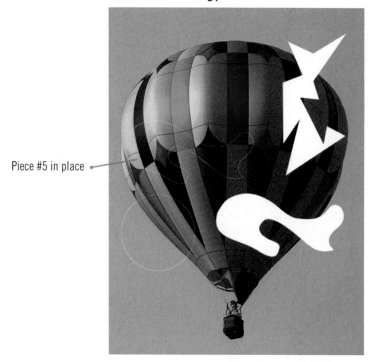

Piece #5 in place

FIGURE B-5: Positioning piece #6

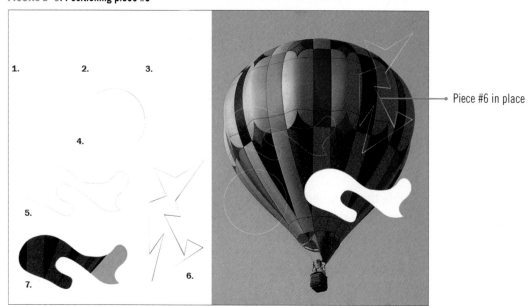

Piece #6 in place

Using the Magic Wand Tool

The Magic Wand tool is a very powerful selection tool. Click any pixel on the canvas, and the Magic Wand tool selects other pixels based on **tolerance**—the similarity of their color. The greater the tolerance value you set for the tool, the more pixels the Magic Wand tool will select. By clicking the Contiguous check box on the Options bar, you can specify that the Magic Wand tool selects only pixels that are **contiguous** to (touching) the area where you click the image. Otherwise, it will select similar pixels throughout the image. For more information about the Magic Wand tool, see the Clues to Use, called Understanding Tolerance, on this page. As with any selection, once you select all of the pixels that you want, you can modify them in many ways—including changing their color in the Hue/Saturation dialog box. Laura tells you to complete the test using the Magic Wand tool, and then to show her a method for changing selected pixels' color using the Hue/Saturation dialog box.

STEPS

Note: Release [Caps Lock] if it is activated.

QUICK TIP

The Magic Wand tool may be hidden behind the Quick Selection tool.

1. Click the Magic Wand tool, then, on the Options bar, change the Tolerance setting to **8** and verify that the Anti-alias and Contiguous check boxes are both checked

2. Click anywhere in the white area that represents the missing piece in the puzzle, then compare your selection to Figure B-6

   The Magic Wand tool selected other white and almost-white pixels, but did not select pixels of the balloon image because they are outside of tolerance. Because the Contiguous option was checked, the white pixels on the left of the canvas are not selected because they are not contiguous—they don't touch the area that you clicked.

QUICK TIP

Once the marquee is close to the #7 piece, zoom in and use the arrow keys to align it precisely.

3. Float over the selected area so that the Magic Wand pointer changes to a white arrow, then drag to move the marquee and align it with the #7 piece on the left of the canvas

4. Click the Move tool, position the #7 piece in the puzzle, deselect, then save your work

5. Open PS B-2.psd, save it as Air Balloon, then click the Magic Wand tool in the center red rectangle of the hot air balloon

   Only a small selection is created because the tolerance setting is low, and there is a variety of red pixels in this area.

6. Deselect, increase the Tolerance value on the Options bar to **48**, then click the same place in the red rectangle

   The increased tolerance value allows for a broader range of reds to be selected. The entire red rectangle is selected, but the selection does not extend into the yellow areas because they are out of tolerance.

7. Deselect, click the Contiguous check box on the Options bar to remove the check mark, click the same place in the red rectangle, then compare your selection to Figure B-7

   With the Contiguous option deactivated, all of the red pixels within tolerance throughout the image are selected.

QUICK TIP

Zooming in on areas of the image that you want to select always helps when making selections

8. Press and hold [Shift], then click unselected red areas in the balloon to add them to the selection

9. Hide the marquee, click Image on the Application bar, point to Adjustments, click Hue/Saturation, then drag the Hue slider to 126

   All of the selected pixels—and only the selected pixels—are changed to a green hue, as shown in Figure B-8.

10. Click OK, save your work, then close Air Balloon.psd and Selections Puzzle.psd

FIGURE B-6: Selecting the white pixels

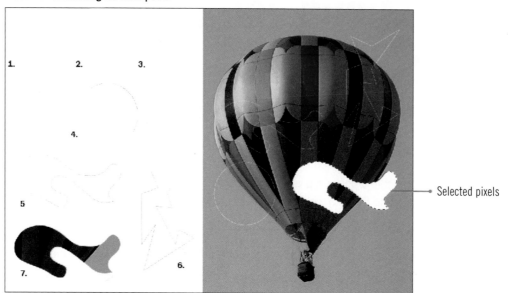

Selected pixels

FIGURE B-7: Selecting pixels without the Contiguous option

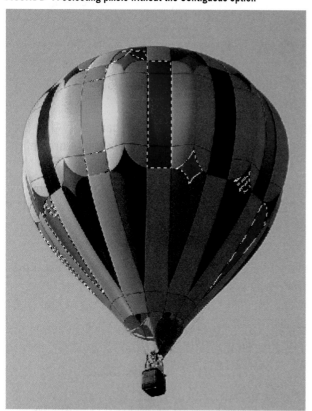

FIGURE B-8: Results of changing the hue of selected pixels

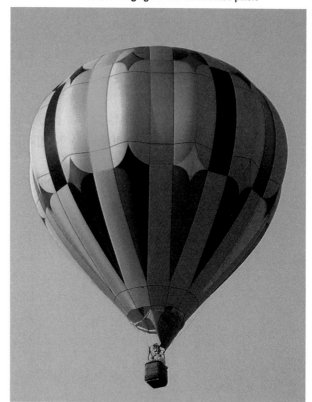

Understanding tolerance

The Magic Wand tool and many other tools in Photoshop do their work based on the function of tolerance. The key to understanding tolerance is to understand that in every Photoshop file, every pixel has a number. The clearest example of that concept can be found in a grayscale image. In a grayscale image, each pixel can be one—and only one—of 256 shades of gray. Tolerance settings work and interact directly with those pixel numbers. For example, let's say you set the tolerance option for the Magic Wand tool to 10. Next, you click the Magic Wand tool on a pixel whose grayscale value is 75. The

Magic Wand tool would select all contiguous pixels whose grayscale value falls within the range of 65—85; ten grayscale values higher and lower than the pixel that you clicked. If the Contiguous option is not activated, the Magic Wand tool would select all the pixels throughout the image whose grayscale values were 65—85. Of course, you don't need to know the number of the pixel you are clicking. Your goal is simply to select pixels of similar color. All you need to do is experiment with different tolerance settings until you get the selection you want.

Saving and Loading Selections

Making selections can be some of the most complex and time-consuming work you'll do in Photoshop, so it makes sense that you can save selections with the Photoshop file. Saving a selection is always a smart idea because you never know when you might want to access the selection again in the future. You've been assigned to work on a design project for a client. Jon explains that the client wants to see color applied to a posterized image. You posterize the file, then create and save four selections in order to load them and fill them with four different colors.

STEPS

Note: Before starting these steps, open the Swatches and Color panels.

1. **Open PS B-3.psd, click Image on the Application bar, point to Adjustments, then click Posterize**

   Posterize is a special effect that is created by reducing the number of colors available for the image.

2. **Drag the Levels slider to 4, then click OK**

   With the Posterize effect set to four, each pixel in the image can be one—and only one—of four available shades of gray: black, dark gray, light gray, or white.

3. **Click Image on the Application bar, point to Mode, then click RGB Color**

   Changing the color mode to RGB Color will allow you to add color to the selections.

4. **Click the Magic Wand tool ⚲, set the Tolerance to 1 on the Options bar, verify that the Anti-alias and the Contiguous check boxes are not checked, then click a white area of the image**

5. **Click Select on the Application bar, click Save Selection, then type White in the Name text box**

   The Save Selection dialog box, shown in Figure B-9, shows that the new selection will be saved with the file PS B-3.psd when you save the file.

6. **Repeat Steps 4 and 5 to make three more selections, named Light Gray, Dark Gray, and Black, by clicking a light gray area, a dark gray area, and a black area with the Magic Wand tool, then saving each selection**

7. **Deselect the last selection by pressing [Ctrl][D] (Win) or ⌘[D] (Mac), click Select on the Application bar, click Load Selection, click the Channel list arrow, click Light Gray, then click OK**

   The saved selection is loaded.

8. **Float the pointer over the Swatches panel, then click the swatch named Pure Yellow Orange, as shown in Figure B-10**

   Pure Yellow Orange becomes the foreground color on the Tools panel.

9. **Click Edit on the Application bar, click Fill, click the Use list arrow, click Foreground Color, verify that the Opacity setting is 100%, if necessary, click OK, then deselect**

   The Light Gray selection is filled with Pure Yellow Orange.

10. **Repeat Steps 7-9 to load the White, Dark Gray, and Black selections, filling each with a color of your choice on the Swatches panel**

    Figure B-11 shows one possible result.

QUICK TIP

Press [Alt] [Backspace] (Win) or [option] [Delete] (Mac) to fill a selection with the foreground color and [Backspace] (Win) or [Delete] (Mac) to fill a selection with the background color.

FIGURE B-9: Save Selection dialog box

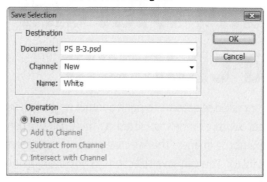

FIGURE B-10: Pure Yellow Orange swatch on the Swatches panel

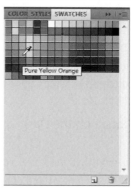

FIGURE B-11: The finished project

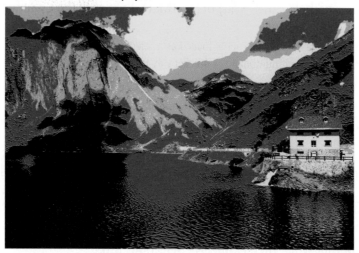

Saving color swatches

There are many ways to change the foreground and background colors. On the Swatches panel, for example, if you click a swatch, the foreground changes to that color. Press [Ctrl] (Win) or ⌘ (Mac) when you click a swatch to change the background color. You can also click the Eyedropper tool and sample any pixel from the image. Doing so changes the foreground color to the color of the pixel. You can also drag the sliders on the Color panel to modify the current foreground color. To save colors that you create, simply float the pointer over a white area of the Swatches panel. The pointer changes to a paint bucket icon. Click and the color will be added as a new swatch. You're even given the option to name it. The new swatch will remain on the Swatches panel for every new file that you create from that point forward. To delete a swatch from the Swatches panel, press and hold [Alt] (Win) or [option] (Mac), then click to delete the swatch.

Working with and Saving Alpha Channels

Alpha channels are saved selections. To put it another way, when you save a selection, the selection is saved as an alpha channel. Alpha channels are listed on the Channels panel in Photoshop. They are displayed as black and white thumbnail images. The selected areas are represented by white, and the areas not selected are represented by black. You can save selections as you are working, but alpha channels are not automatically saved when you save the file. You must specify that they be saved when you save the file. Now that you have four new alpha channels, you view them in the Channels panel. You load the Dark Gray alpha channel, change its color, then save the Dark Gray alpha channel with the file.

STEPS

1. **Click Window on the Application bar, then click Channels**

   The Channels panel holds four default channels: the "composite" RGB channel, and one channel each for Red, Blue, and Green. In addition are the four alpha channels representing the selections you saved: White, Light Gray, Dark Gray, and Black.

2. **Click the Channel thumbnail on the Dark Gray channel, then compare your canvas to Figure B-13**

   The alpha channel is the selection that you saved. The dark gray pixels that you selected are represented by white pixels. Everything that wasn't selected is represented by black pixels.

3. **Click the Channel thumbnails for the other three alpha channels that you saved, then click the RGB channel thumbnail to see the composite image with all of its colors**

4. **Press and hold [Ctrl] (Win) or [⌘] (Mac), then click the Channel thumbnail of the Dark Gray alpha channel**

   The Dark Gray alpha channel is loaded as a selection. Pressing and hold [Ctrl] (Win) or [⌘] (Mac) while clicking a channel thumbnail is a quicker way to load a selection.

5. **In the Swatches panel, click Pure Yellow Green**

   Pure Yellow Green becomes the foreground color.

6. **Fill the selection with the foreground color, deselect, then compare your result to Figure B-14**

7. **Click File on the Application bar, click Save As, type Save Selections in the Name text box, verify that the Alpha Channels check box is checked, as shown in Figure B-15, then click Save**

   All of the saved selections—the alpha channels—are saved with the file. Every time you save a selection and add a channel to a file, you are increasing the file size substantially. Delete alpha channels when you no longer need them.

8. **Save your work, then close Save Selections.psd**

Working with the foreground and background colors

In Photoshop, although you have millions of colors at your disposal, at any given time you are working with just two colors: the foreground and background colors on the Tools panel. As shown in Figure B-12, these are the colors you paint with and fill selections with. You can click the Switch Foreground and Background Colors button or press [X] to switch the foreground and background colors. Click the Default Foreground and Background Colors button or press [D] to revert the foreground and background colors to black and white.

FIGURE B-12: Foreground and Background colors

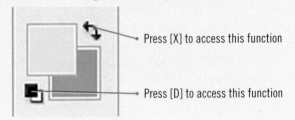

Press [X] to access this function

Press [D] to access this function

FIGURE B-13: The Dark Gray alpha channel

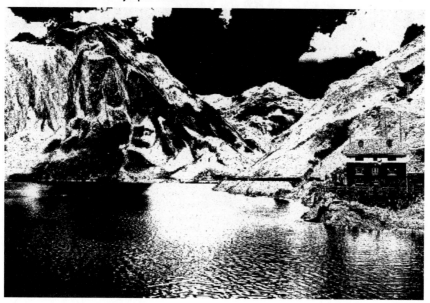

FIGURE B-14: Filling the loaded selection with a new color

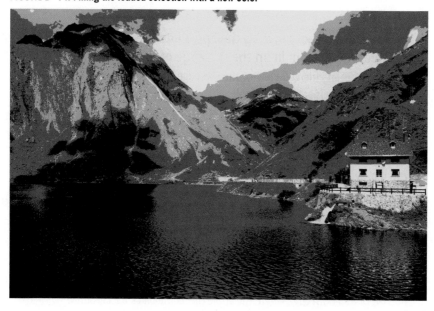

FIGURE B-15: Save Alpha Channels option in the Save As dialog box

Alpha Channels
check box

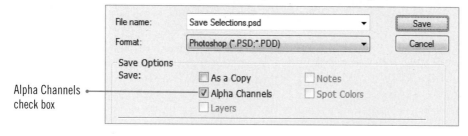

Understanding Anti-Aliased Edges

The outline of a selection is called the **edge** of a selection; the type of edge that you choose will have a big impact on how your work appears. The edge of a selection is always either aliased or anti-aliased. An **aliased edge** is a hard edge—the hard "stair-stepped" pixels are very obvious. The edge is noticeably blunt. This is why aliased edges are seldom used. An **anti-aliased edge** is a crisp but smoother edge. With an anti-aliased edge, Photoshop creates a smooth transition between the edge and its background using many shades of the edge pixel color. Jon provides you with an image he needs for an educational poster. He asks you to try to improve the appearance of an apple against a blue background. You apply an aliased edge and an anti-aliased edge to compare the difference between the two.

STEPS

1. Open PS B-4.psd, then save it as Apple Edges
2. Press and hold [Ctrl] (Win) or ⌘ (Mac), then click the yellow swatch (RGB Yellow) in the top row on the Swatches panel

   The background color changes to RGB Yellow.

QUICK TIP
You will need to make more than one selection to select the entire apple.

3. Click the Magic Wand tool ✨, set the Tolerance value to 72, verify that the Anti-alias check box is *not* checked and that the Contiguous check box *is* checked, then select the entire apple
4. Click the Move tool ⊹, drag the apple into the black area on the right, hide the marquee, then zoom in on the top edge of the apple

   Figure B-16 is an enlarged view of the top edge of the apple and shows the hard aliased edge; the square shapes of the pixels are clearly visible.

5. Double-click the Hand tool ✋ to fit the page in the window, then note on the left of the canvas that the yellow background color fills the remaining area after the move and has the same aliased edge
6. Click Edit on the Application bar, click Undo Move, then deselect

QUICK TIP
You will need to make more than one selection to select the entire apple.

7. Click the Magic Wand tool ✨, click the Anti-alias check box on the Options bar, then select the apple
8. Click the Move tool ⊹, drag the apple into the black area, hide the marquee, then zoom in on the top edge

   As shown in Figure B-17, the apple has an anti-aliased edge. Edge pixels of various shades of green create the illusion of a smooth edge where the apple meets the black background.

9. Click the Hand tool ✋, then move the canvas to the right so that you can examine the edge where the yellow fill meets the blue background

   The anti-aliased edge creates a crisp and smooth transition between the solid yellow and the almost-solid blue background.

10. Save your work, then close Apple Edges.psd

FIGURE B-16: Viewing the aliased edge

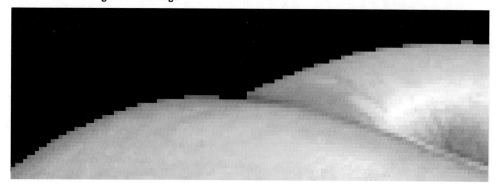

FIGURE B-17: Viewing the anti-aliased edge

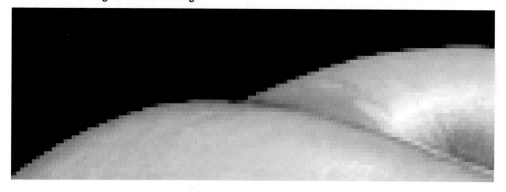

How anti-aliasing works

As we've said before, a Photoshop image is made up of pixels, and pixels are square. By definition, a square does not have a soft edge. So think about this: How do you create a soft edge for a curved object using only squares? The answer is that you can't create a soft edge with squares; squares have right-angle corners. All you can do is create the *illusion* of a soft edge. That's what an anti-aliased edge is: an illusion. Anti-aliasing manipulates the color of edge pixels in a selection to create a visual transition between the selected object and the background. So the soft edge is an optical illusion made by manipulating color—the color of square pixels.

Computer monitors and viewing edges

Your computer monitor acts as the middleman between you and the Photoshop image. Everything you are seeing is through your monitor. Monitors also use red, green, and blue pixels of transmitted light. Using these three colors, your monitor is able to show you millions of colors—more than your eye can differentiate. Monitors have resolution as well: most have a resolution of 72 pixels per inch. This fact has a big impact on how you view your Photoshop image, because at all times the monitor's resolution is trying to match the image's resolution. When you're viewing your image at less than 100%, your monitor is not giving you an accurate visual representation of the pixels in your image. When you're analyzing subtle components of your image—like selection edges!—be sure that you're viewing your canvas at least at 100%.

Working with a Feathered Edge

A **feathered edge** is a blended edge. Photoshop creates a blend at the edge of a selection between the selected pixels and the background image. Photoshop offers settings for controlling the length of the blend at the edge. The feather value is equal to the length of the feathered edge. When you apply a feathered edge to a selection, the edge is equally distributed inside and outside the selection edge. In Photoshop, vignettes are created with feathered edges. A **vignette** is a visual effect in which the edge of an image—usually an oval—gradually fades away. A MegaPixel client has sent in a picture and asked that you create a vignette effect. You create an oval with a feathered edge, preview it in Quick Mask Mode, then save the selection.

STEPS

1. Open PS B-5.psd, then click the Default Foreground and Background Colors button ⬛

2. Click the Elliptical Marquee tool ⭕, type 32 in the Feather text box on the Options bar, then verify that the Anti-alias check box is checked

3. Position the pointer on the jewelry at the woman's neck, press [Alt] (Win) or [option] (Mac), then draw an oval from the center that resembles the shape and size of the one shown in Figure B-18

4. Click the Edit in Quick Mask Mode button ◻ on the Tools panel to preview the selection
   Quick Mask Mode provides a preview of how the feathered edge will appear when you save the selection. The Quick Mask Mode feature shows the selected pixels and hides or "masks" unselected pixels. As shown in Figure B-19, the 32-pixel blend created a very soft and smooth edge that progressively fades out the edge of the selected image. The Quick Mask is very helpful because without it, you would not be able to see the result of the feathered edge until after you saved the selection. To learn more information about Quick Mask Mode, see the Clues to Use below called Understanding Quick Mask Mode.

5. Click the Edit in Standard Mode button ◻ to return to the standard view

6. Save the selection as Vignette, then deselect
   The selection is now an alpha channel saved in the Channels panel.

7. Open the Channels panel, then click the Vignette channel thumbnail to view the saved selection
   In this selection, which transitions gradually from selected pixels to unselected pixels, the alpha channel transitions gradually from white to black. See the Clues to Use called Understanding gray pixels in alpha channels.

8. Click the RGB channel thumbnail, then load the Vignette selection

9. Click the Move tool ⛟, then drag the selected pixels into the green area on the right
   Figure B-20 shows the moved pixels with the feathered edge and also the feathered edge remaining after the move.

10. Save the file with its alpha channels as Vignette, then close Vignette.psd

FIGURE B-18: Drawing the feathered oval selection

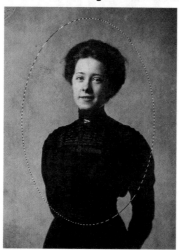

FIGURE B-19: Previewing the selection in Quick Mask Mode

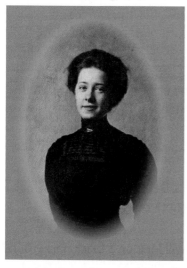

FIGURE B-20: The selected pixels relocated

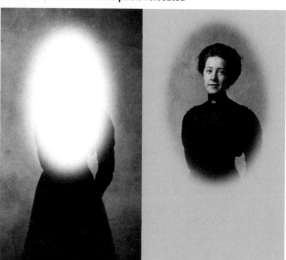

Understanding Quick Mask Mode

Many graphic arts professionals refer to alpha channels as "masks" because the non-selected areas are "masked" by the black areas in the alpha channel. Quick Mask works with the same concept as alpha channels. Quick Mask is a visual aid that gives you a preview of your selection. It helps you to see your selection by "masking out" the areas that aren't selected and showing only the areas that are. You can increase or decrease the opacity of the Quick Mask by double-clicking the Edit in Quick Mask Mode button on the Tools panel. The Quick Mask Options dialog box opens. In this dialog box, you can change the color and the opacity as well as decide whether you want the color to indicate the masked area or the selected area. You can toggle between Quick Mask Mode and Standard Mode by pressing [Q].

Understanding gray pixels in alpha channels

How does Photoshop save a selection? It saves it by creating an alpha channel. Selected areas are white, and non-selected areas are black. But what if the selection has a feathered edge? The only way an alpha channel can render that is with gray pixels. This is the concept of **opacity**. Here's the easiest way to understand this concept in relation to alpha channels: The feathered edge makes the image fade away to nothing outside the selection. In the case of the previous lesson, the center of the oval is where the pixels have 100% opacity—they are fully visible, and they are represented by 100% white pixels in the alpha channel. The pixels completely outside the selection have 0% opacity—they are completely transparent, and they are represented by 100% black pixels in the alpha channel. In a feathered edge, the opacity fades from 100% to 0%, so in the alpha channel, that area fades from white to black. For example, the pixels smack in the middle of the feathered edge would be 50% black; in other words, gray. Pixels closer to the outer edge would be dark gray—almost black and therefore fading out to nothing.

Refining Selection Edges

The **Refine Edge dialog box** offers you a number of useful options for viewing and refining the edge of a selection. The two key options in this dialog box are the Feather slider, which you can use to dynamically feather a selection while you preview the result, and the Contract/Expand slider, which you can use to reduce or enlarge a selection. The Contrast slider is especially useful for removing halos from the edge of a selection. ■■■■ MegaPixel's city zoo client has asked that you create a preliminary design that involves a silhouette of a bird's head on a black background. You decide to make a quick selection and tweak it in the Refine Edge dialog box.

STEPS

1. **Open PS B-6.psd, then save it as** Eagle Silhouette

2. **Press and hold the** Magic Wand tool ▨, **click the** Quick Selection tool ▨, **click the** Brush **list arrow on the Options bar, then set the Diameter to 20 px**

   The Quick Selection tool is selection tool that you use by dragging the tool pointer over the item you wish to select until you have all of it selected. The Quick Selection tool selects pixels based on their similarity, but there's no option to set a tolerance value. Instead, the Quick Selection tool offers you the Add to selection and Subtract from selection tools that you can use to either enlarge an existing selection or remove unwanted areas from a selection. In addition, you can reduce the brush size to select smaller or more specific areas.

3. **Position the Quick Selection tool pointer at the top of the eagle's head, then drag the brush slowly down over the eagle's white feathers and then down over the eagle's brown feathers**

   Compare your result to Figure B-21. To learn more about the Quick Selection tool, see the Clues to Use below called Using the Quick Selection tool.

4. **Click** Select **on the Application bar, click** Refine Edge, **click** Default **to reset the default settings in the dialog box, then verify that the Preview check box is checked**

   Your dialog box should match the one shown in Figure B-22.

5. **Click the** On Black button ▨ **to preview how the eagle will look on a black background**

   The four other preview buttons are called Standard, Quick Mask, On White, and Mask. See Table B-1 for some useful quick keys to use in the Refine Edge dialog box.

QUICK TIP

Results of moving Contract/Expand slider can take a moment to preview.

6. **Drag the** Feather slider **to 5, then drag the** Contract/Expand slider **to +15%**

   The Feather slider allows you to experiment with different feather values while previewing the selection edge. Using the Contract/Expand feature can be useful with a feathered edge to include the feathering on the *outside* of the original selection.

7. **Drag the** Smooth slider **to 0, then click** OK

   The Smooth option will reduce bumps and stair-stepping at the edges of the selection. In this case, we want to keep the detail of the eagle's feathers, not smooth them out.

8. **Click** Select **on the Application bar, then click** Inverse

   Everything outside of the eagle selection is selected. The background is selected making it possible to fill it with black.

9. **Click** Edit **on the Application bar, click** Fill, **click the** Use list arrow, **click** Black, **then click** OK

   The original background is now filled with black.

10. **Deselect, compare your canvas to Figure B-23, save your changes, then close Eagle Silhouette.psd**

FIGURE B-21: Quick selection made from the Quick Selection tool

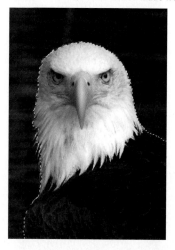

FIGURE B-22: The Refine Edge dialog box

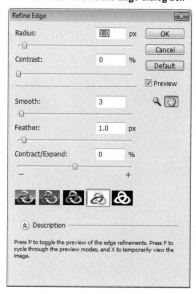

FIGURE B-23: The silhouette of the eagle against black

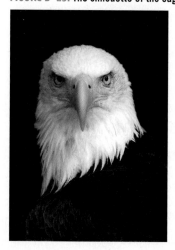

TABLE B-1: Useful keyboard commands for the Refine Edge dialog box (Win & Mac)

keyboard	action	keyboard	action
[P]	Toggles the Preview option on and off	[Shift][F]	Cycles backward through the five preview modes
[F]	Cycles through the five preview modes	[X]	Temporarily displays the entire image

Practice

▼ CONCEPTS REVIEW

FIGURE B-24

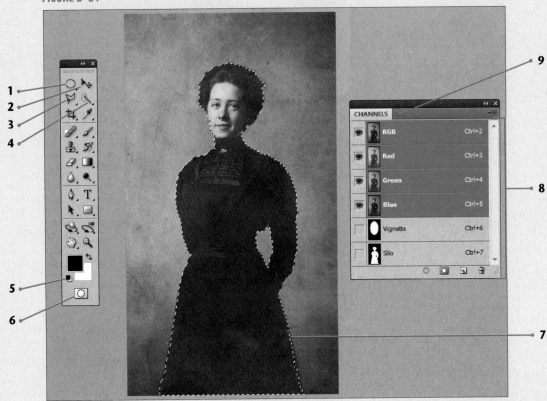

1. Which item points to channels?
2. Which item is used to set default colors on the Tools panel?
3. Which item points to the Move tool?
4. Which item points to a marquee tool?
5. Which item points to a lasso tool?
6. Which item points to a selection?
7. Which item points to the Edit in Quick Mask Mode button?
8. Which item points to the Quick Selection tool?

Match each term with the statement that best describes it.

9. Alpha channel
10. Quick Mask Mode
11. Aliased edge
12. Anti-aliased edge
13. Tolerance
14. Feather
15. Posterize
16. Vignette

a. Hard edge showing pixels stair-stepping
b. Setting that controls the Magic Wand tool
c. Useful for previewing selections
d. Blended edge
e. To reduce the colors in an image
f. Created whenever a selection is saved
g. Effect made with a feathered edge
h. Smooth and crisp edge

Select the best answer from the list of choices.

17. **Which of the following offers the hardest edge for a selection?**
    a. Alias
    b. Anti-alias
    c. Feather
    d. Tolerance

18. **Which of the following would be the best tool for selecting an image of a stop sign?**
    a. Rectangular Marquee tool
    b. Elliptical Marquee tool
    c. Lasso tool
    d. Polygonal Lasso tool

19. **Which of the following is not true about saved selections?**
    a. Saving a selection creates an alpha channel
    b. An alpha channel is a selection
    c. Alpha channels are saved automatically when you save a file
    d. Saving alpha channels increases file size

20. **Which of the following is true about alpha channels?**
    a. White pixels represent selected pixels
    b. Saving a selection with a feathered edge results in an alpha channel with gray pixels
    c. The Load Selection command is the only way to load a saved selection
    d. Both a & b but not c

21. **Which of the following quick keys is used to fill a selection with the foreground color?**
    a. [Alt][Enter] (Win) or [option][return] (Mac)
    b. [Alt][Backspace] (Win) or [option][Delete] (Mac)
    c. [Shift][Enter] (Win) or [Shift][return] (Mac)
    d. [Backspace] (Win) or [Delete] (Mac)

22. **What are the default foreground and background colors in Photoshop?**
    a. Black over White
    b. White over Black
    c. Black over Black
    d. White over White

▼ SKILLS REVIEW

1. **Use the marquee tools.**
   a. Open PS B-7.psd, save it as **Shapes**, zoom in on the #1 piece, then click the Rectangular Marquee tool.
   b. Press [D] to access the default colors on the Tools panel.
   c. Position the center of the crosshair on the upper-left corner of the #1 puzzle piece, drag downward until the center of the crosshair is on the lower-right corner, then release the mouse pointer.
   d. Fit on screen, click the Move tool, drag the piece to the corresponding position in the puzzle on the right, then deselect. You will be positioning puzzle pieces 2, 3, and 4 for the remainder of this lesson. Each time you select a puzzle piece, zoom in on the piece, select it, zoom out, move it to the correct position on the puzzle on the right, then deselect.
   e. Click the Rectangular Marquee tool, select the top square in the #2 piece, press and hold [Shift], position the crosshair over the lower-right corner, drag a second marquee that overlaps the first, then release the mouse pointer.
   f. Select the outer square in the #3 piece, press and hold [Alt] (Win) or [option] (Mac), then select the blue inner rectangle so that it is removed from the selection.
   g. Using the same method, click the Elliptical Marquee tool, verify that the Feather value on the Options bar is 0, press and hold [Alt] (Win) or [option] (Mac), then remove the circle from the selection.
   h. Press [Ctrl][H] (Win) or [⌘][H] (Mac) to hide the marquee, then move the piece into position.
   i. Deselect, then save your work.

2. **Use the lasso tools.**
   a. Zoom in on the #4 piece, then click the Lasso tool.
   b. Click and drag to select just an interior section of the piece.
   c. Use the [Shift] key in conjunction with the Lasso tool to keep adding to the selection until the entire shape is selected.
   d. Press [Alt] (Win) or [option] (Mac) while using the Lasso tool to remove unwanted selected areas you might have created outside of the shape.
   e. Move the piece into place in the puzzle on the right.

f. Zoom in on the #5 piece, click the Polygonal Lasso tool, then press [Caps Lock] so that the Lasso tool icon is a precise crosshair.

g. Position the crosshair at the tip of the upper-right point of the shape, click, release the mouse button, then move the mouse pointer to the next corner on the shape and click.

h. Using the same method, move your mouse around the shape, clicking on the remaining corners of the shape.

i. Float over the original point you clicked so that the Polygonal Lasso tool icon appears with a small "o" beside it, then click to close the selection.

j. Move the piece into place in the puzzle on the right, then deselect.

3. Use the Magic Wand tool.

a. Verify that Caps Lock is not active, then click the Magic Wand tool.

b. Change the Tolerance setting to 4.

c. Verify that the Anti-alias check box is checked.

d. Verify that the Contiguous check box is checked.

e. Click anywhere in the #6 puzzle piece to select it.

f. Click the Move tool, move the piece into position, and keep the piece selected.

g. Hide the marquee, click Image on the Application bar, point to Adjustments, click Hue/Saturation, then drag the Hue slider to –112.

h. Click OK, then compare your screen to Figure B-25.

i. Save your work, then close Shapes.psd.

FIGURE B-25

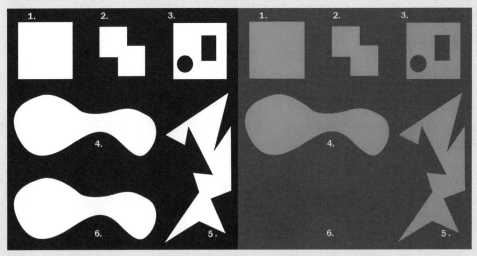

4. Save and load selections.

a. Open PS B-8.psd.

b. Click Image on the Application bar, point to Adjustments, then click Posterize.

c. Drag the Levels slider to 4, then click OK.

d. Click Image on the Application bar, point to Mode, then click RGB Color.

e. Click the Magic Wand tool, set the tolerance to **1**, then verify that the Anti-alias check box is not checked and that the Contiguous check box is not checked.

f. Click a white area of the image.

g. Click Select on the Application bar, click Save Selection, type **White** in the Name text box, then click OK.

h. Save three new selections named Light Gray, Dark Gray, and Black.

i. Click Select on the Application bar, click Load Selection, click the Channel list arrow, click Light Gray, then click OK.

j. Float your cursor over the Swatches panel so that it changes to the Eyedropper, then click Pure Yellow Orange to make it the foreground color.

k. Click Edit on the Application bar, click Fill, click the Use list arrow, click Foreground Color, then click OK.

l. Using the same methodology, load and fill the three other saved selections with different colors. Figure B-26 shows one possible result.

FIGURE B-26

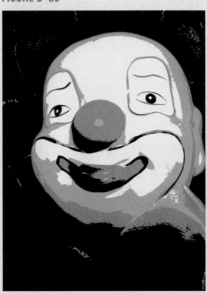

5. **Work with and save alpha channels.**

a. On the Channels panel, click the Dark Gray channel thumbnail to view the channel itself.

b. Click the thumbnails for the three other alpha channels that you saved, then click the RGB channel to return to the image on the canvas.

c. On the Swatches panel, choose Pure Green as a new foreground color.

d. Press and hold [Ctrl](Win) or ⌘(Mac) then click the Dark Gray channel thumbnail.

e. Fill the selection with the foreground color.

f. Click File on the Application bar, click Save As, type **Clown Posterize** in the Name text box, then verify that the Alpha Channels check box is checked.

g. Click Save, then close Clown Posterize.psd.

6. **Understand anti-aliased edges.**

a. Open PS B-9.psd, then save it as **Skills Edges**.

b. On the Swatches panel, press and hold [Ctrl](Win) or ⌘(Mac), then click the RGB Yellow swatch in the top row to make it the background color.

c. Click the Magic Wand tool, set the Tolerance value to 4, verify that the Anti-alias check box is not checked and that the Contiguous check box is not checked, then click the center of any orange shape.

d. Click the Move tool, then drag the selected pixels into the white area on the right.

e. Hide the selection, then examine the edges of various shapes.

f. Undo the move, deselect, click the Magic Wand tool, check the Anti-alias check box, then select all the shapes again.

g. Move the selected pixels into the white area, then hide the selection marquee.

h. Zoom in and examine the edges of various shapes.

i. Examine the edges where the yellow fills meet the blue background on the left of the canvas.

j. Undo the move, then save your work.

7. Work with a feathered edge.

  a. Verify that all pixels are deselected, then set the foreground and background colors in the Tools panel to the default colors.

  b. Click the Magic Wand tool, then click the center of any orange shape.

  c. Click Select on the Application bar, point to Modify, then click Feather.

  d. Type 12 in the Feather Radius text box, then click OK.

  e. Click the Edit in Quick Mask Mode button on the Tools panel to preview the selection.

  f. Click the Edit in Standard Mode button to return to Standard view.

  g. Click the Move tool, then drag the selected pixels into the white area on the right.

  h. Hide the selection, then examine the edges of the shapes on the right and left.

  i. Compare your results with Figure B-27.

  j. Save your work, then close Shape Edges.psd.

FIGURE B-27

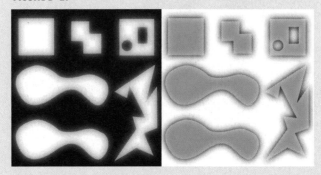

8. Refine selection edges.

  a. Open PS B-10.psd, then save it as **Apple Silhouette**.

  b. Press and hold the Magic Wand tool, click the Quick Selection tool, click the Brush list arrow on the Options bar, then set the Diameter to 20 px.

  c. Click and drag the brush slowly over the apple until the entire apple is selected.

  d. Click Select on the Application bar, click Refine Edge, click Default to reset the default settings in the dialog box, then verify that the Preview check box is checked.

  e. Drag the Feather slider to 5, drag the Contract/Expand slider to –15, then drag the Smooth slider to 77.

  f. Drag the Contrast slider to 43, click the On Black button to preview how the apple will look on a black background, then click OK.

  g. Click the Move tool, then move the selected pixels into the black space on the right part of the canvas.

  h. Deselect, compare your canvas to Figure B-28, save your work, then close Apple Silhouette.psd.

FIGURE B-28

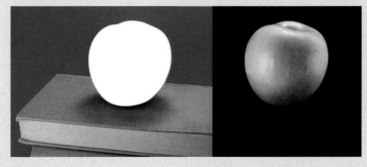

▼ INDEPENDENT CHALLENGE 1

The Estonia Travel and Tourism Board has sent you a great image of a hot air balloon to promote sightseeing around Tallinn. They tell you that they love the image, but they don't like the colors of the balloon—they think the primary palette of yellow, red, and blue is "not exciting or magical." They ask that you change the colors of the balloon to something more interesting. You realize that you'll need to make a really good selection of the balloon so that the color changes won't show.

a. Open PS B-11.psd, then save it as **Magic Wand Mask**.

b. Click the Magic Wand tool.

c. Set the Tolerance to 8, then verify that the Anti-alias and Contiguous check boxes are both checked.

d. Use the Magic Wand tool to select the sky. (*Hint*: You will likely need to click multiple times with the Magic Wand tool to select the entire sky.)

e. Click Select on the menu, then click Inverse.

f. Use the Lasso tool to remove the basket from the selection so that only the balloon is selected.

g. Click Select on the Application bar, then click Refine Edge.

h. Click the Default button, then click the On Black preview button. (*Hint*: The selection is clearly outside of the edge of the balloon, so you need to contract it.)

i. Set the Feather to 0. (*Hint*: The edge of the selection should be crisp against the sky, not soft.)

j. Set the Contract/Expand value to –50%.

k. Set the Smooth value to 10, then scroll around the image itself to preview the edges.

l. Click OK, then hide the selection marquee.

m. Click Image on the Application bar, point to Adjustments, then click Hue/Saturation.

n. Drag the Hue slider to –37, then click OK.

o. View the image at 100%, then scroll around to examine the edges.

p. Save your work, compare your screen to Figure B-29, then close Magic Wand Mask.psd.

FIGURE B-29

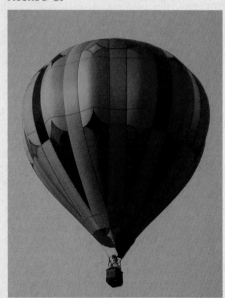

▼ INDEPENDENT CHALLENGE 2

Your client has called, asking that you modify a file that shows balloons against the sky. They tell you that they would like you to posterize the balloons and change their color so that the yellow balloons are orange. They have created and saved a selection of the balloons to make your work easier.

a. Open PS B-12.psd, then save it as **Orange Balloons**.

b. Posterize the image to 4 levels.

c. Open the Channels panel.

d. Press and hold [Ctrl](Win) or [⌘](Mac), then click the Balloons channel thumbnail to load the selection.

e. Click Image on the Application bar, point to Adjustments, then click Hue/Saturation.

f. Drag the Hue slider to –29, then click OK.

g. Compare your result to Figure B-30.

h. Save your work, then close Orange Balloons.psd.

FIGURE B-30

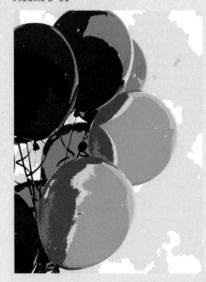

▼ INDEPENDENT CHALLENGE 3

Your company has a client that specializes in online IQ tests. You've worked on producing more than 100 visual puzzles in the last month. Two of the puzzles have come back with requests for changes. The client has supplied two low-res examples of the changes for you to match.

    a. Open PS B-13.psd, then save it as **IQ Test**.

    b. Open PS B-14.psd. (*Hint*: If you can, make room on your screen for both files. You need to make IQ Test.psd match the small file.)

    c. Use the Rectangular Marquee tool to drag one marquee around all four red boxes—be precise.

    d. Draw one marquee around the four blue squares to deselect that entire area.

    e. Use the Magic Wand tool to remove the black squares from the selection with one click.

    f. Use the same method to remove the red squares from the selection.

    g. Fill the remaining selection with the 50% gray swatch on the Swatches panel.

    h. Deselect.

    i. Click the first yellow swatch on the Swatches panel to make it the foreground color.

    j. Fill the white squares in the center with the yellow color.

    k. Fill the blue squares with the first green swatch on the Swatches panel.

    l. Fill the red squares with the same yellow you used in Step j so that your screen resembles Figure B-31.

Advanced Challenge Exercise

    ■ Expand the Swatches panel so that you can see all the swatches.

    ■ Float your cursor in the gray area beneath the swatches so that your cursor turns into a paint bucket icon.

    ■ Click the mouse pointer.

    ■ Type **Yellow I Used** in the Name text box, then click OK.

    m. Close PS B-14.psd.

    n. Save your work, then close IQ Test.psd.

FIGURE B-31

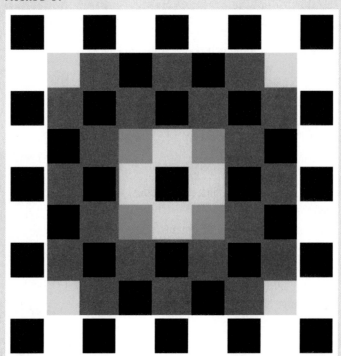

▼ REAL WORLD INDEPENDENT CHALLENGE

Your sister has just bought a new condo and has lots of wall space to fill. You have a great photo of her and decide to apply an "Andy Warhol" effect to the photo and give it to her to enlarge and frame.

a. Open PS B-15.psd, then posterize the file to 6 levels.

b. Click Image on the Application bar, point to Mode, then click RGB Color.

c. Open the Channels panel and keep it visible while you work.

d. Click the Magic Wand tool, set the Tolerance to 8, then verify that the Anti-alias check box is not checked and that the Contiguous check box is not checked.

e. Click the lightest gray area in the woman's cheek.

f. Save the selection as **Lightest Gray**.

g. Save three new selections named **Light Gray**, **Dark Gray**, and **Darkest Gray**. (*Hint*: Don't select any of the white areas or the black areas.)

h. Use the Channels panel to load the Lightest Gray selection.

i. Fill the selection with a color of your choice.

j. Load and fill the three other saved selections with different colors. Figure B-32 shows one possible solution.

Advanced Challenge Exercise

- Load the Lightest Gray selection.
- Double-click the Edit in Quick Mask Mode button.
- Click the Color box and set the color to R255/G0/B0.
- Set the Opacity to 100%.
- Click OK.
- Click the Edit in Standard Mode button.

k. Save the file with the alpha channels as **Posterized Woman**.

l. Close Posterized Woman.psd.

FIGURE B-32

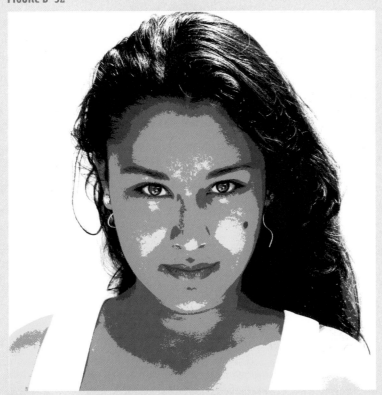

▼ VISUAL WORKSHOP

Open PS B-16.psd, then save it as **Visual Solution.** Create a feathered selection so that the canvas resembles Figure B-33.

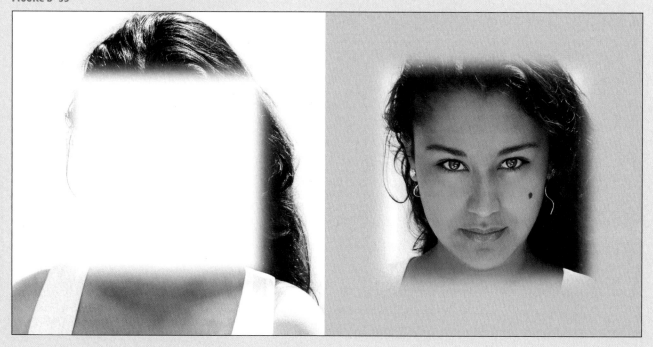

Working with Layers

Files You Will Need:

PS C-1.psd
PS C-2.psd
PS C-3.psd
PS C-4.psd
PS C-5.psd
PS C-6.psd
PS C-7.psd
PS C-8.psd
PS C-9.psd
PS C-10.psd

The Layers panel is one of Photoshop's greatest features because it allows you to segregate various art components onto different virtual layers within a single document. Working with layers allows you to apply various effects—like drop shadows or glows—to individual art components without affecting others. Layers give you options for positioning artwork in relation to other artwork and allow you to move that artwork without affecting the content on other layers. At MegaPixel, you're given artwork for a print ad for a local jewelry retailer. The artwork involves a **montage**: multiple art components overlapping to create a single composition. You prepare yourself to work extensively with layers and the Layers panel.

OBJECTIVES

Work with the Layers panel

Merge layers and manipulate opacity

Duplicate layers, delete layers, and paste new layers

Scale artwork

Flip and rotate artwork

Add an Outer Glow layer style

Add a Drop Shadow layer style

Work with a layer mask

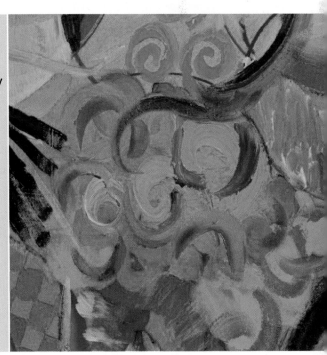

Working with the Layers Panel

The Layers panel houses all the layers in a document and offers you many options for manipulating those layers. Some basic operations you can do with the Layers panel and layered artwork is to hide or show various art components and move them independently of one another. 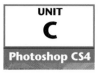 Jon asks that you spend a few minutes examining the supplied document. He asks that you examine the layer structure and move items around just to get a sense of how the montage has been built.

STEPS

Note: Before starting these steps, verify that the Tools panel and the Layers panel are the only two panels showing.

1. Open PS C-1.psd, then save it as Roman Holiday 1

2. Click the Layers panel list arrow, click Panel Options, click the medium Thumbnail Size option button, then click OK

   The thumbnails in the figures throughout this unit are the medium size.

3. Press and hold [Alt] (Win) or [option] (Mac), then click the Indicates layer visibility button 👁 on the Passport layer

   Only the artwork on the Passport layer is visible. Pressing and holding [Alt] (Win) or [option] (Mac) and clicking the Indicates layer visibility button shows only that layer and hides all other layers.

4. Click the Indicates layer visibility button 👁 on the Coin and Colosseum layers, then compare your screen to Figure C-1

   The artwork on the two layers becomes visible.

5. Make all the remaining layers visible

6. Click the Move tool ⯈⊹, click the Pen layer on the Layers panel, then click and drag the pen artwork to move it to the left side of the canvas

   Only the artwork on the selected layer moves.

7. Click the Couple layer to select it, press and hold [Ctrl] (Win) or ⌘ (Mac), then click the Couple Shadow layer so that both are selected

   Pressing and holding [Ctrl] (Win) or ⌘ (Mac) allows you to select multiple layers on the Layers panel.

8. Drag the Couple and Couple Shadow artwork to the upper-right corner of the canvas

   Because both layers are selected on the Layers panel, the artwork on both layers moves as you drag.

9. Target the Coin layer, then move the Coin artwork down so that its bottom edge is behind the title

   Compare your screen to Figure C-2. Your results will vary from the figure.

10. Click File on the Application bar, then click Revert

FIGURE C-1: Viewing the visible layers

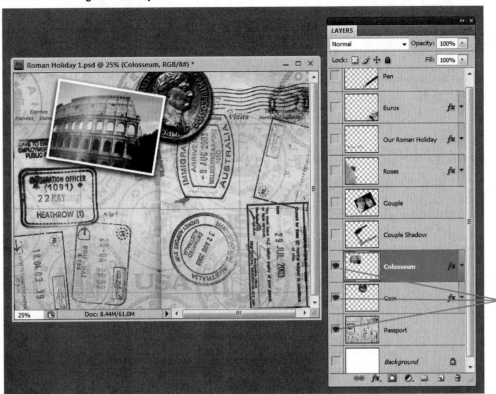

Three layers showing

FIGURE C-2: Canvas with repositioned artwork

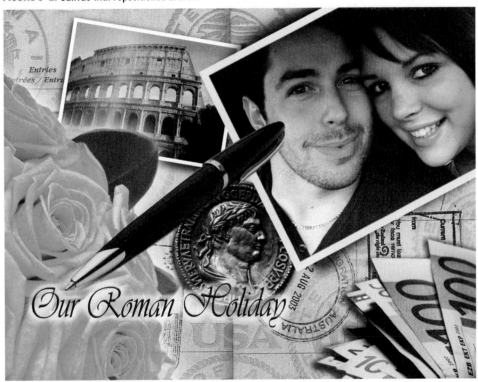

Life without layers

It seems quite hard to believe now, but in the early versions of Photoshop, there were no layers! It was possible to overlap various components of artwork, but once you deselected, those components would become embedded in the canvas. So, if the montage we worked on in this lesson was created in Photoshop 2.0, all of the elements would have existed on one canvas, one bed of pixels. If you think about that for a moment, you get a real sense of the true benefit of working with layers: the options to edit, rethink, and redesign.

Merging Layers and Manipulating Opacity

On the Layers panel, artwork on a top layer appears *in front* of artwork on layers beneath it. Thus, artwork on the bottom layer would be behind the artwork on layers above it. You can use the Layers panel to reorder layers and also to merge layers. When you merge multiple layers, separate artwork on those layers is merged onto one layer and can no longer be manipulated individually. In Photoshop, the term **opacity** refers to how opaque artwork is. For example, if artwork has 100% opacity, it is completely opaque—no part of it is transparent. Conversely, artwork with 0% opacity is completely transparent and thus invisible. In between the two extremes, artwork with 50% opacity would be visible, but any artwork on a layer or layers beneath it would be visible *through* it. ▆▆▆▆ You decide to experiment with reordering the layers in hopes of improving the impact of the montage. You also experiment with merging layers and reducing the opacity of various artwork components.

STEPS

1. Verify that all layers are visible on the Layers panel, then target the Coin layer

2. Drag the Coin layer above the Colosseum layer on the Layers panel until you see a horizontal black line, as shown in Figure C-3, then release the mouse pointer
    The coin artwork appears in front of the Colosseum artwork.

3. Click the Pen layer on the Layers panel, then drag it down below the Euros layer so that your canvas resembles Figure C-4

4. Target both the Coin and the Colosseum layers, click the Layers panel list arrow, then click Merge Layers
    The artwork is merged onto one layer as one piece of art.

5. Click the Move tool ▸⊕, then click and drag to move the artwork in any direction
    Both the Coin and Colosseum artwork move because they are now one piece of art on the same layer.

6. Click Edit on the Application bar, click Undo Move, then drag the Opacity slider on the Layers panel to 50%
    The Coin and Colosseum artwork becomes 50% transparent. The Opacity slider can set a layer's opacity to any percentage between 0% and 100%.

7. Target the Couple Shadow layer, then reduce the opacity to 75%

8. Target the Passport layer, then press [5]
    The opacity of the Passport layer is reduced to 50%.

9. Compare your canvas to Figure C-5, save your work, then close Roman Holiday 1.psd

FIGURE C-3: Moving the Coin layer above the Colosseum layer

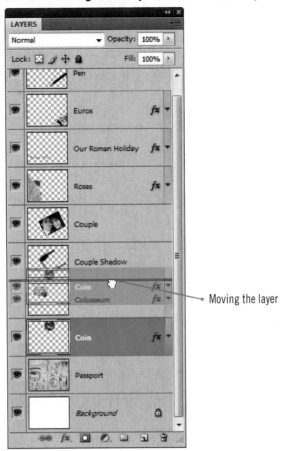

Moving the layer

FIGURE C-4: Moving the Pen layer beneath the Euros layer

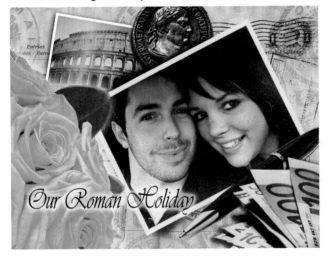

FIGURE C-5: Canvas with transparent artwork

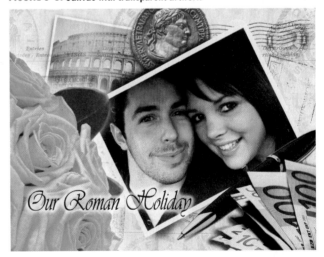

Merging layers and memory

The more layers in a file, the larger the file size. It follows logically that merging layers reduces file size. Remember though that merging layers is a commitment: once artwork is merged onto a single layer, it can't be unmerged later on in the project (other than by undoing, reverting, or using the History panel). For example, if you merge two layers then quit Photoshop, there will be no way to unmerge that artwork. Generally speaking, it's best to keep artwork segregated on different layers simply to keep your options open for any modifications you might need to make as your project evolves.

Duplicating, Deleting, and Pasting New Layers

Layers are created in Photoshop in a variety of ways. You can click the Create a new layer button on the Layers panel or use the New Layer command on the Layers panel menu. However, some of the most common ways that new layers are created in Photoshop are when you duplicate an existing layer or when you paste artwork copied from another file. Now that you've studied the layers in the document and made some changes to them, you decide to duplicate one layer to make a more interesting montage. Then Jon asks you to remove one piece of artwork and replace it with artwork from another file.

STEPS

1. **Open PS C-2.psd, save it as** Roman Holiday 2, **target the** Coin layer, **click the** Layers panel list arrow, **then click** Duplicate Layer

2. **Type** Top Coin **in the As text box, then click** OK

   A duplicate of the original artwork is created in the same position on a layer immediately above the targeted layer.

3. **Use the Move tool** ⬚ **or the arrow keys to reposition the Top Coin artwork as shown in Figure C-6**

QUICK TIP
Pressing [Ctrl][J] (Win) or ⌘[J] (Mac) is the fastest and easiest way to duplicate a layer.

4. **With the Top Coin layer still targeted, press [Ctrl][J] (Win) or** ⌘**[J] (Mac)**

   The layer is duplicated.

5. **Double-click the** Top Coin copy name, **type** Bottom Coin **to rename the layer, press [Enter] (Win) or [return] (Mac), drag the** Bottom Coin layer **beneath the Couple Shadow layer, then reposition the Bottom Coin artwork, as shown in Figure C-7**

QUICK TIP
Click the Don't show again check box in the warning dialog box if you don't want to be asked to confirm that you want to delete future layers.

6. **Target the** Colosseum layer, **click the** Delete layer button 🗑 **on the Layers panel, then click** Yes **to confirm that you want to delete the layer**

7. **Open Colosseum.psd, then view each layer separately to understand how the file was built**

8. **Show both layers, select all, click** Edit **on the Application bar, then click** Copy Merged

   Clicking Copy Merged copies the visible image on the canvas as a single image. In other words, Copy Merged copies a combined, or "merged," result of all the visible layers.

9. **Close Colosseum.psd without saving changes, return to the Roman Holiday 2.psd file, target the** Euros layer, **click** Edit **on the Application bar, then click** Paste

   The artwork is pasted as a new layer, named Layer 1, directly above the targeted Euros layer.

10. **Name the new layer** Colosseum, **move it to the position shown in Figure C-8, then save your work**

Pasting new layers

Whenever you copy artwork and then paste, the copied artwork is always pasted onto a new layer. That new layer is always created above the targeted layer on the Layers panel. This is a great feature in Photoshop, because you can always be confident that when you paste artwork, the new artwork will always be isolated on its own layer and will not directly affect any existing artwork in the file. If you use the Fit on Screen command on the View menu so that your entire canvas is visible before you paste, when you paste, the pasted artwork will be centered on the canvas. This knowledge can be very useful for alignment considerations.

FIGURE C-6: Repositioning the Top Coin artwork

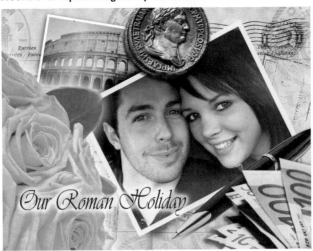

FIGURE C-7: Repositioning the Bottom Coin artwork

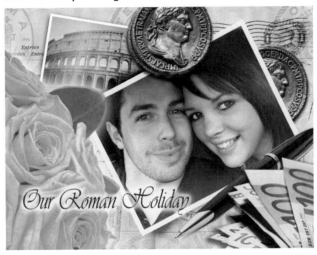

FIGURE C-8: Positioning the Colosseum artwork

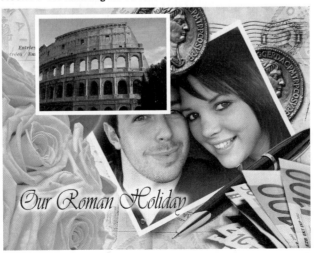

Scaling Artwork

One of the great features of Photoshop is the ability to **transform** artwork—move, scale, rotate, flip, and distort artwork. Transforming skills become important especially when creating a montage, because montages involve specific positioning relationships between elements. **Scaling**—a term for resizing artwork— is one of the most basic transformations and one you'll use often. Now that the montage contains all of the elements that you want to work with, Jon asks you to reduce the size of the Colosseum and the Bottom Coin images.

QUICK TIP

Throughout this lesson, keep an eye on the W and H text boxes on the Options bar to see the percentage of enlargement or reduction you are making to the width and height of the selected artwork.

QUICK TIP

If you activate the Maintain aspect ratio button (the Lock icon) between the W and H text boxes, any change you make to one will automatically be made to the other.

QUICK TIP

Press [Enter] (Win) or [return] (Mac) to apply a transformation quickly.

QUICK TIP

[Ctrl][T] (Win) or [⌘][T] (Mac) are the quick keys for accessing the Transform command.

1. **Verify that the Colosseum layer is targeted, click Edit on the Application bar, point to Transform, then click Scale**

   The transform bounding box appears around the artwork. The bounding box has a square handle at each corner that you click and drag to transform artwork. The handles are sometimes referred to as resizing handles.

2. **Position the mouse pointer on the lower-right corner handle until a double-headed arrow appears, click and drag in many directions to modify the image, then release the mouse pointer**

   Clicking and dragging the corner handle allows you to enlarge, reduce, and/or distort the image.

3. **Undo your last step, position the mouse pointer on the lower-right corner handle, press and hold [Shift], click and drag in different directions, then release the mouse pointer**

   The [Shift] key constrains the scale proportionately. You can enlarge or reduce the artwork, but you can't modify the proportional relationship between the width and height.

4. **Undo the move, then note the crosshair icon in the middle of the bounding box**

   The crosshair icon is automatically positioned at the center of the bounding box and therefore at the center of the artwork.

5. **On the Options bar, double-click the W text box, type 80, press [Tab], type 80 in the H text box, press [Tab], then compare your screen to Figure C-9**

   The artwork is scaled 80% from at the crosshair, which is at the artwork's center point. By default, when you enter a scale value in the W and/or H text boxes on the Options bar, the artwork is scaled using the crosshair icon as the point of origin for the scale.

6. **Click the Move tool ▸⊕, then click Apply to apply the scale**

   You can press [Esc] to cancel a transformation.

7. **Target the Bottom Coin layer, press [Ctrl][T] (Win) or ⌘[T] (Mac), then drag the crosshair icon to the position shown in Figure C-10**

8. **Press and hold [Shift][Alt] (Win) or [Shift][option] (Mac), position the mouse pointer over the lower-left handle, drag to experiment with resizing the coin artwork, then release the mouse pointer**

   Pressing and holding the [Alt] (Win) or [option] (Mac) key ensures that any transformation will be executed using the location of the crosshair as the point of origin. The [Shift] key is used in this step to constrain the width/height proportion of the artwork while scaling.

9. **Undo the move, double-click the W text box on the Options bar, type 67, press [Tab], type 67 in the H text box, press [Tab], then compare your screen to Figure C-11**

10. **Click the Move tool ▸⊕, click Apply, then save your work**

FIGURE C-9: Using the Options bar to scale the artwork

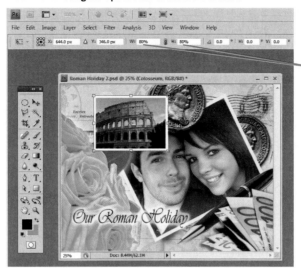

Width and Height text boxes on the Options bar

FIGURE C-10: Moving the crosshair icon

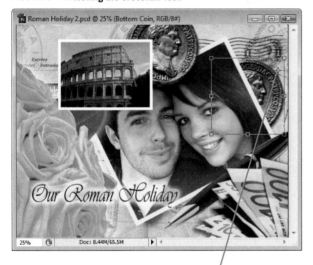

Crosshair icon determines the point of origin for a transformation

FIGURE C-11: Scaling the artwork from the relocated crosshair icon

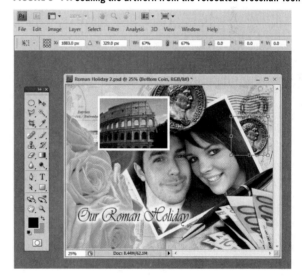

Understanding the point of origin in a transformation

The point of origin defines the point from which a transformation occurs. For example, let's say you created a 2" × 2" square and you reduced it by 50% using its center point as the point of origin. In this case all four sides of the square would move equally towards the center until the new size of the square was 1" × 1". Before you transform, move the crosshair icon to the point that you want to remain fixed, then transform the artwork using that point as the point of origin for the transformation.

Remember that the crosshair icon determines the point of origin automatically only when you enter values directly into the Control panel. If you transform by hand by clicking and dragging the bounding box, you must press and hold [Alt] (Win) or [option] (Mac) to transform using the location of the crosshair as the point of origin.

Flipping and Rotating Artwork

Flipping and rotating are two transformations that can be very useful when creating a montage of various images. **Flipping** artwork creates a mirror image of the artwork. You can flip images horizontally or vertically. **Rotating** moves an object clockwise or counterclockwise around its center point, much like a pinwheel spins. You can rotate an image by hand or by entering a specific rotation value on the Options bar. ▓▓▓ Jon directs you to flip the main image in the montage and asks that you rotate the coins in the image so that it is not so obvious that they are duplicate images.

STEPS

1. Target the Colosseum layer, click Edit on the Application bar, point to Transform, then click Rotate

   The transform bounding box appears around the artwork.

2. Position the mouse pointer outside of the bounding box so that a curved double-arrow icon appears, click and drag to rotate the artwork to various rotations, then release the mouse pointer

> **QUICK TIP**
> Entering a positive value in the Set rotation text box rotates artwork in a clockwise direction. Entering a negative value in the Set rotation text box rotates artwork in a counterclockwise direction.

3. Undo the move, type 17 in the Set rotation text box on the Options bar, apply the transformation, then compare your result to Figure C-12

   The image is rotated 17° around its center point.

4. Drag the Colosseum layer down so that it is immediately above the Passport layer in the Layers panel

5. Target both the Couple and the Couple Shadow layers, click Edit on the Application bar, point to Transform, then click Flip Horizontal

   The artwork on both layers is flipped horizontally.

6. Verify that the Couple and Couple Shadow layers are still selected, add the Bottom Coin layer to the selection, then move the artwork down slightly to the position shown in Figure C-13

> **QUICK TIP**
> Pressing and holding [Shift] when rotating rotates the artwork in 15° increments.

7. Click the Bottom Coin layer so that it is the only targeted layer, press [Ctrl][T] (Win) or ⌘[T] (Mac), press and hold [Shift], then click and drag to rotate the bottom coin −45 degrees

   The bottom coin is rotated and no longer appears as an obvious duplicate of the larger coin.

8. Apply the rotation, then compare your artwork to Figure C-14

9. Save your work

Rotating vs. flipping

Rotating and flipping are two very different transformations that produce different results. You can compare rotating artwork with the tire on your car turning on a specific point. By default, artwork in Photoshop is rotated around its center point unless you move the crosshair icon to a new location. When you flip artwork, you create a mirror image of the artwork. Photoshop offers you the ability to flip artwork horizontally—across an imaginary vertical axis—or vertically—across an imaginary horizontal axis. Flipping an image can produce odd results, especially when the image shows peoples' faces. Nobody's face is perfectly symmetrical, and flipping a face can yield unflattering results. Also remember, if there's text anywhere in an image when flipped, that text is going to read backwards, which is a dead giveaway that the image has been flipped! If you want to flip an image, target the layer that the image is on, click Edit on the Application bar, point to Transform, then click Flip Horizontal or Flip Vertical.

FIGURE C-12: Rotating the Colosseum artwork

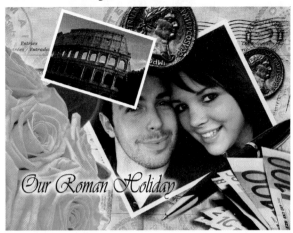

FIGURE C-13: Moving the artwork on three layers

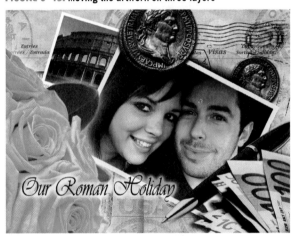

FIGURE C-14: Rotating the bottom coin artwork

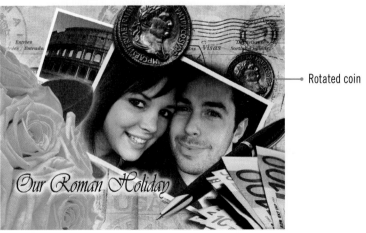

Rotated coin

Adding an Outer Glow Layer Style

Layer styles are built-in effects that you can apply to layers; they include glows, shadows, bevels, embosses, and chiseled edges, among many others. When you apply a layer style to a layer, all the artwork on that layer inherits the layer style. Layer styles are listed on the Layers panel beneath the layer they've been applied to, and as with all layers, they can be hidden or shown. Jon asks you to apply a gold outer glow to the pen artwork, similar to the glow around the bouquet of roses.

STEPS

1. **Target the Pen layer, click Layer on the Application bar, point to Layer Style, then click Outer Glow**

   The Layer Style dialog box opens. Note that on the left side is a list of all the available layer styles and that Outer Glow is checked and highlighted. The settings you see in the dialog box are settings for an outer glow.

   QUICK TIP

   Move the Layer Style dialog box to the side, if necessary, so that you can see the pen artwork on the canvas.

2. **Enter the values shown in Figure C-15 and verify that the Preview check box is checked**

   QUICK TIP

   You can also choose a glow color by placing the mouse pointer over the canvas and then clicking a color with the eyedropper pointer when the Color Picker dialog box is open.

3. **Click the Set color of glow square, type 253 in the R text box, type 226 in the G text box, type 162 in the B text box, click OK to close the Color Picker, then click OK to close the Layer Style dialog box**

4. **Compare your canvas and Layers panel to Figure C-16**

   The Outer Glow layer style is listed on the Layers panel as a component of the Pen layer; the Indicates layer effects icon appears on the layer, indicating a layer style has been applied to it.

   QUICK TIP

   Click the small black triangle to the right of the layer to hide or show the layer effects for that layer.

5. **Hide and show the Outer Glow layer style on the Layers panel to hide and show the effect**

6. **Double-click the Outer Glow layer style on the Layers panel to open the Layer Style dialog box**

   The Layer Style dialog box opens with the Outer Glow layer style settings.

7. **Drag the Opacity, Spread, and Size sliders to see the effect that each has on the outer glow effect, then click Cancel to close the Layer Style dialog box without saving the changes**

8. **Save your work**

FIGURE C-15: Settings for an Outer Glow layer style

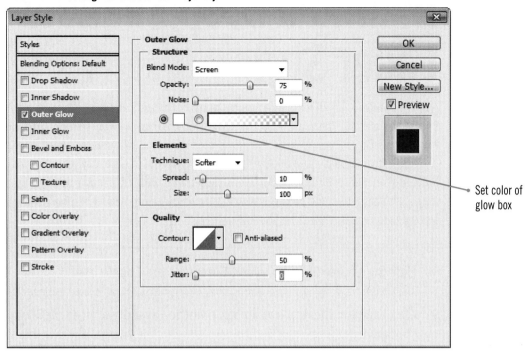

Set color of glow box

FIGURE C-16: Viewing the layer style on the canvas and in the Layers panel

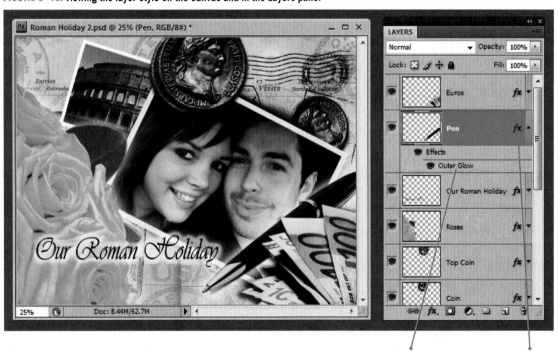

Outer Glow layer style
listed on Layers panel

Indicates layer effects icon

Adding a Drop Shadow Layer Style

A **drop shadow**, an effect where artwork appears to cast a shadow, is one of the most commonly used Photoshop effects. There are many methods for creating a drop shadow, and one method is to use Photoshop's Drop Shadow layer style. One of the many great features about layer styles is that you can copy them from one layer to another, which can save lots of time and speed up your work. See Table C-2 for an explanation of Drop Shadow layer style settings. Jon asks that you use a Drop Shadow layer style as an alternate to the drop shadow that is already being used for the main artwork in the montage. He also asks that you apply a Drop Shadow layer style to the Colosseum artwork.

STEPS

1. **Hide the Couple Shadow layer, then target the Couple layer**
   The Couple Shadow layer is not a drop shadow layer style. It was created using the Brush tool.

2. **Click Layer on the Application bar, point to Layer Style, then click Drop Shadow**
   The Layer Style dialog box opens, showing settings for the Drop Shadow layer style.

3. **Verify that the Preview check box is checked, then enter the values shown in Figure C-17**

4. **Click OK, then compare your canvas to Figure C-18**

5. **Hide and show the Drop Shadow layer style on the Layers panel to hide and show the effect**

6. **Press and hold [Alt] (Win) or [option] (Mac), drag the Indicates layer effects icon 𝑓𝑥 to the Colosseum layer, then release the mouse pointer when a black frame surrounds the Colosseum layer**
   As shown in Figure C-19, the drop shadow appears behind the Colosseum artwork, and the Drop Shadow layer style is added to the Colosseum layer.

7. **Double-click the Drop Shadow layer style on the Colosseum layer to open the Layer Style dialog box, change the Spread value to 12 and the Size value to 40, then click OK**
   The drop shadow on the Colosseum artwork is updated.

8. **Save your work**

TABLE C-2: Drop Shadow layer style options

setting	purpose
Angle	Determines the lighting angle at which the effect is applied to the layer
Distance	Specifies the offset distance for the shadow—how far it is away from the artwork
Spread	Determines the size of the shadow effect before the edge blurs
Size	Controls the size of the blur at the edge of the effect

FIGURE C-17: Settings for a Drop Shadow layer style

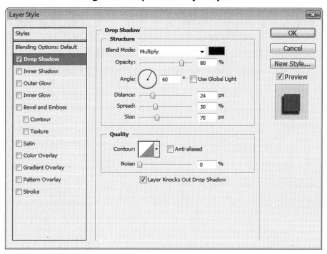

FIGURE C-18: Viewing the Drop Shadow layer style on the canvas and in the Layers panel

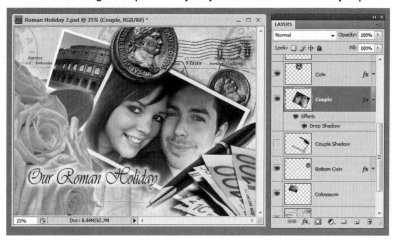

FIGURE C-19: Viewing the Drop Shadow layer style behind the Colosseum artwork and in the Layers panel

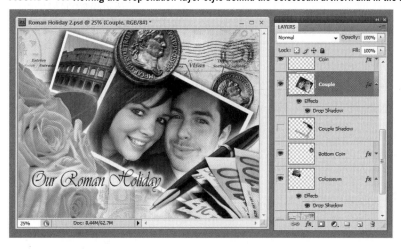

Working with a Layer Mask

A **layer mask** allows you to define which areas of artwork on a single layer are visible, not visible, or partly visible. The basic concept of a layer mask is very simple: White areas of the layer mask represent art on the layer that is 100% visible. Black areas of the layer mask represent art on the layer that is 100% **masked** and therefore invisible. Gray areas of the layer mask represent art on the layer that is semi-transparent. You can use many methods to apply black, white, or gray to a layer mask. One common method is to use the Brush tool to paint in the layer mask, thus adjusting the opacity of the artwork by hand. You can set size and hardness options for the Brush tool on the Options bar. Jon feels that the green leaves on the bouquet of roses might be distracting to the overall color palette of the montage. He asks that you use a layer mask to provide the client with two alternative montages: one with the leaves and one without the leaves.

STEPS

1. **Target the Roses layer, click Layer on the Application bar, point to Layer Mask, then click Reveal All**

   As shown in Figure C-20, a layer mask is added to the layer. By default the new layer mask is targeted, which is indicated by the double-lined black border around the mask. When you click Reveal All, an all-white layer mask is added to the layer; therefore, all of the artwork on the layer remains visible, or revealed. The Hide All type of layer mask creates an all-black layer mask in which all of the artwork is hidden.

2. **Click the small black triangle on the Roses layer to reveal the layer effects, then hide the Outer Glow layer style on the Roses layer**

3. **Click the Default Foreground and Background Colors button 🔲 on the Tools panel, verify that the foreground color is set to black, then click the Brush tool 🖌**

4. **On the Options bar, verify that the Opacity setting is 100%, click the Brush list arrow to open the Brush Preset picker, set the Master Diameter to 15 px, then set the Hardness to 30%**

5. **Zoom in so that the top green leaf in the bouquet is large on your screen, then paint over the leaf until the entire leaf is no longer visible**

   As you paint, the areas you paint become invisible because you are painting black in the layer mask. It is important that you understand that because the layer mask is targeted in the Layers panel, you are painting in the layer mask, not on the canvas itself.

6. **Scroll, then paint to mask out the bottom leaf**

   Your canvas and Layers panel should resemble Figure C-21.

7. **Press and hold [Alt] (Win) or [option] (Mac), click the layer mask thumbnail on the Layers panel, then compare your canvas and Layers panel to Figure C-22**

   Pressing and holding [Alt] (Win) or [option] (Mac) and clicking the layer mask thumbnail displays the layer mask on the canvas.

8. **Click the Roses Layer thumbnail to the left of the layer mask thumbnail**

   The canvas displays the artwork on the layer. The layer mask is no longer targeted, but it is still active.

9. **Press and hold [Shift], then click the layer mask thumbnail on the Roses layer**

   As shown in Figure C-23, the layer mask is inactive, and the green leaves are visible once again.

10. **Save your work, close Roman Holiday 2.psd, then exit Photoshop**

FIGURE C-20: Layer mask added to the Roses layer

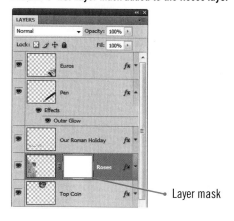

Layer mask

FIGURE C-21: Artwork with both leaves masked out

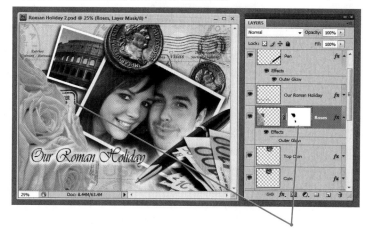

Masked pixels in the layer
mask and on the artwork

FIGURE C-22: Viewing the layer mask

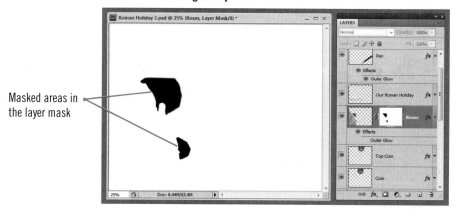

Masked areas in
the layer mask

FIGURE C-23: Deactivating the layer mask

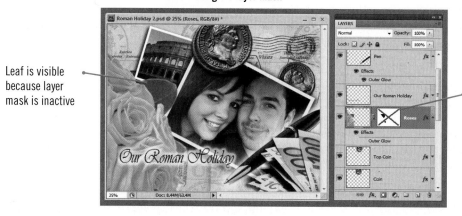

Leaf is visible
because layer
mask is inactive

Red X indicates layer
mask is inactive

Three Brush tool techniques

When you click the Brush tool on the Tools panel, you can practice these three techniques that will make you much more effective with the brush:

1. Press the right bracket key repeatedly to increase the brush size.

2. Press the left bracket key repeatedly to decrease the brush size.

3. [Shift]-click the brush to cover large areas. Click the brush once anywhere on the canvas. Move the brush pointer to a different location. Press and hold [Shift], then click the brush at the new location. The Brush tool will paint from the first click and connect to the second click.

Practice

▼ CONCEPTS REVIEW

FIGURE C-24

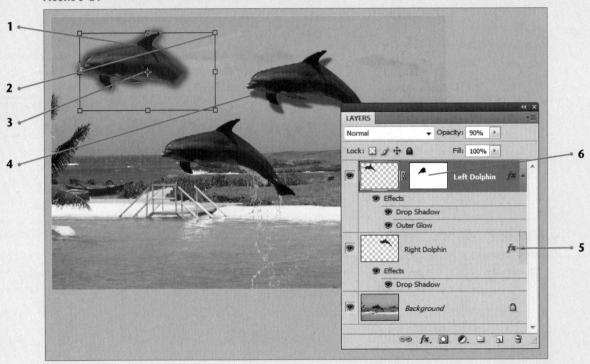

1. Which item points to a selection handle?
2. Which item points to a drop shadow effect?
3. Which item points to the Indicates layer effects icon?
4. Which item points to an outer glow effect?
5. Which item points to a layer mask?
6. Which item points to the point of origin icon?

Match each term with the statement that best describes it.

7. **Transform**
8. **Layer style**
9. **Layer mask**
10. **Opacity**
11. **Flipping**
12. **Merging**
13. **Indicates layer effects icon**

a. Used to affect image opacity in specific areas
b. Appears when layer styles are applied
c. Transformation that creates a mirror image
d. The measure of how opaque artwork is
e. Effects such a drop shadow or an outer glow
f. Condensing layered artwork onto one layer
g. To move, scale, or rotate an image

Select the best answer from the list of choices.

14. Which of the following is not a benefit of using layers?

a. Organization

b. Segregation

c. Editing ability

d. None of the above

15. Which of the following is not a layer style?

a. Outer Glow

b. Blur

c. Drop Shadow

d. Inner Shadow

16. Which of the following is not a transformation option?

a. Rotate

b. Blend

c. Scale

d. Move

17. Which of the following is not true about the Opacity slider?

a. It can be applied to specific areas of a layer.

b. It can be applied at 52%.

c. It can be used to make pixels semitransparent.

d. It is manipulated only in the Layers panel.

18. Which of the following is not true about a layer mask?

a. It can be used to manipulate opacity in specific areas of a layer.

b. One layer mask affects all areas of the layer.

c. It is created by default when you create a new layer.

d. It can be shown and hidden.

19. Which of the following is true about a layer mask?

a. An all-black layer mask means all the artwork on the layer is visible.

b. An all-white layer mask means all the artwork on the layer has 0% opacity.

c. Pixels in a layer mask are either black or white.

d. A light gray layer mask means all the artwork on the layer is semitransparent.

▼ SKILLS REVIEW

1. Work with the Layers panel.

a. Open PS C-3.psd, then save it as **Shining Future 1**.

b. Click the Layers panel list arrow, click Panel Options, choose the medium Thumbnail Size option button, then click OK.

c. Press and hold [Alt] (Win) or [option] (Mac), then click the Indicates layer visibility button on the Flower layer.

d. Click the Indicates layer visibility button on the Background and Flower Shadow layers.

e. Make all the remaining layers visible.

f. Click the Move tool, click the Moon layer on the Layers panel, then drag the moon artwork to move it to the right side of the canvas behind the flower.

g. Click the Child layer to select it, press and hold [Ctrl] (Win) or ⌘ (Mac), then click the Child Shadow layer so that both are selected.

h. Drag to move the Child and Child Shadow artwork up so that the child is "standing" in the water.

i. Target the Type artwork, then move it to the left so it is outside of the flower's shadow.

j. Save your work, then close Shining Future 1.psd.

2. Merge layers and manipulate opacity.

a. Open PS C-4.psd, then save it as **Shining Future 2**.

b. Verify that all layers are visible, then target the Moon layer on the Layers panel.

c. Drag the Moon layer down below the Flower Shadow layer on the Layers panel.

d. Click the Type layer, then drag it to the top of the Layers panel so that it is the top layer.

e. Target both the Flower and the Purple Center layers, click the Layers panel list arrow, then click Merge Layers.

f. Click the Move tool, then drag the merged artwork to the right of the canvas.

g. Undo the move, target the Moon layer, then drag the Opacity slider on the Layers panel to 50%.

h. Target the Dolphin layer, then reduce the Opacity to 75%.

i. Verify that the Move tool is selected, then press [0].

j. Save your work, then close Shining Future 2.psd.

3. Duplicate layers, delete layers, and pasting new layers.

   a. Open PS C-5.psd, save it as **A Bright Shining Future**, target the Moon layer, click Layer on the Application bar, then click Duplicate Layer.

   b. Type **Middle Moon** in the Name text box, then click OK.

   c. With the Middle Moon layer still targeted, press [Ctrl][J] (Win) or ⌘[J] (Mac).

   d. Double-click the Middle Moon Copy name, then rename the layer as **Little Moon**.

   e. Target the Purple Center layer, click the Delete layer button on the Layers panel, then click Yes to confirm that you want to delete the layer.

   f. Open Globe.psd, then note that the file has three layers.

   g. Click Select on the Application bar, click Load Selection, click the Channel list arrow, click Globe Only, then click OK.

   h. Click Edit on the Application bar, then click Copy Merged.

   i. Close Globe.psd without saving changes, return to the A Bright Shining Future.psd file, target the Flower layer, then paste.

   j. Name the new layer **Globe**, move it to the position shown in Figure C-25, then save your work.

4. Scale artwork.

   a. Verify that the Little Moon layer is targeted, click Edit on the Application bar, point to Transform, then click Scale.

   b. Position the mouse pointer over the lower-right corner handle until a double-headed arrow appears, click and drag in many directions to modify the image, then release the mouse pointer.

   c. Undo the move, position the mouse pointer over the lower-right corner handle, press and hold [Shift], click and drag in different directions, then release the mouse pointer.

   d. Undo the move, then note the crosshair icon in the middle of the bounding box.

   e. On the Options bar, double-click the W text box, type **10**, press [Tab], type **10** in the H text box, then press [Tab].

   f. Click the Move tool, then click Apply to apply the scale.

   g. Target the Middle Moon layer, then press [Ctrl][T] (Win) or ⌘[T] (Mac).

   h. Press and hold [Shift][Alt] (Win) or [Shift][option] (Mac), position the mouse pointer over the lower-right selection handle, click and drag to experiment with different sizes, then release the mouse pointer.

   i. Undo the move, double-click the W text box, type **28**, press [Tab], type **28** in the H text box, press [Tab], then apply the scale.

   j. Click the Move tool, move the Little Moon and Middle Moon artwork to the positions shown in Figure C-26, then save your work.

5. Flip and rotate artwork.

   a. Target the Middle Moon layer, click Edit on the Application bar, point to Transform, then click Rotate.

   b. Position the mouse pointer outside of the bounding box so that a curved double-arrow icon appears, click and drag to rotate the artwork to various rotations, then release the mouse pointer.

   c. Undo the move, type **27** in the Set rotation text box on the Options bar, then apply the transformation.

   d. Target both the Child and the Child Shadow layers, click Edit on the Application bar, point to Transform, then click Flip Horizontal.

   e. Target the Little Moon layer, press [Ctrl][T] (Win) or ⌘[T] (Mac), press and hold [Shift], then drag the rotate pointer to rotate the artwork –45 degrees.

   f. Apply the rotation, then save your work.

6. Add an Outer Glow layer style.

   a. Target the Dolphin layer, click Layer on the Application bar, point to Layer Style, then click Outer Glow.

   b. Verify that the Preview check box is checked, set the Blend mode to screen, set the Opacity to 75%, set the Noise to 0, set the Spread to 27%, then set the Size to 40.

   c. Click the Set color of glow square, type **255** in the R text box, **200** in the G text box, **255** in the B text box, click OK to close the Color Picker, then click OK to close the Layer Style dialog box.

d. Hide and show the Outer Glow layer style on the Layers panel to hide and show the effect on the artwork.

e. Double-click the Outer Glow layer style on the Layers panel to open the Layer Style dialog box.

f. Drag the Opacity, Spread, and Size sliders to see the effect that each has on the outer glow effect, then click Cancel to close the Layer Style dialog box without applying the changes.

g. Save your work, then compare your screen to Figure C-27.

7. Add a Drop Shadow layer style.

a. Target the Type layer.

b. Click Layer on the Application bar, point to Layer Style, then click Drop Shadow.

c. Verify that the Preview check box is checked, set the Blend Mode to Multiply, set the Opacity to 100%, set the Distance to 9, set both the Spread and Size to 0, then click OK.

d. Toggle the Drop Shadow layer style on and off in the Layers panel to hide and show the effect.

e. Target the Dolphin layer, press and hold [Alt] (Win) or [option] (Mac), click and drag the Indicates layer effects icon to the Globe layer, then release the mouse pointer when a black frame appears around the Globe layer.

f. Save your work.

8. Work with a layer mask.

a. Target the Moon layer, click Layer on the Application bar, point to Layer Mask, then click Reveal All.

b. Click the Default Foreground and Background Colors button on the Tools panel, then click the Brush tool.

c. On the Options bar, verify that the Opacity setting is 100%, click the Brush list arrow to open the Preset Brush picker, set the Master Diameter to 125 px, then set the Hardness to 40%.

d. Paint over the bottom third of the moon so that it is no longer visible.

e. Press and hold [Alt] (Win) or [option] (Mac), then click the layer mask thumbnail in the Layers panel to view the mask.

f. Click the Moon layer thumbnail to the left of the layer mask thumbnail to view the artwork again.

g. Press and hold [Shift], then click the layer mask thumbnail on the Moon layer to make it inactive.

h. Press and hold [Shift], then click the layer mask thumbnail on the Moon layer to make it active.

i. Compare your results to Figure C-27.

j. Save your work, close A Bright Shining Future.psd, then exit Photoshop.

FIGURE C-25

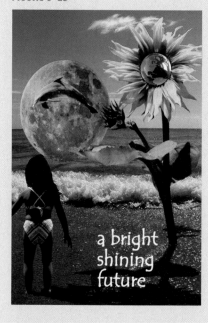

FIGURE C-26

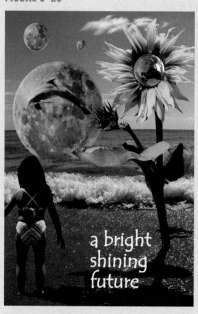

FIGURE C-27

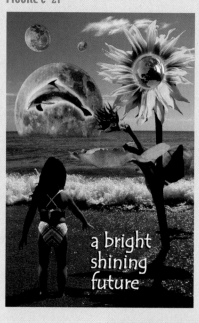

▼ INDEPENDENT CHALLENGE 1

The Web Design department at your advertising agency has asked you to create a drop shadow to create a "white on white" effect that they will be using for graphics on a Web site they are building.

a. Open PS C-6.psd, then save it as **Roman Numerals**.

b. Hide the Background layer to see the contents of the XVII layer, show the Background layer again, then target the XVII layer.

c. Click Layer on the Application bar, point to Layer Style, then click Drop Shadow.

d. Verify that the Preview check box is checked, set the Opacity to 75%, set the Distance to 34, set the Spread to 0, set the Size to 40, then click OK.

e. Click Layer on the Application bar, point to Layer Style, then click Stroke.

f. Experiment with the Size slider to see the effect on the XVII artwork.

g. Enter the values shown in Figure C-28 then click OK.

h. Save your work, compare your result to Figure C-29, then close Roman Numerals.psd.

FIGURE C-28

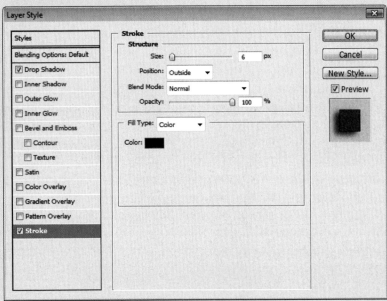

FIGURE C-29

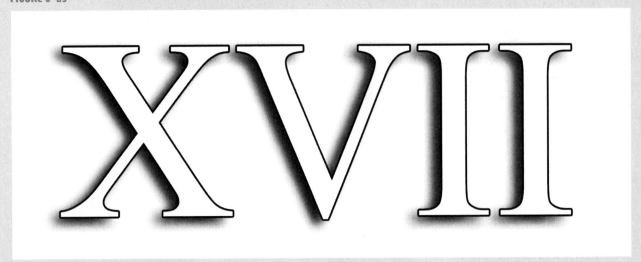

▼ INDEPENDENT CHALLENGE 2

The Web design department at your advertising agency is designing a splash page for a Web site that shows an image of a dolphin in front of a large moon. You are asked to copy the dolphin image into the moon file, then use a layer mask to remove the background from the dolphin image.

a. Open PS C-7.psd, then save it as **Dolphin Moon**.

b. Open Dolphin Sky.psd, select all, copy, then close Dolphin Sky.psd.

c. Return to Dolphin Moon.psd, paste, then name the new layer **Dolphin**.

d. Click Layer on the Application bar, point to Layer Mask, then click Reveal All.

e. Show the default colors on the Tools panel, then click the Brush tool.

f. On the Options bar, verify that the Opacity is set to 100%, change the Master Diameter to 40 px, then set the Hardness to 80%.

g. Paint over the big areas of blue sky to mask them out.

h. Zoom in on the dolphin's head, reduce the Master Diameter of the Brush to 7 px, then paint along the edges of the dolphin to remove the sky completely. (*Hint*: Use the Brush skills from the Clues to Use in Lesson 8 to help you work more effectively. Use the Hand tool to scroll around the magnified image.)

i. Compare your result to Figure C-30, save your work, the close Dolphin Moon.psd.

FIGURE C-30

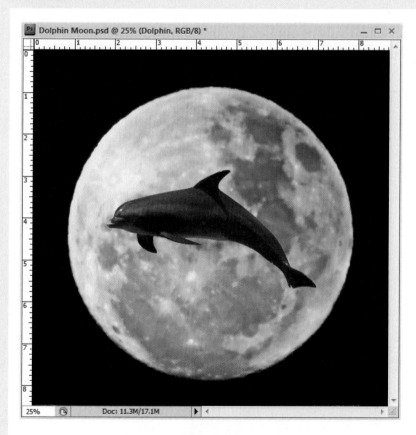

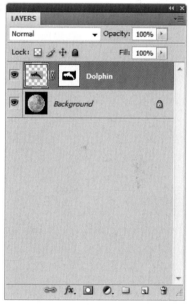

▼ INDEPENDENT CHALLENGE 3

You have been asked to take over the design of a splash page for an important client. You are given the artwork that the Web Design department has created so far, along with notes on how to finish the job.

a. Open PS C-8.psd, then save it as **Double Dolphins**.

b. Drag the Green Moon layer beneath the Purple Moon layer.

c. Target the Dolphin layer, then duplicate the layer.

d. Rename the new layer **Small Dolphin**.

e. Click the Move tool, press and hold [Shift], then click and drag the Small Dolphin artwork straight down and center it over the Green Moon artwork.

f. Select both the Green Moon layer and the Small Dolphin layer.

g. Scale the artwork 50%.

h. Save your work, then compare your canvas to Figure C-31.

Advanced Challenge Exercise

- Target the Small Dolphin and Green Moon layers.
- Rotate them 180 degrees.
- Target the Dolphin and Purple Moon layers.
- Flip them horizontally.

i. Close Double Dolphins.psd, then exit Photoshop.

FIGURE C-31

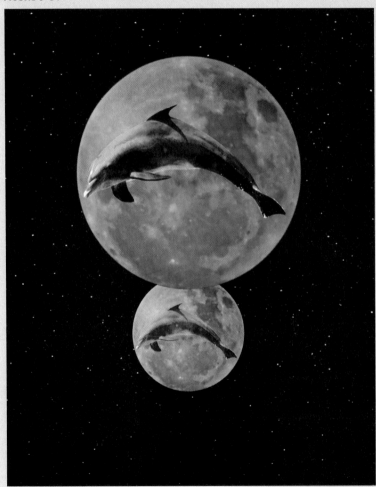

▼ REAL WORLD INDEPENDENT CHALLENGE

It's the end of the summer and you have some great photos to share with family and friends. Rather than just send out an individual photo, you decide to make a montage of three photos, two of them inset into a larger photo.

a. Open PS C-9.psd, then save it as **Sisters Postcard**.

b. Open Jenny.tif, select all, copy, then close Jenny.tif.

c. Paste the artwork into Sisters Postcard.psd, then rename the layer **Jenny**.

d. Open Annie.tif, select all, copy, then close Annie.tif.

e. Paste the artwork into Sisters Postcard.psd, then rename the layer **Annie**.

f. Move the Jenny artwork to the upper-right corner.

g. Scale the Jenny artwork so that it fits into the upper-right corner without overlapping the girls in the main image.

h. Move the Annie artwork to the lower-left corner.

i. Scale the Annie artwork so that it fits into the lower-left corner over the girl's legs.

j. Add a light yellow outer glow layer style to the Jenny artwork.

k. Copy the layer style from the Jenny artwork to the Annie artwork.

Advanced Challenge Exercise

■ Double-click the Outer Glow layer on the Annie layer, then drag the Layer Style dialog box to the right so that you can see the canvas.

■ Click the Set color of glow box in the Layer Style dialog box.

■ Position the eyedropper pointer over the pink stripe in the little girl's dress, then click.

■ Close the Color Picker dialog box, then close the Layer Style dialog box.

l. Compare your result to Figure C-32, then save your work.

FIGURE C-32

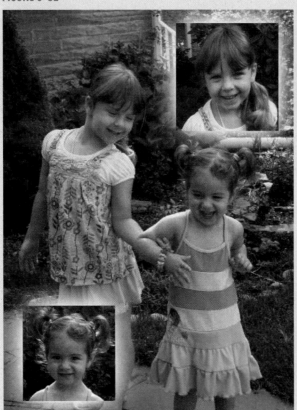

▼ VISUAL WORKSHOP

Open PS C-10.psd, then save it as **Three Glowing Globes**. Reorder the layers and move the globes to the position shown in Figure C-33. Add a gold Outer Glow layer style to the large gold globe. Copy the Outer Glow layer style from the Gold Globe layer to the Pink Globe and the Blue Globe layers. Change the color of the glow on the two smaller globes to match the figure.

FIGURE C-33

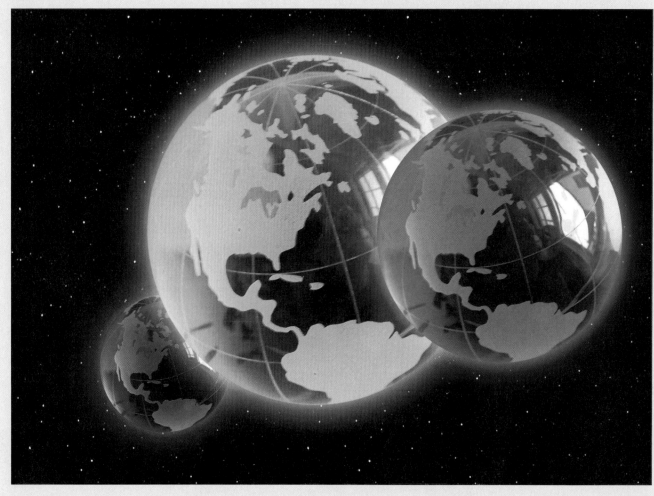

Working with Type and Gradients

When people think of Photoshop, usually their first thought is of images, photographs, and special effects. But another great Photoshop feature is the ability to create sophisticated typographical effects. Photoshop makes it easy to create classic effects like beveled and embossed text, chiseled text, and text that shines as though it were made of chrome. Even better, you can combine type with photographic images to produce truly unique typographical designs. When you start working extensively with type, you often find yourself working with gradients as well. **Gradients** are blends between two or more colors, and they are really effective with type and typography. A white-to-black gradient can add weight to a title, or a green-to-yellow gradient can make for a vibrant headline that appears to glow. Gradients offer so many more options than a simple solid color for filling type. 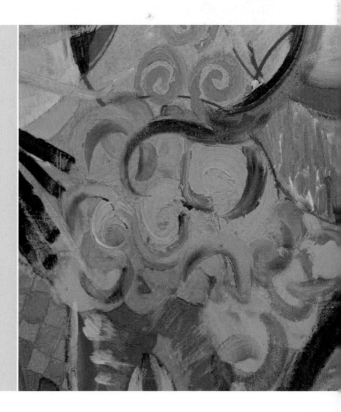 Jon gives you a number of different Photoshop projects that all involve working with type.

OBJECTIVES

Set type

Lock transparent pixels

Create bevel and emboss effects on type

Apply gloss contours to layer styles

Create a double emboss effect

Apply a gradient

Create a new gradient

Clip a gradient into type

Clip imagery into type

Fade type

Setting Type

Adobe has outfitted Photoshop with all the text editing capabilities you'd expect from any top-notch word processing or layout package. When you create type in Photoshop, it is "live type" just like in any other application; you can select it, copy it, paste it, and so on. The **Character panel** is command central for formatting type in Photoshop. You can do what you need to do all in one place: set the typeface, the size, the tracking, the kerning—all the formatting happens on the Character panel. Jon tells you about a new Web client that will be working with your agency. He tells you to be prepared to design lots of different headlines for the different areas of their site. He asks to you to start by setting a simple headline in Photoshop.

STEPS

1. **Open PS D-1.psd, then save it as Set Type**

2. **Click the workspace switcher on the Application bar, then click Typography**

    The Typography workspace offers many panels that are used commonly when working with type.

3. **Click the Type tool** T., **then click the cursor at the left of the canvas**

    A blinking type cursor appears, prompting you to begin typing. A type layer appears on the Layers panel.

4. **Type Typography**

> **QUICK TIP**
>
> The type layer is automatically named with the word(s) that you typed, as shown in Figure D-1.

5. **Click the Move tool**

6. **On the Character panel, click the Set the font family list arrow, then choose Garamond or a similar typeface**

7. **Click the Set the font style list arrow, click Bold, click the Set the font size list arrow, then click 60 pt**

8. **Drag the type to center it on the canvas, click Window on the Application bar, then click Swatches to open the Swatches panel**

> **QUICK TIP**
>
> You cannot use the Fill command to fill type.

9. **Click the blue swatch in the top row named RGB Blue, then press [Alt][Delete] (Win) or [option][Delete] (Mac) to fill the text on the Typography layer with the foreground color**

    Pressing [Alt][Delete] (Win) or [option][Delete] (Mac) fills a selection with the foreground color. Pressing [Delete] fills a selection with the background color. When you fill a text layer, only the text is filled with the color, not the entire canvas.

10. **Compare your canvas to Figure D-2**

FIGURE D-1: Type layer

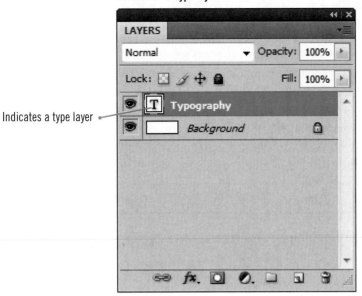

Indicates a type layer

FIGURE D-2: Filling text with a color

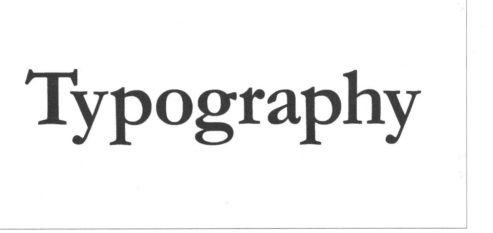

Working with the Character panel

Figure D-3 shows the Character panel and identifies the many options available to you when working with type. The Tracking and Kerning options are used to perfect the appearance of typography in terms of spacing. Tracking controls the overall spacing between letters in a given word or paragraph. Kerning controls the spacing between any two specific letters. The Horizontal and Vertical scale options resize selected text, making it wider or taller, respectively. Be sure to experiment with the formatting buttons at the bottom of the panel, which are very convenient for making all caps, small caps, superscripts, and other classic examples of typographical formatting.

FIGURE D-3: Character panel

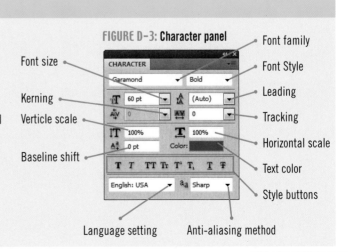

Font size

Kerning

Verticle scale

Baseline shift

Font family

Font Style

Leading

Tracking

Horizontal scale

Text color

Style buttons

Language setting   Anti-aliasing method

Locking Transparent Pixels

When you create a new layer in Photoshop, you'll see no changes to the artwork on your canvas. This is because each new layer is automatically a transparent layer; it's empty, because it has no artwork in it. You can apply color to any of the pixels on the layer—for example, you could fill the entire layer with color—but until you do, you can think of the pixels on the layer as being transparent, or "empty." This idea that a layer contains **transparency** is an important concept to understand, especially when working with type. On a type layer, the pixels on the layer that *aren't* used to render the type are transparent by default. To protect a pixel's transparency, you can lock the transparent pixels on a layer. Jon has asked you to create an interesting effect with type using black and red fill colors.

STEPS

1. **Verify that the Typography type layer is targeted, click Layer on the Application bar, point to Rasterize, then click Type**

   The term **rasterize** means "convert to pixels." The contents of the layer are converted from type to pixels. The type icon disappears from the layer on the Layers panel, and the layer is no longer editable as type. To learn more about rasterizing type, read the Clues to Use on this page called *"What's the purpose of rasterizing type?"*

QUICK TIP
By default, transparent areas of a layer are displayed as a grid of gray and white squares. You can change the grid size and grid color in the Transparency & Gamut category of the Preferences dialog box.

2. **Hide the Background layer**

   As shown in Figure D-4, many pixels on the Typography layer are transparent.

3. **Press [D] to access the default foreground and background colors**

4. **Press [Alt][Delete] (Win) or [option][Delete] (Mac) to fill with the black foreground color**

   All the pixels on the layer—transparent and non-transparent—are filled with black.

5. **Undo the fill, then click the Lock transparent pixels icon on the Layers panel, as shown in Figure D-5**

   Locking the transparent pixels on the layer ensures that they will remain transparent when other pixels are being modified.

6. **Fill the layer with the black foreground color**

   The transparent pixels on the layer are not filled with black.

7. **Click the RGB Red swatch on the Swatches panel, click the Brush tool , set the Master Diameter to 50 px, then set the Hardness to 100%**

8. **Paint different areas of the type red, then compare your result to Figure D-6**

   Because transparent pixels are locked, only the black pixels are affected by the Brush tool.

9. **Show the Background layer, save your work, then close Set Type.psd**

FIGURE D-4: Identifying transparent pixels

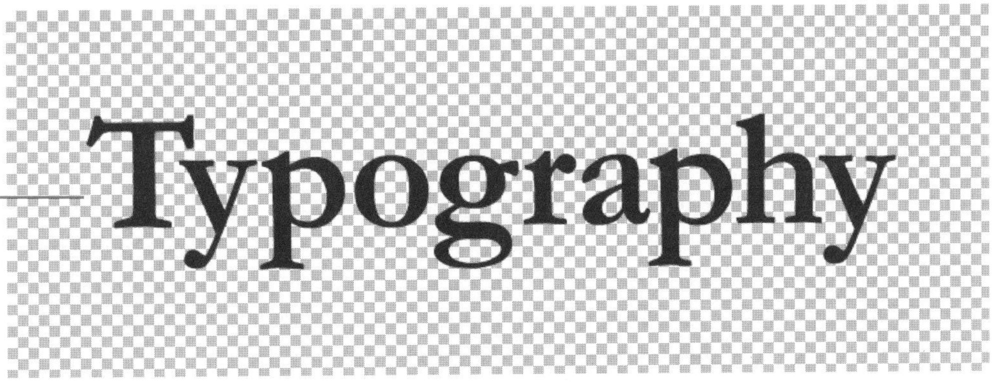

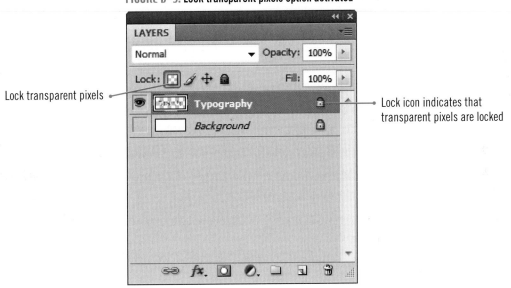

Transparent pixels represented by gray and white checker-board

FIGURE D-5: Lock transparent pixels option activated

Lock transparent pixels

Lock icon indicates that transparent pixels are locked

FIGURE D-6: Painting in a layer with locked transparent pixels

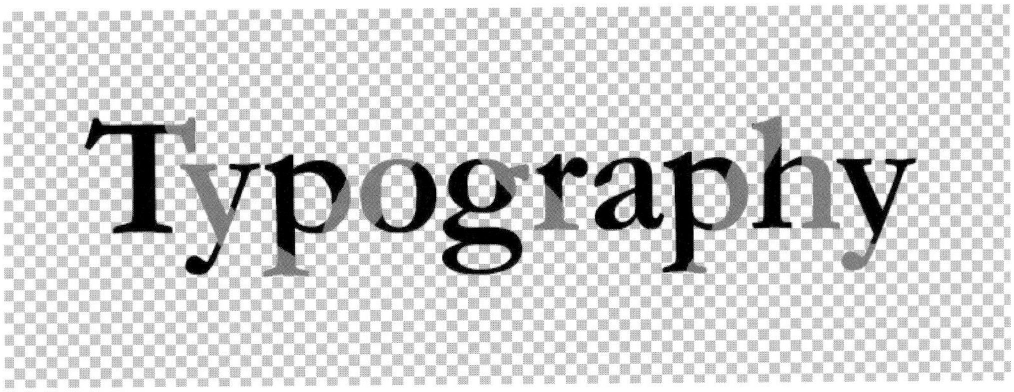

What's the purpose of rasterizing type?

The term **rasterize** means to convert to pixels. When you rasterize a type layer, you convert it from "live" type—type that is selectable and editable—to pixels. Its appearance doesn't change, but functionally, it is really not live anymore. You can't select it, and you can't modify it.

Rasterizing type is a commitment. Once you do so, other than using the Undo command or reverting the file, you can never go back and convert the rasterized text back into live type. So why rasterize type in the first place? The biggest reason for rasterizing type is to avoid font issues. When you share a Photoshop file that includes font information, the person that opens your file will need the same font installed on their computer to render the type. When type is rasterized, you no longer need the font installed because it's not type anymore, it's just pixels.

Creating Bevel and Emboss Effects on Type

Prepare to fall in love with the Bevel and Emboss layer style, especially when you use it to design type. Bevel and Emboss is a layer style—a built-in effect that you can apply to layers—just like the layer styles you first learned in Unit C. Bevel and Emboss is especially effective for type, because you can use it to create classic effects like raised text and chiseled text. And it's not just a one-trick pony layer style: the dialog box features a number of different styles and techniques that you can use to create all kinds of different bevel and emboss effects. It's a great place to experiment and play just to see the different looks you can achieve. ░░░░░ Jon supplies you with type to use to create sample headline effects for your client's Web site. He asks that you start with a Bevel and Emboss effect and asks that you experiment with a couple of different looks.

STEPS

1. Open PS D-2.psd, save it as Bevel Type, then click the HEADLINE layer on the Layers panel
2. Click Layer on the Application bar, point to Layer Style, then click Bevel and Emboss
   The Layer Style dialog box opens with the default Bevel and Emboss settings selected.
3. Set the Style to Emboss, set the Technique to Smooth, then set the Depth slider to 100%
4. Set the Size slider to 24 px, set the Soften slider to 0 px, then click OK
   Your canvas should resemble Figure D-7.
5. Double-click the Bevel and Emboss layer style on the Layers panel to open the Layer Style dialog box
6. Set the Style to Inner Bevel, set the Technique to Chisel Hard, then set the Depth slider to 120%

QUICK TIP
Note how the layer
style creates the
interesting effect on
the letter "J"

7. Set the Size slider to 44, set the Soften slider to 0, then click OK
   As shown in Figure D-8, the modified settings produce an entirely different bevel and emboss effect.
8. Save your work

FIGURE D-7: Smooth Emboss effect

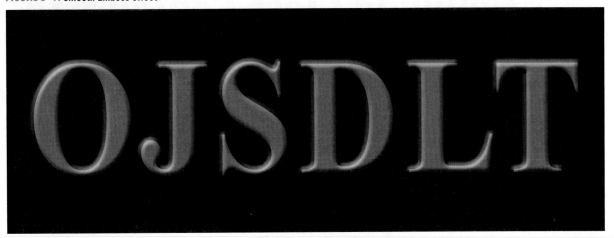

FIGURE D-8: Inner Bevel Chisel Hard effect

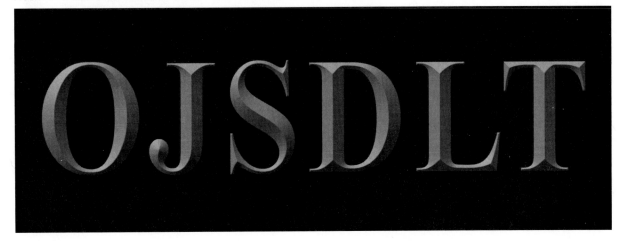

Using a Stroke Emboss layer style

A stroke is a basic artistic element that places an outline on an object or on type. For example, you can apply a black fill to type, then apply a colored stroke as an outline. In Photoshop, the best method for applying a stroke is to apply it as a layer style. This method allows you to apply the stroke, choose its color and its size, and—as with all layer styles—you can modify it or remove it at any time.

Once you've applied the Stroke layer style, you can then apply a Bevel and Emboss layer style to the stroke. To do this, click the Style list arrow in the Bevel and Emboss dialog box, then choose Stroke Emboss. As a result, only the stroke will be beveled and embossed.

Applying Gloss Contours to Layer Styles

Gloss contours are a set of 12 preset adjustments that affect the brightness and contrast of a layer style to create dramatic lighting effects. They are available for many different kinds of layer styles, not just Bevel and Emboss. Gloss contours fall into the "pick and choose" category of Photoshop features: you simply click through them to see what they do and how they affect the current artwork you're working with, and choose the one you like best. After a while, you'll get a sense of what to expect from each of them. However, the gloss contours will produce different results for different types of artwork. Jon tells you he likes the chiseled type effect you came up with for the type, but says he'd like to see you "jazz it up." He suggests you apply a gloss contour to the layer style.

STEPS

1. Double-click the Bevel and Emboss layer style on the Layers panel to open the dialog box

2. Move the Layer Style dialog box out of the way, if necessary, so that you can see at least one of the letters on your canvas

3. Click the Gloss Contour list arrow, then position the mouse pointer over the third square in the second row: Ring – Double
   As shown in Figure D-9, a tool tip appears, revealing the name of the gloss contour.

4. Click Ring – Double to see the effect on the artwork, then click each of the remaining 11 gloss contours to see its effect on the type artwork

5. Click the gloss contour named Cone

6. Click the Anti-aliased check box beside the Gloss Contour list arrow, then click OK
   Your artwork should resemble Figure D-10.

7. Save your work

FIGURE D-9: Gloss Contours in the Layer Style dialog box

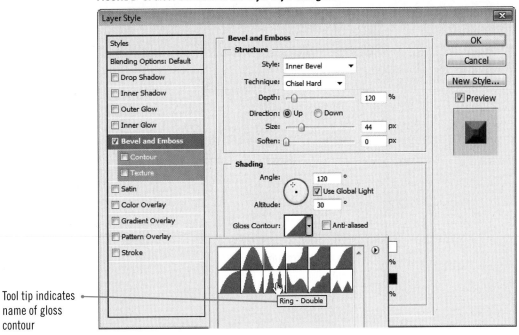

Tool tip indicates name of gloss contour

FIGURE D-10: Cone gloss contour applied to artwork

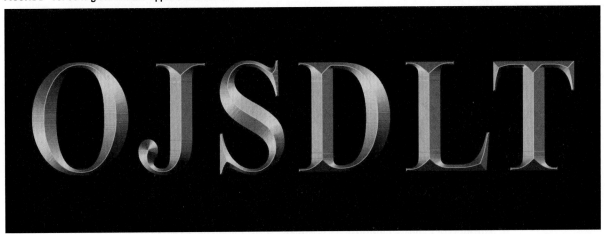

Understanding the Use Global Light option

Many layer styles create the effects that they do by adjusting the brightness and contrast of the artwork they're applied to. The effect is often created with a "light source" meaning that the artwork appears to be brightened from a certain direction. For example, if you apply a Bevel and Emboss layer style to chiseled text and set the light source to light the artwork from the right, you will create interesting shadows on the left side of the artwork.

You will find that you will apply multiple layer styles to artwork when working in Photoshop. The Use Global Light option exists as a simple solution to help you maintain a consistent light source for multiple layer styles. With the Use Global Light option checked, all of your layer styles will create their individual effects using "light" from the same direction.

Consistency is great when you want it, and if you want a consistent light source, the Use Global Light feature is a great option. But don't think that you *must* have a consistent light source. Sometimes different layer styles applied to the same artwork look even more interesting when they strike the artwork from different angles or light sources. You can turn off the Use Global Light option and manually set the angle and the altitude of the light source by dragging the Direction of light source icon in the Shading section of the Layer Style dialog box.

Creating a Double Emboss Effect

Layer styles are a lot of fun and they produce interesting and useful effects. But at some point, you're bound to feel that you're not really *creating* artwork with a layer style, because the result is something anyone could achieve by dragging the sliders to the same settings that you did. That is the truth about layer styles: they are canned effects, manufactured by Adobe Systems and packaged with the program. As a designer, it's your job to see past this built-in limitation of layer styles and figure out how to create *unique* artwork with these effects. The key to doing so is to understand the concept that unique and effective Photoshop artwork is created with *many* layer styles and other built-in effects combined in inspired and insightful ways to produce artwork that is unexpected and brand-new. ▨▨▨ Jon tells you that he thinks your headline style is heading in the right direction, but that you need to take it to the next level and create a bevel and emboss headline that is unique, not just one layer style applied to one piece of artwork.

STEPS

1. **Duplicate the Headline layer, rename the new layer Inner Bevel, then hide the Inner Bevel layer**

   In this exercise we are hiding the Inner Bevel layer style so that you can see the Outer Bevel layer style being built. However, if you were designing this type in a real-world project, you would probably want to show the Inner Bevel layer style to see the final effect of both layer styles together.

2. **Target the Headline layer, then rename it Outer Bevel**

3. **Drag the Indicates layer effects icon ▣ on the Outer Bevel layer to the Delete layer button 🗑 on the Layers panel**

   The layer style is removed. Instead of deleting the layer style, we could have double-clicked it to open the dialog box and changed the inner bevel layer style to an outer bevel layer style. This method, however, allows you to see the outer bevel effect being built from scratch. Your Layers panel should resemble Figure D-11.

4. **Click Layer on the Application bar, point to Layer Style, then click Bevel and Emboss**

5. **Set the Style to Outer Bevel, set the Technique to Chisel Hard, then set the Depth slider to 100%**

6. **Set the Size slider to 13, then set the Soften slider to 0**

7. **Apply the Cove – Deep gloss contour, then click the Anti-aliased check box**
   Your Layer Style dialog box should resemble Figure D-12.

8. **Click OK, then take a moment to view the effect**

9. **Show the Inner Bevel layer, then compare your canvas to Figure D-13**

10. **Save your work, then close Bevel Type.psd**

FIGURE D-11: Viewing the Layers panel after deleting a layer style

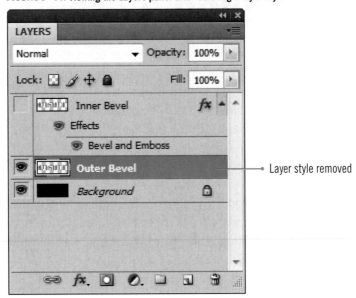

Layer style removed

FIGURE D-12: Creating an Outer Bevel layer style

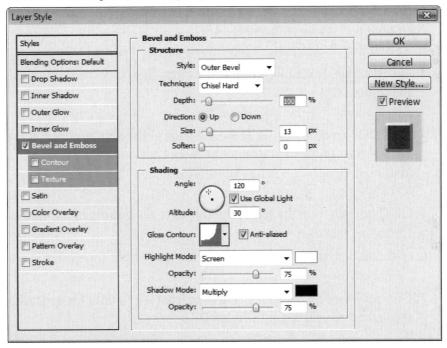

FIGURE D-13: Viewing the effect of combining layer styles

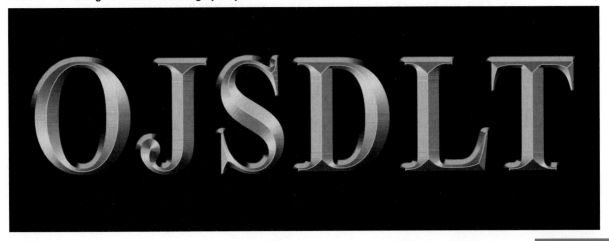

Applying a Gradient

A **gradient** is a blend between two or more colors. Often, a gradient between two colors creates a third distinct color. For example, any gradient between red and yellow will produce orange somewhere in between. Photoshop comes loaded with preset gradients of different colors that are available for you to apply with the Gradient tool. The Gradient tool is the single tool that you use to apply gradients, and the Gradient tool determines the placement and the length of the gradient. The tool works by clicking, dragging, and releasing. Where you click determines where the gradient begins, where you drag determines the length of the gradient, and where you release determines where the gradient ends. In addition, the Gradient tool comes with options that allow you to determine the *type* of gradient you are applying. A **linear** gradient blends straight from one color to another in a linear fashion. A **radial** gradient blend radiates outward from one color to another, like a series of concentric circles. Jon tells you that the Web client's headline graphics call for a number of gradient effects and asks you to experiment with some of Photoshop's default gradients.

STEPS

1. **Open PS D-3.psd, then save it as** Making the Gradient

2. **Click the** Gradient tool **, then click the** Click to open Gradient Picker list arrow **on the Options bar, shown in Figure D-14**
   A list of default gradient swatches becomes available.

3. **Click the** Blue, Yellow, Blue gradient swatch, **then click the** Linear Gradient button **on the Options bar**
   Table D-1 describes the five types of gradients.

4. **Position the mouse pointer at the left edge of the canvas, click and drag to the right edge of the canvas, then release the mouse button**
   As shown in Figure D-15, a linear gradient is created from the left edge of the canvas to the right edge of the canvas.

5. **Click and drag from the top of the canvas to the bottom of the canvas**
   The gradient is re-created from top to bottom

6. **Click and drag from the upper-left to the lower-right corner of the canvas**
   The gradient is re-created diagonally from the upper-left to the lower-right corner of the canvas.

7. **Click anywhere on the canvas and drag from left to right for approximately one inch, then compare your result to Figure D-16**
   The length of the entire gradient is approximately one inch long. Any pixels outside of the one-inch range are filled with the solid start and end color, which in this case is blue.

8. **Click the** Radial Gradient button **on the Options bar**

9. **Repeat Step 7, then compare your result to Figure D-17**
   A radial gradient follows the same rules as a linear gradient: the gradient starts where you click and ends where you release. With a radial gradient, however, the gradient "radiates" out from a center point, like concentric circles.

10. **Save your work**

FIGURE D-14: **Gradient swatches**

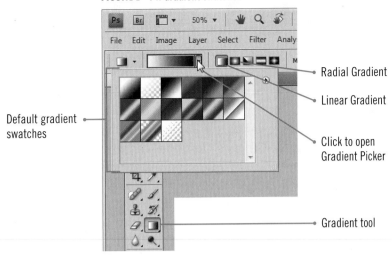

Default gradient swatches

Radial Gradient

Linear Gradient

Click to open Gradient Picker

Gradient tool

FIGURE D-15: **Linear gradient across the canvas**

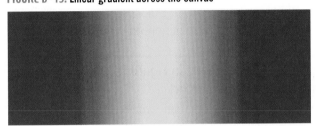

FIGURE D-16: **Shortened linear gradient**

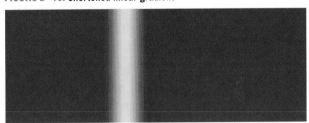

FIGURE D-17: **Radial gradient**

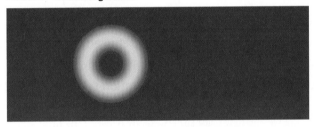

TABLE D-1: **Five types of gradients**

type of gradient	button icon	description
Linear	▦	Blends from the starting point to the ending point in a straight line.
Radial	▦	Blends from the starting point to the ending point in a circular pattern.
Angle	◪	Blends in a counterclockwise sweep around the starting point. Think of an angle gradient as the big hand and the little hand being in the same place on a clock, like at midnight. The gradient is created from background to the foreground color from the big hand to the little hand in a counterclockwise direction.
Reflected	▭	Blends using symmetric linear gradients on either side of the starting point. Think of a reflected gradient as a mirror. Click and drag from your foreground to background color and it creates a linear gradient *plus* a mirror image of that gradient at the point where you first clicked. Practically speaking, this type of gradient would be useful for making something that looks like a lead pipe or some other kind of metal tube.
Diamond	◈	Blends from the starting point outward in a diamond pattern. The ending point defines one corner of the diamond. The result appears to be concentric squares, with the starting color being in the center. The result is very 3D and could be useful for Web graphics especially.

Creating a New Gradient

In addition to the preset gradients that come with Photoshop, you can create your own customized gradients in the Gradient Editor dialog box. The colors that make up a gradient are called **color stops**. In the Gradient Editor dialog box, you create a customized gradient on the **gradient ramp** in the dialog box. You can create gradients between two color stops or between multiple color stops. You add color stops simply by clicking the gradient ramp, and you remove them by dragging them down and off of the gradient ramp. You determine the length of the gradient between color stops by moving color stops closer to each other or farther away. The **Location** text box below the gradient ramp identifies a selected color stop's location, from left to right, on the gradient ramp. You tell Jon that you'd prefer to design the client's headline graphics with customized gradients rather than those that come prepackaged with Photoshop. He agrees and asks that you start by creating a simple three-color gradient.

STEPS

QUICK TIP

The gradient fill box on the Options bar is also called *Click to edit the gradient box.*

1. **Click the gradient fill on the Options bar, as shown in Figure D-18**

   The gradient fill on the Options bar is the last gradient fill used. It appears when you select the Gradient tool. Clicking the gradient fill on the Options bar opens the Gradient Editor dialog box. The Blue, Yellow, Blue gradient appears in the gradient ramp in the dialog box. The color stops on the gradient ramp represent blue, yellow, and blue.

2. **Drag the left color stop all the way to the left, as shown in Figure D-19, then click the Color box below the Gradient Ramp to open the Color Picker**

   The name of the gradient in the Name text box changes to "Custom" once you begin to modify the existing gradient.

3. **Type 255 in the R text box, type 0 in the G and B text boxes, then click OK**

   The color stop on the gradient ramp has changed to red.

4. **Drag the last color stop all the way to the right, then change its color to 0R/255G/0B**

QUICK TIP

To delete a color stop, drag it straight down and off of the gradient ramp.

5. **Click right below the gradient ramp between the first and second color stops**

   A new color stop is added to the gradient ramp where you click

6. **Drag the new color stop until the Location text box reads 25%**

   The Location text box indicates where, from left to right, a color stop is positioned on the gradient ramp. For example, at 25%, the new color stop is exactly between the first stop at 0% and the middle stop at 50%.

7. **Change the color of the new color stop to 255R/150G/0B**

8. **Type Red, Orange, Yellow, Green in the Name text box, then click the New button**

   As shown in Figure D-20, the new gradient is added to the group of presets in the Gradient Editor.

9. **Click OK, save your work, then close Making the Gradient.psd**

FIGURE D-18: Clicking the active gradient fill

Gradient fill

When the Gradient tool is selected, the last gradient fill used appears on the Options bar

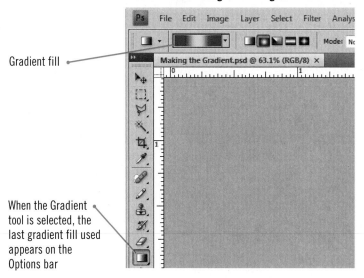

FIGURE D-19: Creating a new gradient

Name changes to Custom once you modify the Blue, Yellow, Blue gradient

Gradient ramp

First color stop

Click to change color of selected stop

Last color stop

Middle color stop

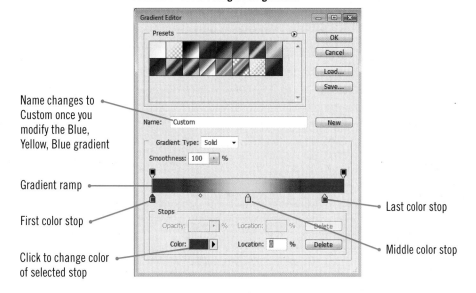

FIGURE D-20: Viewing the new gradient in the Gradient Editor

New gradient swatch

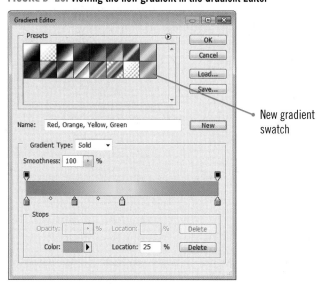

Clipping a Gradient into Type

Clipping refers to using artwork on one layer to mask the artwork on a layer above it. The artwork that functions as the mask is referred to as a **clipping mask**. The simplest example of clipping and a clipping mask would be of a type layer with a layer above it filled with a gradient. If you target the gradient layer and then create a clipping mask, the gradient will be clipped into the type layer beneath it and will be visible only within the type. The transparent areas of the type layer will mask the gradient artwork. The layer functioning as the clipping mask—the type layer in the above example—is referred to as the **base layer**. For artwork to be clipped, it must be immediately above the base layer. Base layers can have multiple layers clipped into them, but all of those layers must be immediately above the base layer on the Layers panel. Jon asks that you clip a gradient into a type headline. You clip the Red, Orange, Yellow, Green gradient into the headline and then move it within the clipping mask to see different parts of the gradient.

STEPS

1. Open PS D-4.psd, then save it as Clip Layers

2. Hide the Effects on the Inner Bevel layer, create a new layer above the Inner Bevel layer, then name the new layer Gradient

3. Click the Gradient tool ▣, then verify that the Red, Orange, Yellow, Green gradient is the active gradient on the Options bar

4. Verify that the Gradient layer is targeted on the Layers panel, position the mouse pointer at the top edge of the canvas, then create a linear gradient from the top to the bottom of the canvas

   Your canvas should resemble Figure D-21.

5. Click the Layers panel list arrow, then click Create Clipping Mask

   As shown in Figure D-22, the Gradient layer is clipped into the Inner Bevel layer, indicated by the black arrow on the Gradient layer. The gradient artwork is visible only where there is artwork on the Inner Bevel layer. The gradient artwork is not visible—it is masked—where there are transparent pixels on the Inner Bevel layer.

6. Click the Move tool ▸⊕, then, in one move, drag the gradient artwork straight down so more of the red in the gradient is visible

   The gradient artwork moves but continues to be masked by the Inner Bevel layer.

7. Undo the move

8. Make the Effects layer visible on the Inner Bevel layer, then compare your canvas to Figure D-23

   The gradient artwork is beveled and embossed. When a layer style is applied to a layer, any artwork that is clipped into the layer will take on the appearance of the layer style.

9. Save your work

FIGURE D-21: Red, Orange, Yellow, Green gradient applied to the canvas

FIGURE D-22: Red, Orange, Yellow, Green gradient masked by the Inner Bevel layer

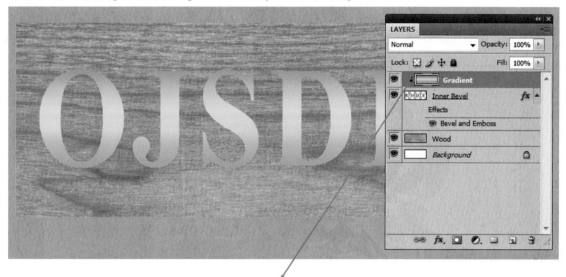

Bent black arrow indicates layer is
being clipped into base layer

FIGURE D-23: Making the layer style effect visible

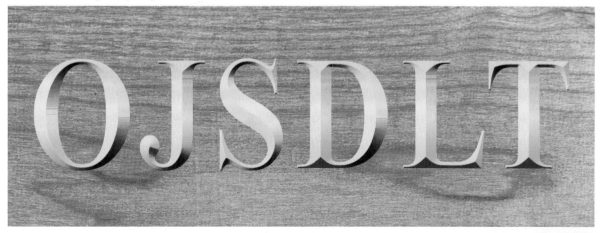

Clipping Imagery into Type

Clipping imagery into type works the same way as clipping a gradient into type, except that you are clipping a picture instead of a gradient fill. A good example of clipping a picture into type would be an old fashioned postcard with the word FLORIDA and different scenes of Floridian attractions inside the letters. Clipping an image into type is a classic type of design that is visually interesting and communicates an idea with strength and clarity. ▪▪▪▪ Jon tells you that some of the client's headlines will involve a nature motif and asks that you clip an image of wood grain into the headline.

1. **Hide the Effects on the Inner Bevel layer**
2. **Move the Wood layer to the top of the Layers panel**
3. **Click the Layers panel list arrow, then click Create Clipping Mask**

   As shown in Figure D-24, the wood artwork is clipped into the Inner Bevel artwork. It's important that you understand that the Wood layer is being clipped into the Inner Bevel layer, not into the Gradient layer immediately beneath it. The gradient artwork has no visual impact on the final artwork because the gradient artwork is beneath the wood artwork.

4. **Show the Effects on the Inner Bevel layer, then compare your canvas to Figure D-25**
5. **Save your work, then close Clip Layers.psd**

FIGURE D-24: Clipping the Wood layer into the Inner Bevel layer

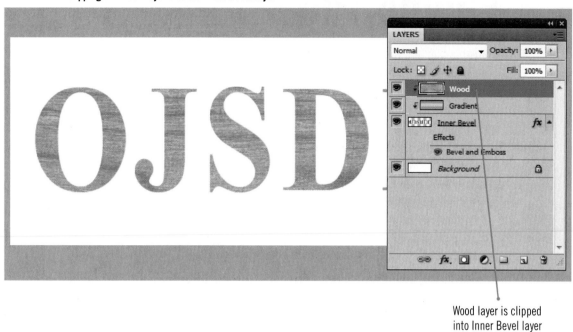

Wood layer is clipped
into Inner Bevel layer

FIGURE D-25: Viewing the artwork with the layer style visible

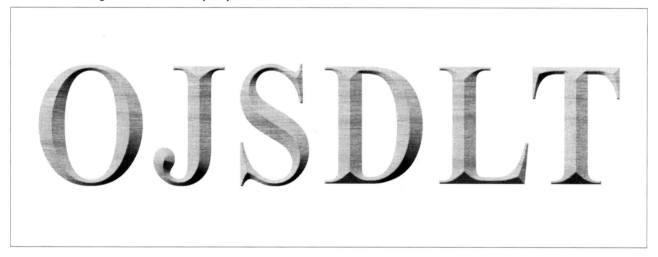

Fading Type

Gradients play an important visual and artistic role when they function as a color element in artwork. Gradients play an important practical role when used in layer masks. The fundamental rule of a layer mask is that white areas of the mask reveal 100% of the related artwork on the layer, and black areas of the mask hide or mask 100% of the related artwork on the layer. Therefore, it follows logically that gradients in a layer mask that blend from white to black affect the related artwork as a blend from "revealed" to "masked." Thus, a gradient in a layer mask becomes a powerful tool for gradually fading artwork on the layer. Jon provides you with a stylized headline for the client's Web site and asks that you use a layer mask to fade it gradually from top to bottom. He tells you to experiment with different fades and to be sure that the headline remains legible even with the fade.

STEPS

1. Open PS D-5.psd, then save it as Fade Type

2. Target the FADE OUT layer, then click the Add layer mask button 🔳 on the Layers panel
   An all-white layer mask is added to the layer.

3. Verify that the foreground color is white and the background color is black
   When you create a new layer mask, the foreground/background colors default to white/black.

4. Click the Gradient tool 🔳, click the Click to open Gradient Picker list arrow on the Options bar, then click the Foreground to Background gradient swatch

5. Verify that the layer mask is targeted on the Fade Out layer, create a gradient from the top of the type down to the bottom of the type, then compare your result to Figure D-26
   Because the layer mask was targeted, you applied the gradient to the layer mask. The layer mask gradates from white to black from the top to the bottom of the type. Thus, the type is fully visible at its top edge, completely invisible at its bottom edge, and gradually fades from top to bottom.

6. Create a gradient from the top of the type down to the bottom of the canvas, then compare your result to Figure D-27

7. Press and hold [Alt] (Win) or [option] (Mac), then click the layer mask to view the layer mask
   The area of the mask that corresponds to the bottom of the type is dark gray, not black. Thus, the type does not fully disappear at its bottom edge.

8. Press and hold [Alt] (Win) or [option] (Mac), then click the layer thumbnail to view the layer artwork

9. Save your work, then close Fade Type.psd

FIGURE D-26: Fading the type completely

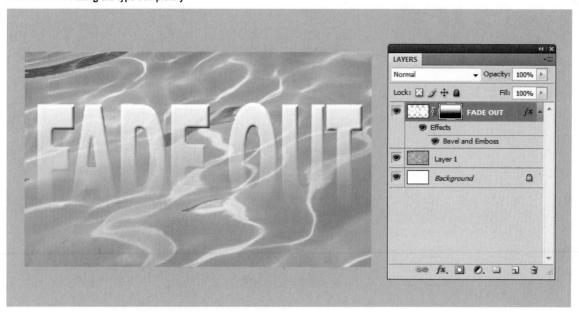

FIGURE D-27: Fading the type, but not completely

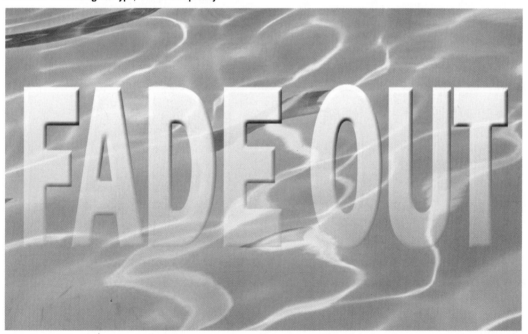

Practice

▼ CONCEPTS REVIEW

FIGURE D-28

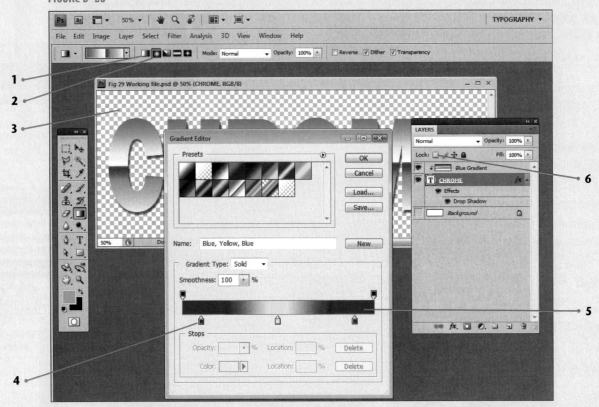

1. Which item points to the gradient ramp?
2. Which item points to the Linear Gradient button?
3. Which item points to the Radial Gradient button?
4. Which item points to the Lock transparent pixels button?
5. Which item points to transparent pixels?
6. Which item points to a color stop?

Match each term with the statement that best describes it.

7. **Gradient**
8. **Gloss contour**
9. **Clipping**
10. **Foreground to Background**
11. **Radial gradient**

a. Color blend that radiates outward from its center
b. Name of a default gradient swatch
c. Using one layer's artwork as a mask for another layer's artwork
d. Preset color adjustment applied to layer style for a visual effect
e. Blend between one or more colors

Select the best answer from the list of choices.

12. **Which of the following is not an option in the Layer Style dialog box for formatting a Bevel and Emboss layer style?**

    a. Gloss contour

    b. Size

    c. Technique

    d. Create clipping mask

13. **Which of the following is a type of style available in the Bevel and Emboss layer style dialog box?**

    a. Chisel Hard

    b. Chisel Soft

    c. Inner Bevel

    d. Smooth

14. **Which of the following is not true about gloss contours?**

    a. They can be used with all styles of bevel and emboss effects.

    b. They can be used only with bevel and emboss layer styles.

    c. They are preset adjustments.

    d. They each have a name.

15. **Which of the following is not true about gradients?**

    a. All gradients are made with at least two colors.

    b. Some gradients are made with more than two colors.

    c. Radial gradients can gradate from left to right on the canvas.

    d. Linear gradients can move from top to bottom on the canvas.

16. **Which of the following is not true about clipping layers?**

    a. Only one layer can be clipped into another layer.

    b. The Layers panel indicates which layers are clipped.

    c. Transparent pixels in the base layer play a role in how other layers appear when clipped.

    d. Clipped layers take on the appearance of layer styles applied to the base layer.

▼ SKILLS REVIEW

1. **Set type.**

    a. Open PS D-6.psd, then save it as **Set Skills Type**.

    b. Click the workspace switcher list arrow on the Application bar, then click Typography.

    c. Click the Type tool, then click on the left side of the canvas.

    d. Type **Type It**.

    e. Click the Move tool, then open the Character panel.

    f. Click the Set the font family list arrow, then choose Impact or a similar typeface.

    g. Set the font size to 96 pt by typing **96** in the Set the font size text box.

    h. Center the type on the page, click the RGB Red swatch on the Swatches panel, then press [Alt][Delete] (Win) or [option][Delete] (Mac) to fill the type.

    i. Save your work.

2. **Lock transparent pixels.**

    a. Verify that the Type It layer is targeted, click Layer on the Application bar, point to Rasterize, then click Type.

    b. Hide the Background layer.

    c. Press [D] to access the default foreground and background colors.

    d. Press [Alt][Delete] (Win) or [option][Delete] (Mac) to fill with the black foreground color.

    e. Undo the fill, then click the Lock transparent pixels icon on the Layers panel.

    f. Fill the layer with the black foreground color.

    g. Click the RGB Red swatch on the Swatches panel, click the Brush tool, set the diameter to 50, then set the Hardness to 100%.

h. Paint different areas of the type red, then compare your result to Figure D-29.

i. Show the Background layer, save your work, then close Set Skills Type.psd.

3. Create Bevel and Emboss effects on type.

FIGURE D-29

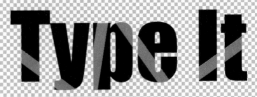

a. Open PS D-7.psd, save it as **Bevel Skills Type**, then click the HEADLINE layer on the Layers panel.

b. Click Layer on the Application bar, point to Layer Style, then click Bevel and Emboss.

c. Set the Style to Emboss, set the Technique to Smooth, then set the Depth slider to 100%.

d. Set the Size slider to 24, set the Soften slider to 0, then click OK.

e. Double-click the Bevel and Emboss layer style on the Layers panel to reopen the dialog box.

f. Set the Style to Inner Bevel, set the Technique to Chisel Hard, then set the Depth slider to 120%.

g. Set the Size slider to 50, set the Soften slider to 0, then click OK.

h. Save your work.

4. Apply gloss contours to layer styles.

a. Double-click the Bevel and Emboss layer style on the Layers panel to open the dialog box.

b. Click the gloss contour named Cone.

c. Click the Anti-aliased check box, then click OK.

d. Save your work.

5. Create a double emboss effect.

a. Duplicate the Headline layer, rename the new layer **Inner Bevel**, then hide it.

b. Target the Headline layer, then rename it **Outer Bevel**.

c. Drag the Indicates layer effects icon on the Outer Bevel layer to the Delete layer button on the Layers panel.

d. Click Layer on the Application bar, point to Layer Style, then click Bevel and Emboss.

e. Set the Style to Outer Bevel, set the Technique to Chisel Hard, then set the Depth slider to 100%.

f. Set the Size slider to 12, then set the Soften slider to 0.

g. Click to apply the Ring gloss contour, then click to activate the Anti-aliased check box, if necessary.

h. Click OK, then show the Inner Bevel layer.

i. Save your work, then close Bevel Skills Type.psd.

6. Apply a gradient.

a. Open PS D-8.psd, then save it as **Gradient Skills.**

b. Click the Gradient tool, click the Linear Gradient button on the Options bar, then click the Click to open Gradient Picker list arrow on the Options bar.

c. Click the Copper swatch.

d. Position the mouse pointer at the left edge of the canvas, click and drag to the right edge of the canvas, then release the mouse button.

e. Click and drag from the top of the canvas to the bottom of the canvas.

f. Click and drag from the upper-left to the lower-right corner of the canvas.

g. Click approximately 1" in from the left edge of the canvas and drag left to right for approximately two inches.

h. Click the Radial Gradient button on the Options bar.

i. Repeat Step g, then save your work.

▼ SKILLS REVIEW (CONTINUED)

7. Create a new gradient.

   a. Click the active gradient fill on the Options bar to open the Gradient Editor dialog box.

   b. Click the Blue, Yellow, Blue swatch.

   c. Drag the left color stop all the way to the left, then click the Color box below the gradient ramp.

   d. Type **0** in the R text box, type **255** in the G text box and **0** in the Blue text box, then click OK.

   e. Click the far right color stop, drag it all the way to the right, then change its color to **0R/255G/255B**.

   f. Click immediately below the gradient ramp between the first and second color stops.

   g. Drag the new color stop so that the Location text box reads 35%.

   h. Change the color of the new color stop to **255R/128G/0B**.

   i. Name the new gradient **Green, Orange, Yellow, Cyan**, as shown in Figure D-30 then click the New button.

   j. Click OK, save your work, then close Gradient Skills.psd.

8. Clip a gradient into type.

   a. Open PS D-9.psd then save it as **Skills Clip Layers**.

   b. Hide the effects on the Inner Bevel layer, create a new layer above the Inner Bevel layer, then name the new layer **Gradient**.

   c. Click the Gradient tool, then verify that the Green, Orange, Yellow, Cyan gradient is the active gradient.

   d. Verify that the new layer is targeted on the Layers panel, position the mouse pointer at the top edge of the canvas, then create a linear gradient from the top to the bottom of the canvas.

   e. Click the Layers panel list arrow, then click Create Clipping Mask.

   f. Click the Move tool, then, in one move, click and drag the gradient artwork straight down so other areas of the gradient become visible.

   g. Undo the move.

   h. Make the effects visible on the Inner Bevel layer, then save your work.

9. Clip imagery into type.

   a. Hide the Effects on the Inner Bevel layer.

   b. Move the Granite layer to the top of the Layers panel.

   c. Click the Layers panel list arrow, then click Create Clipping Mask.

   d. Show the effects on the Inner Bevel layer, then compare your result to Figure D-31.

   e. Save your work, then close Skills Clip Layers.psd.

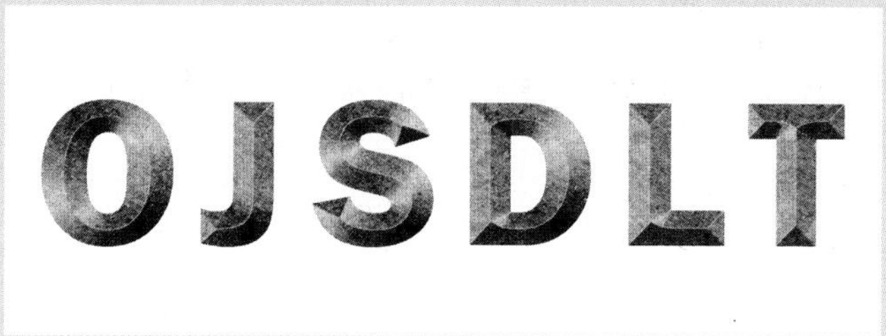

10. Fade type.

   a. Open PS D-10.psd then save it as **Fade Skills Type**.

   b. Target the FADE AWAY layer, then click the Add layer mask button on the Layers panel.

   c. Press [D] to access default foreground and background colors, then click the Switch foreground and background colors button so that your foreground color is white and your background color is black.

   d. Click the Gradient tool, click the Click to edit gradient list arrow, then click the Foreground to Background gradient swatch.

   e. Verify that the layer mask is targeted in the FADE AWAY layer, then create a gradient from the left edge of the letter F to the right edge of the letter Y.

FIGURE D-30

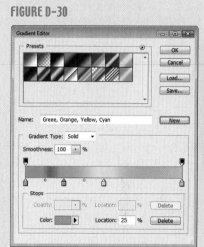

FIGURE D-31

OJSDLT

f. Create a gradient from the middle of the letter "D" to the right edge of the canvas, then compare your result to Figure D-32.

FIGURE D-32

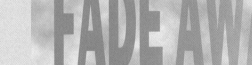

g. Press and hold [Alt] (Win) or [option] (Mac), then click the layer mask to view the layer mask.

h. Press and hold [Alt] (Win) or [option] (Mac), then click the layer thumbnail to view the layer artwork.

i. Save your work, then close Fade Skills Type.psd.

▼ INDEPENDENT CHALLENGE 1

A clothing line named Black On Blue has asked your company to design a simple sign for them to use at a trade show. The client asks that you use just a "basic" typeface and to do something with color to "make it a little bit more interesting" than just black type on a white background.

a. Open PS D-11.psd, then save it as **Black On Blue**.

b. Press [D] to access the default foreground and background colors.

c. Click the Type tool, then type the words **BLACK ON BLUE** in all uppercase letters.

d. Click the Move tool, then open the Character panel.

e. Apply the Impact font or a similar bold font.

f. Change the font size to 54 pts.

g. Fill the type with the RGB Blue swatch.

h. Rasterize the type.

i. Click the Rectangle Marquee tool, then create a rectangular marquee around the entire top half of the rasterized type.

j. Press [D] to access the default foreground and background colors.

FIGURE D-33

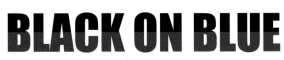

k. Lock the transparent pixels, then fill the selection with the black foreground color.

l. Compare your result to Figure D-33.

m. Save your work, close Black On Blue.psd, then exit Photoshop.

▼ INDEPENDENT CHALLENGE 2

One of your luxury hotel clients has asked your firm to design a postcard for one of their daily evening events. The only design advice that they give you is that they want something "eye-catching."

a. Open PS D-12.psd, then save it as **Sunset Gradient**.

b. Fill the Background layer with black, then lock transparent pixels on both of the type layers.

c. Fill the type on the two type layers with white.

d. Open the Gradient Editor dialog box.

e. Click the Red, Green gradient swatch.

f. Change the color of the left color stop to **255R/228G/0B**.

g. Change the color of the right color stop to **0R/0G/0B**.

h. Add a third color stop between the first and second color stops.

i. Change the color of the new color stop to **255R/0G/0B**, then change its location to 85%.

j. Add a new color stop between the first color stop and the new color stop.

k. Change the color of the new color stop to **255R/132G/0B**, change its location to 50%.

▼ INDEPENDENT CHALLENGE 2 (CONTINUED)

l. Name the new gradient **Sunset Gradient**, click New, then click OK.

m. Create a new layer above the Sunset type layer, then name the new layer **Sunset Gradient**.

n. Click the Gradient tool, then verify that Sunset Gradient is the active gradient on the Options bar.

o. Position your cursor at the top edge of the SUNSET type, then create a linear gradient from the top of the SUNSET type to the bottom of the SUNSET type.

p. Click the Layers panel list arrow, then click Create Clipping Mask.

q. Compare your canvas to Figure D-34.

r. Save your work, close Sunset Gradient.psd, then exit Photoshop.

FIGURE D-34

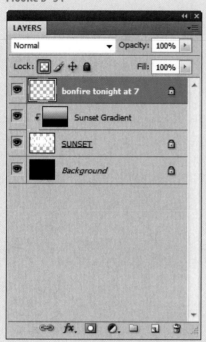
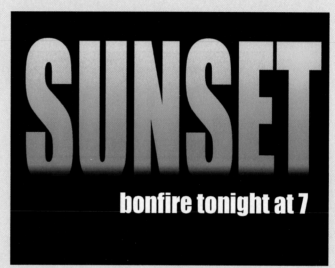

▼ INDEPENDENT CHALLENGE 3

Your firm's hotel client calls and says that they would like you to make changes to a postcard you previously designed for them. They request that you define the type a little better by adding a stroke. They ask for "something interesting," not just a "boring white stroke."

a. Open PS D-13.psd, then save it as **Sunset Stroke Emboss**.

b. Click the SUNSET layer on the Layers panel.

c. Click Layer on the Application bar, point to Layer Style, then click Stroke.

d. Click the Set color of stroke swatch, type **128** in the R, G, and B text boxes, then click OK.

e. Set the Size to 10, then set the Position to Center.

f. In the Styles column at the left of the dialog box, click the words Bevel and Emboss.

g. Set the Style to Stroke Emboss, set the Technique to Chisel Hard, then set the Depth slider to 100%.

h. Set the Size slider to 2, then set the Soften slider to 0.

▼ INDEPENDENT CHALLENGE 3 (CONTINUED)

i. Click the Gloss Contour list arrow, click the Gaussian gloss contour, then verify that the Anti-aliased check box is checked.

j. Click OK, then compare your result to Figure D-35.

Advanced Challenge Exercise

- Double-click the Bevel and Emboss layer style on the Layers panel.
- Drag the Highlight Mode opacity slider to 100%.
- Click the Set color for highlight swatch, type **255R/255G/0B**, then click OK.
- Click OK to close the Layer Style dialog box.

k. Save your work, then close Sunset Stroke Emboss.psd.

FIGURE D-35

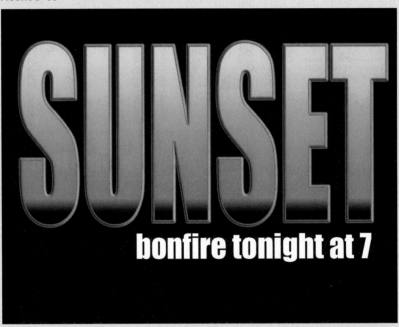

▼ REAL WORLD INDEPENDENT CHALLENGE

Your best friend is getting married and has planned many activities during the weekend leading up to the wedding ceremony. He asks you to help him create an invitation for a special bonfire on the beach two nights before the wedding. You choose an image of a beach scene, duplicate it to create a sunset scene, then clip the sunset artwork into type.

a. Open PS D-14.psd, then save it as **Sunset Clipped**.

b. Verify that only the Background and Original layers are showing on the Layers panel.

c. Hide and show the Sunset layer, comparing the artwork to the Original artwork. (*Hint*: The Sunset artwork is a duplicate of the Original artwork. It has been colorized orange, and sunset artwork has been added at the center.)

d. Show all layers, then drag the Sunset layer above the HEADLINE layer.

e. Clip the Sunset layer into the HEADLINE layer.

f. Add a white layer mask to the Sunset layer.

g. Set the foreground and background colors to white and black.

h. Click the Gradient tool, then click the Foreground to Background gradient swatch.

i. Position the mouse pointer halfway up from the base of the letter N.

▼ REAL WORLD INDEPENDENT CHALLENGE (CONTINUED)

j. Drag down, releasing the mouse button at the base of the letter N.

k. Duplicate the Original layer.

l. Drag the Original copy layer above the HEADLINE layer.

m. Duplicate the Sunset layer, then drag the Sunset copy layer to the top of the Layers panel.

n. Delete the layer mask on the Sunset copy layer.

o. Clip the Sunset copy layer into the type layer beneath it.

p. With the Sunset copy layer still targeted, drag the Opacity slider on the Layers panel to 75%.

q. Compare your Layers panel and your artwork to Figure D-36.

Advanced Challenge Exercise

- Double-click the Bevel and Emboss layer style on the Layers panel.
- Click the Use Global Light check box to remove the check mark.
- Change the Angle to 180°.
- Click OK to close the Layer Style dialog box.

r. Save your work, then close Sunset Clipped.psd.

FIGURE D-36

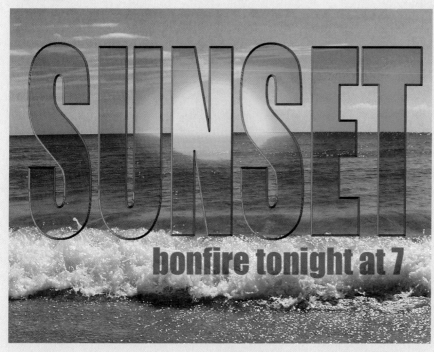

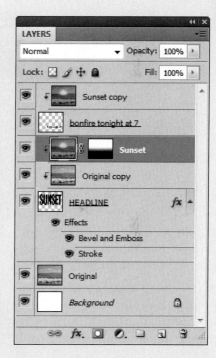

Open PS B-15.psd, then save it as **Radial Gradient.** Create and apply a gradient so that your canvas resembles Figure D-37.

FIGURE D-37

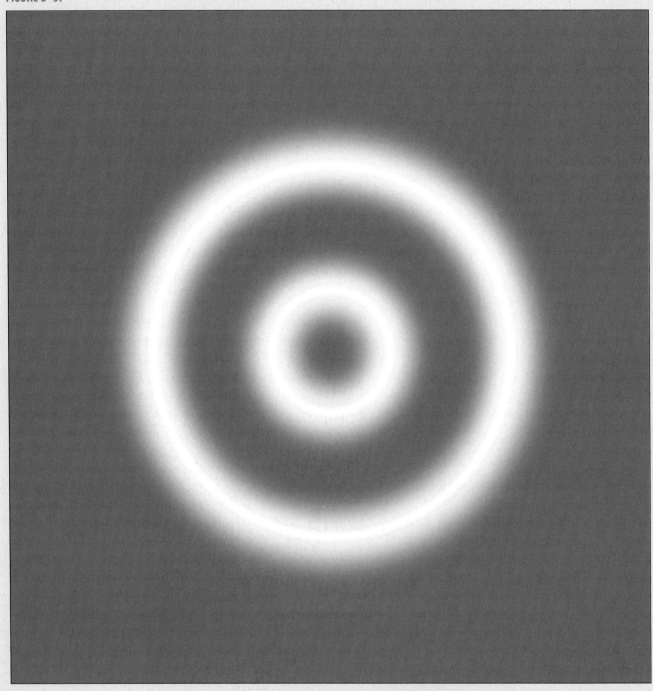

Improving Images with Adjustment Layers

In our digital world, images can come from just about anywhere. Photoshop offers many practical operations like the ability to improve characteristics of images: their color, their contrast, their overall effect. An adjustment layer allows you to apply adjustments to images without directly affecting the artwork.

An adjustment layer is called "non-destructive" because it exists as a layer on the Layers panel. Brightness/Contrast, Levels, and Color Balance are three common, powerful, and highly useful adjustments for improving the overall appearance of an image. When you understand the basics of Grayscale and RGB color modes, then you're ready and able to dramatically improve your images with adjustments. Jon asks you to improve the appearance of a number of grayscale and RGB images using adjustments.

OBJECTIVES

Understand grayscale

Investigate a grayscale image

Use the Brightness/Contrast adjustment

Adjust black and white points with levels

Adjust the midpoint with levels

Investigate an RGB image

Use the Color Balance adjustment

Use the Vibrance adjustment

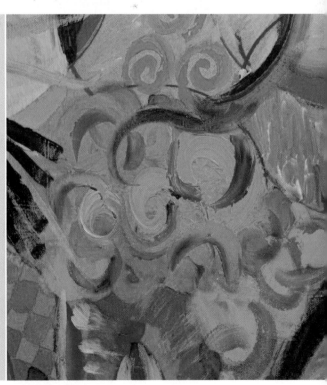

Understanding Grayscale

A **grayscale** image refers to a digital image in which each pixel can be one—and only one—of 256 shades of gray. With 256 shades of gray available per pixel, the illusion of a continuous tone image can be created. The grayscale range is 0–255. Pixels with a grayscale value of 0 are black. Pixels with a grayscale value of 255 are white. Any number in between 0 and 255 is gray—light gray or dark gray—with 128 being the middle point in the grayscale range. Jon tells you about a new client who will be supplying imagery that will require lots of analysis and correction for quality and color. He gives you a grayscale image and asks that you analyze it.

STEPS

1. Open PS E-1.psd, then save it as Grayscale

2. Click Image on the Application bar, point to Mode, then note that Grayscale is checked
    This image has been saved in Grayscale mode, meaning that one of 256 shades of gray is available per pixel.

3. Open the Info panel, click the Info panel list arrow, click Panel Options, enter the settings shown in Figure E-1, then click OK
    When you set the readouts on the Info panel to RGB, they indicate the grayscale value of each pixel, from 0–255. The three readouts—R, G, and B—will always be the same for a grayscale image; you can think of them as a single number.

    > **QUICK TIP**
    > Identifying pixel information in the Info panel is referred to as **sampling** pixels.

4. Click the Eyedropper tool, then position it over different areas of the image, noting the readouts on the Info panel

5. Position the Eyedropper tool at the very bottom of the gradient on the right, then move slowly to the top of the gradient
    The pixels in the gradient range from 0 at the bottom to 255 at the top.

6. Sample areas in the man's shoulder to see the grayscale information for the darker areas of the image, then see if you can find pixels with a value of 0, the darkest pixels in the grayscale range

7. Sample areas in the white stripe in the hat and parts of the hood to find mid-range areas of the image, then see if you can find pixels with a value near 128, which is the exact middle of the grayscale range

8. Position the Eyedropper tool over the man's cheek and the light area at the lower right to find light areas of the image
    Figure E-2 identifies some of the lightest pixels in the image.

FIGURE E-1: Info panel settings

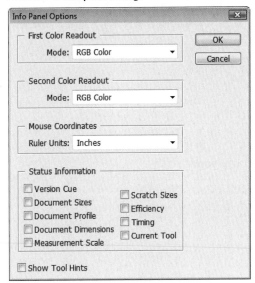

FIGURE E-2: Sampling the lightest pixels in the image

Very light pixels

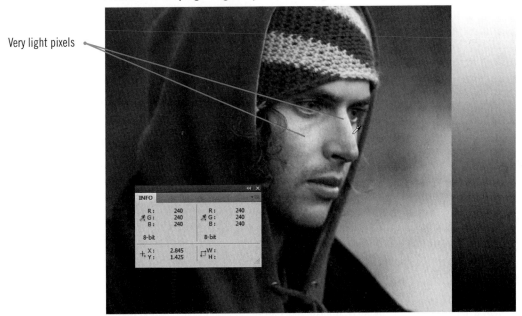

Choosing settings on the Info panel

Why do you set the readouts on the Info panel to RGB if you are sampling a pixel in a grayscale image? Adobe has designed the Info panel so that the Grayscale readouts sample pixels in *ink percentages*. Note the word *ink*. In other words, the readout provides information for what *would* be a printed reproduction of the image. In a printed piece, a pixel with the value of 100% is a black printed dot. 0% means no ink, and on a white paper, where there's 0% ink, that area remains white. So the Grayscale readout on the Info panel would identify white areas as 0%. In a grayscale image, each pixel can be one of 256 shades of gray. Use the RGB readouts on the Info panel to identify grayscale values for pixels.

Investigating a Grayscale Image

The first step in analyzing the appearance of any image is to identify the highlights, midtones, and shadows. **Highlights** are the lightest areas of the image and are represented by pixels whose value falls in the upper third of the grayscale range. **Shadows** are the darkest areas represented by pixels in the low third of the grayscale range. **Midtones**, as the name suggests, fall into the middle range of the grayscale.

When you look at a digital image, you don't see individual pixels, you see the illusion of **continuous tone**: a smooth transition from shadows to midtones to highlights. In order to create this illusion, a sufficient number of grays must be available per pixel so that the eye perceives smooth transitions between tones. 🔳🔳 Jon asks you to continue working with the image to identify the basic overall shadow, midtone, and highlight areas.

STEPS

1. **On the Layers panel, make the Chart layer visible, then compare your canvas to Figure E-3**

   The chart uses a gradient to identify the shadow, midtone, and highlight areas of the grayscale image.

2. **Look at the image of the man and try to see it not as a picture but as a range of tones from shadows to midtones to highlights**

3. **Using the chart as a guide, sample different areas of the image to identify shadows, midtones, and highlights**

4. **Target the Background layer on the Layers panel**

5. **Move the Info panel to the upper-left corner of the canvas, click Image on the Application bar, point to Adjustments, click Posterize, drag the Levels slider to 3, and continue to keep the Posterize dialog box open**

6. **Drag the Posterize dialog box to the left, then compare your image and the gradient on the right to Figure E-4**

   At this posterize setting, only three shades of gray are available per pixel: 0, 148, and 255. This image now has one color for highlights, one for midtones, and one for shadows. In the same way that those three shades are unable to render a smooth gradient on the right, they are unable to render the image as a smooth continuous-tone image.

7. **Position the pointer over the image and note the readouts on the Info panel**

8. **In the Posterize dialog box, change the Levels value to 16, then compare your result to Figure E-5**

   At this setting, 16 shades of gray are available per pixel. The image has clearly improved, but not nearly enough to create the illusion of continuous tone. The effect on the gradient at the right of the window mirrors the effect of the image. Just as the gradient shows distinct steps between grays, the image shows the same effect, especially in the hood and in the image background areas on the right side. However, note that at a very quick glance, your eye might accept the appearance of the knitted hat and—to some degree—the man's face as continuous tone.

9. **Change the Levels value to 200**

   At this level—still inferior to the standard 256 levels available in a grayscale image—the eye cannot identify any stair-stepping effect in the image; it appears to be continuous tone. The gradient on the right, however, still shows some signs of stair-stepping.

10. **Click Cancel, hide the Chart layer on the Layers panel, save your work, then close Grayscale.psd**

QUICK TIP

The readouts in the Info panel now show before and after information. The number on the left refers to the original grayscale value of a given pixel, and the number on the right refers to the value with the posterize adjustment applied; this value can only be 0, 148, or 255.

QUICK TIP

The appearance of the gradient in this figure is called **stair-stepping**, which refers to the idea that you can see each step in the transition from black to white.

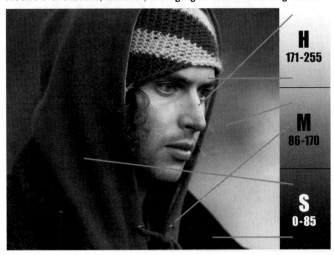

FIGURE E-3: Shadows, midtones, and highlights identified on the gradient

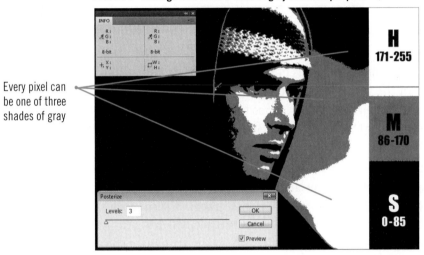

FIGURE E-4: Image with three shades of gray available per pixel

Every pixel can be one of three shades of gray

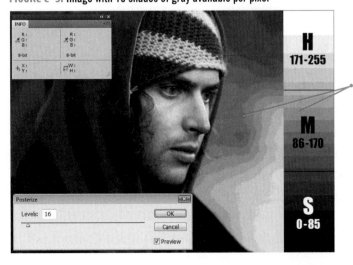

FIGURE E-5: Image with 16 shades of gray available per pixel

Background and gradient show stair-stepping

Using the Brightness/ Contrast Adjustment

Adjustments are operations you do that affect the appearance of an image, such as manipulating brightness and contrast. You can make adjustments directly to pixels on a layer, but you can't go back and re-adjust at a later time. **Adjustment layers** are adjustments you make that exist as layers on the Layers panel. Once created, they affect the image, but they can be manipulated at a later time. You can hide an adjustment layer or show it, and you can delete it at any time.

The Brightness/Contrast adjustment, as the name suggests, affects the brightness and contrast in an image. **Brightness** is defined by a pixel's grayscale value: the higher the number, the brighter the pixel. **Contrast** is represented by the relationship between the highlights and shadows. When the highlights aren't bright enough and the shadows aren't dark enough, the image will lack contrast and appear "flat" in its tonal range. Good contrast is created when highlights and shadows are distinctly different in tonal range: bright vs. dark. Jon gives you an image that overall is too dark and has poor contrast. He asks that you use the Brightness/Contrast adjustment to improve the tonal range of the image.

STEPS

1. **Open PS E-2.psd, save it as Adjust Brightness Contrast, duplicate the Background layer, then rename the new layer After**

2. **Sample the highlight areas of the face, including the whites of the eyes, to get a general range of the values of the highlights in the image**

   The values are generally 140–170, far too low for highlights, which should be over 200. Really, there are no highlights in the image, as the brightest areas of the image fall into the midtone range. This image is not bright enough.

3. **Sample the hair and the image background area to the left of the face to get an idea of the general range of the shadows in the image**

   The values are generally 40–70, which puts them at the high end of the shadow range. The image lacks contrast because the highlight values are too close to the shadow values.

4. **Press and hold [Alt] (Win) or [option] (Mac), click the Create new fill or adjustment layer button 🖉 on the Layers panel, then click Brightness/Contrast**

   The New Layer dialog box and the Adjustments panel open.

QUICK TIP
Because it is clipped, the adjustment will affect only the After layer, not the Background layer.

5. **Click the Use Previous Layer to Create Clipping Mask check box, then click OK**

   As shown in Figure E-6, the Adjustments panel shows Brightness and Contrast sliders, and a clipped Brightness/Contrast layer appears on the Layers panel.

6. **Drag the Brightness slider on the Adjustments panel and sample the image until the pixels in the face fall into the 200–225 range, then compare your result to Figure E-7**

   The Brightness setting in the figure is set to 75. The appearance of the image improves dramatically.

7. **Drag the Contrast slider on the Adjustments panel to 80**

   The shadows darken and the highlights brighten. The shadows are improved dramatically, especially in the hair and the dark details of the face, like the pupils and the eyelashes.

8. **Reduce the Brightness to 65, then compare your result to Figure E-8**

   The reduced brightness deepens the shadows and increases the visible details of the face. Note the freckles. The face pixels still fall into the highlight range and are bright enough to give the image stunning contrast.

9. **Hide and show the Brightness/Contrast adjustment layer**

10. **Save your work, then close Adjust Brightness Contrast.psd**

FIGURE E-6: Brightness/Contrast adjustment layer on the Layers panel

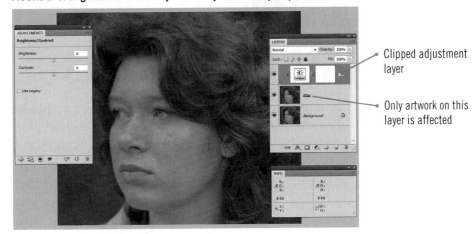

Clipped adjustment layer

Only artwork on this layer is affected

FIGURE E-7: Increasing the brightness

Shadow areas very light

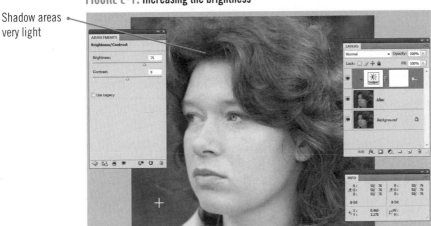

FIGURE E-8: Before and after the adjustment

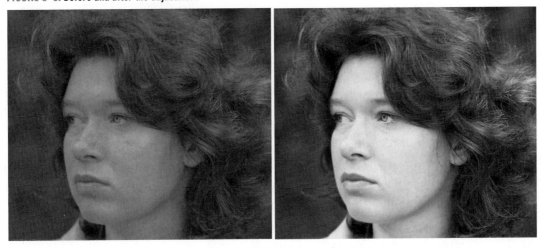

Extreme working behavior

A key to making adjustments is to sometimes walk the fine line between going far enough to make the adjustment the best it can be and going too far. When making adjustments, the first thing many designers do is push the adjustment to the extreme to see what the adjustment looks like when it's too much. When you work this way, seeing what you don't want can make it easier to find what you do want. Experiment with adjustments to see them at their extreme first. You're training your eye to recognize when an image looks its best, and recognizing when an image looks bad is a big part of that training.

Adjusting Black and White Points with Levels

In addition to shadows, midtones, and highlights, every image has a **black point**, representing the darkest pixel in the image, and a **white point**, representing the brightest pixel in the image. In other words, the black and white points represent the start and the end of the tonal range of the image.

Black and white points have a substantial effect on contrast. Often, photographers will capture an image with settings defined that the darkest pixel be no darker than, say, 15, and the brightest no lighter than 240. This forces the camera not to make shadows too dark or highlights too white. It results in an image that has a smooth tonal range from shadow to highlight but still lacks contrast because the darkest shadows aren't dark enough and the whitest highlights aren't white enough. This can be fixed using a Levels adjustment. For more information about levels, read the Clues to Use on the next page titled *How the Levels adjustment works.* ▨▨▨▨ Jon gives you an image with poor contrast and says he suspects the problem is with the black and white points.

STEPS

1. **Open PS E-3.psd, then save it as** Adjust White and Black Points

2. **Take a moment to make a visual analysis of the image and its tonal range**

   The image looks good, with a smooth range from shadow to highlight. However, it lacks contrast: it lacks "snap," and it's "flat."

3. **Sample the image to find the darkest and lightest pixels in the image**

   The darkest pixels are in the low 20s and the lightest pixels are around 230. No pixels have a grayscale value of 0–19 or 234–255.

4. **Click the** Create new fill or adjustment layer button ⬕. **on the Layers panel, then click** Levels

   The Adjustments panel displays settings for the Levels adjustment layer.

5. **Click the** Switch panel to Expanded View button ⬕ **on the Adjustments panel, then compare your Adjustments panel to Figure E-9**

   The histogram, shown on the panel, reflects exactly what you learned when sampling the image. The **histogram** is a visual reference of every pixel in the image (or in a selection). The black point on the histogram is represented by the black triangle, and the white point is represented by the white triangle.

   The tonal range of the image does not use the entire grayscale, represented by the gradient ramp below the histogram. Note how far to the right of the black triangle the histogram begins, and how far it ends from the white triangle.

> **QUICK TIP**
> The repositioned black and white triangles determine the new range of the histogram. The pixels at the far left of the histogram now have a grayscale value of 0, and those at the far right now have a grayscale value of 255.

6. **Drag the** black triangle **immediately beneath the histogram towards the right to the beginning of the histogram, drag the** white triangle **towards the left to the end of the histogram, then compare your result to Figure E-10**

7. **Hide and show the Levels 1 adjustment layer on the Layers panel to see the before and after view of the image**

   The *lengthened* tonal range is a stunning improvement in overall contrast for the image.

8. **Save your work**

FIGURE E-9: Adjustments panel with Levels adjustment layer settings

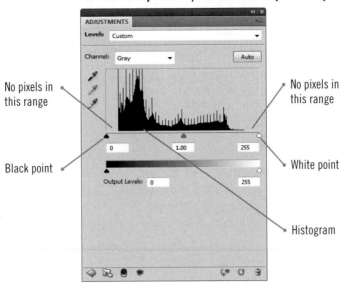

No pixels in this range

No pixels in this range

Black point

White point

Histogram

FIGURE E-10: Adjusting the black and white points

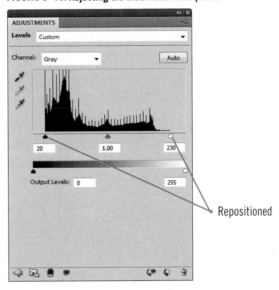

Repositioned

How the Levels adjustment works

The Levels type of adjustment, shown in Figure E-11, is a powerful adjustment option for affecting the tonal range of images. The most striking component of the Levels adjustment is the histogram.

Imagine that the histogram has 256 "slots," one for each of the 256 available colors in the grayscale image. The slot for the 0-value pixels is on the left, and the slot for the 255-value pixels is on the right. Now imagine that there are a total of 1000 pixels in the image with a grayscale value of 64. Using a black marble to represent each pixel, imagine that you drop 1000 marbles into the 64 slot on the slider. Next, imagine that the image contains 1500 pixels with a grayscale value of 72, and you drop 1500 black marbles into the 72 slot. Imagine that you do this for each of the 256 slots on the slider. Your result would be the histogram—exactly what you see in the Levels dialog box. The height of the histogram, from left to right, shows the relative number of pixels that the whole file—or a selection of pixels—has for each of the 256 grayscale values.

You adjust the image by manipulating the sliders at the bottom of the histogram. The black triangle represents the 0 on the grayscale. The white triangle represents 255 on the grayscale. The gray triangle represents the 128 midpoint. When you move any of the triangles, you readjust how the histogram relates to the full grayscale range, from shadow to highlight.

FIGURE E-11: Levels adjustment options on the Adjustments panel

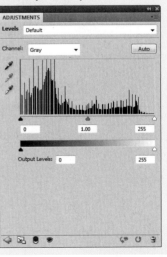

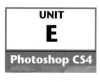

Adjusting the Midpoint with Levels

Adjusting the tonal range of an image is a lot like knowing which fork to use in fine dining: You start at the outside and work your way in. First, you set your black and white points—the extremes. Then, you verify that there's satisfactory contrast between the highlight and shadow range. Once those are established, you are ready—if you want to—to adjust the midpoint. The **midpoint** defines which areas of the image fall into the middle range of the available grayscale. In other words, it separates the bright half from the dark half. Moving the midpoint darkens or lightens the image. Interestingly, a midpoint adjustment is often only subjective—do you like the image better if it's brighter or darker? Jon thinks you've been very successful adjusting the black and white points. He tells you to "play" with the midpoint and "see what you come up with."

STEPS

1. **Take a moment to note the overall "feel" of the image, then relate that impression to the histogram on the Adjustments panel**

   Overall, the image has more dark areas than light areas. The hood is such a big part of the image and overall falls into the mid-upper shadow range. This is represented in the histogram, which shows significantly more pixels to the left of the midpoint than to the right.

2. **Drag the gray midpoint triangle left until the text box reads 1.20**

   Moving the midpoint triangle left by definition places more of the histogram to the right of the midpoint. Now, pixels that were in the lower half of the histogram are being defined as the midpoint of the grayscale.

3. **Evaluate the feel of the adjusted image, then compare your image to Figure E-12**

   Brightened, the image feels less heavy, but it also has less tension overall. The midpoint adjustment also makes the face too bright.

4. **Drag the gray midpoint triangle right until the text box reads .70**

   Artistically, this was a much better move than brightening the midpoint. The darkening has given great intensity to the face and the eyes. But it has also made the shadow areas so dark that they no longer show any detail, and this is not acceptable.

5. **Set the foreground color to black, click the Brush tool , then on the Options bar set the Master Diameter to 300 px and the Hardness to 0%**

6. **Click the Opacity list arrow on the Options bar, then change the Opacity to 10%**

7. **Target the layer mask on the Levels adjustment layer, then paint to lighten the shoulders and darkest areas of the jacket**

   Because the opacity of the brush is set to only 10%, you are essentially painting with a light gray. You are masking the adjustment very gradually.

8. **Compare your result to Figure E-13, save your work, then close Adjust White and Black Points**

FIGURE E-12: Brightening the midtones

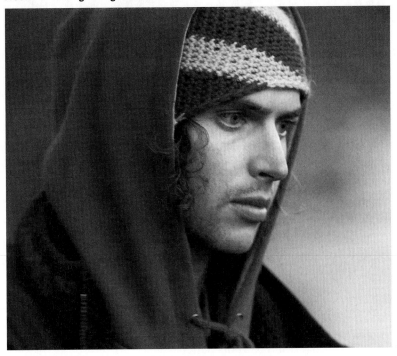

FIGURE E-13: Masking areas of the image from the adjustment

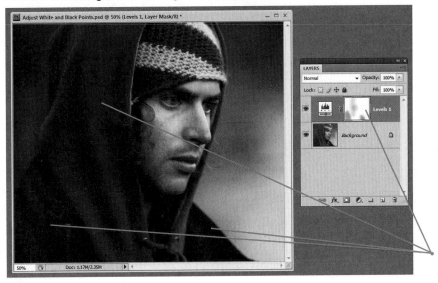

Adjustment is reduced
in these areas

Using layer masks with adjustments

When you create an adjustment layer—like the Levels adjustment layer—it is created automatically with a layer mask. It's a smart idea to think of the layer mask as less of an option and more of an essential component of working with adjustment layers. Sometimes, you will make an adjustment that you can apply completely to the artwork beneath, but more often, you will want to use the layer mask to apply the adjustment selectively in different strengths to different areas of the artwork.

When you set a low percentage of opacity on the Brush tool and then paint in the layer mask, the brush has reduced impact. In other words, if you set the brush to 10% opacity and paint in the layer mask with a black foreground color, each stroke of the brush will mask the artwork very gradually. This allows you to show or mask the adjustment very subtly and to be very specific as to how you want to affect the artwork beneath. Some designers automatically mask the adjustment completely then use a low-opacity brush to paint white in the mask, thus "brushing in" the adjustment gradually in specific areas. Remember, once you learn how to do it, it's easy to apply an adjustment layer. The layer mask allows you to apply it in a way that is unique and expresses your artistic vision.

Investigating an RGB Image

First and foremost, we could write an entire book on RGB color. With that in mind, let's focus on the essentials of what you need to know about RGB to work effectively in Photoshop. That starts with your monitor, which displays color with light. Like a TV screen, your monitor is a light source. Red, green, and blue are the **additive primary colors** of light. What that means is that red, green, and blue light can combine to produce all the other colors in the spectrum. The colors you see on your monitor—the purples, oranges, limes, yellows—all of them are created by mixing varying strengths and combinations of red, green, and blue.

In the early lessons in this book, we examined grayscale in a black-and-white image as being 256 shades of gray available per pixel to render the image. To apply the concept to an RGB image, simply take that concept and multiply by three! In an RGB image, there are 256 shades of red, 256 shades of green, and 256 shades of blue available per pixel. Remember, the resulting pixel is just one color—say, baby blue—but it is a combination of red, green, and blue. Jon tells you about a new client who will be supplying imagery that will require lots of analysis and correction for quality and color. He gives you an RGB image and asks that you analyze it.

STEPS

1. **Open PS E-4.psd, save it as RGB, then click the Default Foreground and Background Colors button ▣ on the Tools panel**

   The file has been saved in RGB Color mode.

2. **Click Edit (Win) or Photoshop (Mac) on the Application bar, point to Preferences, click Interface, click the Show Channels in Color check box to activate it, if necessary, then click OK**

3. **Verify that the two readouts in the Info panel are set to RGB color, click the Eyedropper tool 🖊, then position it over different areas of the image**

   The Info panel shows different values of R, G, and B per pixel. Each pixel can be one of 256 shades of red, 256 shades of green, and 256 shades of blue.

   QUICK TIP

   Because only the Red channel is displayed, all three readouts in the Info panel show info for the Red channel.

4. **Click Window on the Application bar, click Channels, then click the Red channel thumbnail**

   As shown in Figure E-14, the Red channel is displayed. Each pixel in the Red channel can be one of 256 shades of red from 0 (black) to 255 (red).

5. **Click the Green channel thumbnail to see the Green channel, click the Blue channel thumbnail to see the Blue channel, then click the RGB channel thumbnail to see the color image**

   The RGB channel is called the **composite** channel because it is the result of combining the R, G, and B channels.

   QUICK TIP

   You can think of the color cyan as being "minus red," because it is created by removing red.

6. **Select the right half of the canvas, fill the selection with white, deselect, then use the Eyedropper tool to sample the white pixels**

   Every white pixel is 255R/255G/255B.

7. **Click the Red channel thumbnail, fill the channel with black, click the RGB thumbnail to see the composite image, then compare your canvas to Figure E-15**

   The pixels on the right side of the canvas change to cyan: 0R + 255G + 255B = Cyan.

   QUICK TIP

   You can think of the color magenta as being "minus green," because it is created by removing green.

8. **Undo the fill to restore the Red channel, fill the Green channel with black, then click the RGB channel thumbnail**

   The pixels on the right side of the canvas change to magenta: 255R + 0G + 255B = Magenta.

   QUICK TIP

   You can think of the color yellow as being "minus blue," because it is created by removing blue.

9. **Undo the fill to restore the Green channel, fill the Blue channel with black, then click the RGB channel thumbnail**

   As shown in Figure E-16, the pixels on the right side of the canvas change to yellow: 255R + 255G + 0B = Yellow.

10. **Save your work, then close RGB.psd**

FIGURE E-14: Viewing the Red channel only

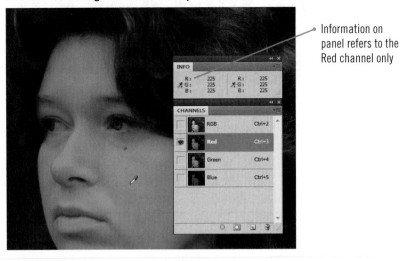

Information on panel refers to the Red channel only

FIGURE E-15: Viewing the image with no red component

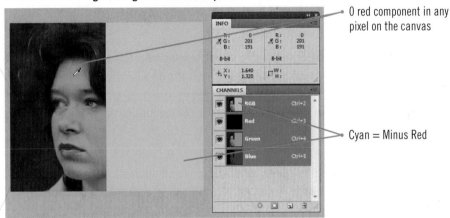

0 red component in any pixel on the canvas

Cyan = Minus Red

FIGURE E-16: Viewing the image with no blue component

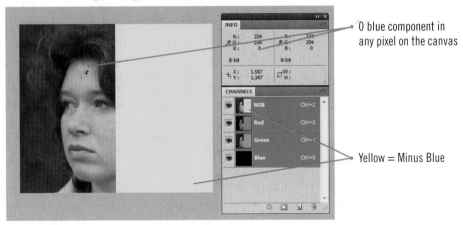

0 blue component in any pixel on the canvas

Yellow = Minus Blue

About cyan, magenta, and yellow

If you've done any professional printing, you know that color printing is done using cyan, magenta, and yellow inks, plus black ink for detail, collectively called CMYK. In fact, cyan, magenta, and yellow are the primary colors for printing. However, it's important that you exclude that information from this discussion. We're looking at color on a monitor, a monitor is a light source, and the primary colors of light are red, green, and blue.

The role of cyan, magenta, and yellow—as per this lesson—is that each is created by removing one of the additive RGB primary colors. This point is the key to manipulating color and doing color corrections in Photoshop. Many of Photoshop's color adjustment dialog boxes manipulate color using RGB and CMY as their basis, which you'll see in the next lesson.

Using the Color Balance Adjustment

Color Balance is an adjustment that allows you to control the balance of red, green, and blue in an image. It's a great tool for adjusting any color problems with an image. For example, many images from a digital camera are often too red. You can use the Color Balance adjustment to fix that. ▰▰▰ Jon asks you to open an image in Photoshop and improve the color by removing blue and green, using the Color Balance adjustment.

STEPS

1. **Open PS E-5.psd, then save it as Color Balance**

2. **Take a moment to look at the image and assess your feelings about what it looks like and how you might think it could be better**

   The image has good contrast but overall is "cold." The colors are muted, and the flesh tone has underlying hints of blue and purple.

3. **Click the Eyedropper tool ✎, position the tool over the background, note the RGB read-outs on the Info panel, then sample the shadows in the hair**

   The background is a natural setting, probably green leaves, so you would expect to see larger concentrations of green in these pixels. However, the shadows in the hair also reflect this green: where the shadows in the hair should be neutral, they show dominance in green.

4. **Sample the whites in the eyes**

   Whites in eyes are great places to sample for midtones and highlights. The RGB values should all be relatively close; in this image, the whites show dominance in blue.

5. **Click the Create new fill or adjustment layer button ◖ on the Layers panel, then click Color Balance**

   The Color Balance dialog box appears, shown in Figure E-17. The sliders represent what you learned in Lesson 6. Cyan is opposite Red, Magenta is opposite Green, and Yellow is opposite Blue.

6. **Experiment with the sliders by dragging them in each direction, noting the effect on the image, then click the Reset to adjustment defaults button ↻ on the Adjustments panel**

7. **Verify that the Midtones option button is selected on the Adjustments panel, drag the Blue slider to –26, then sample the white of the eye on the left side of the screen**

   With the adjustment, the values are all much closer: 187/197/197. Thus, the blue dominance is reduced.

8. **Click the Shadows option button on the Adjustments panel, then drag the Green slider left to –16**

   The move has a dramatic improvement on the image. Colors become more vibrant, and the face becomes a warmer pink, because reducing green increases the magenta balance. Green is much less dominant in the shadows in the hair.

9. **Click Window on the Application bar, click Adjustments to close the panel, hide and show the Color Balance 1 adjustment layer to see the before and after view of the image as shown in Figure E-18, then save your work**

FIGURE E-17: Color Balance adjustment

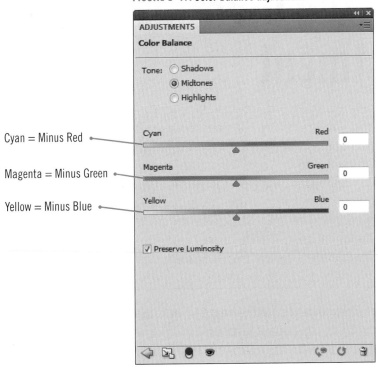

Cyan = Minus Red

Magenta = Minus Green

Yellow = Minus Blue

FIGURE E-18: Before and after the adjustment

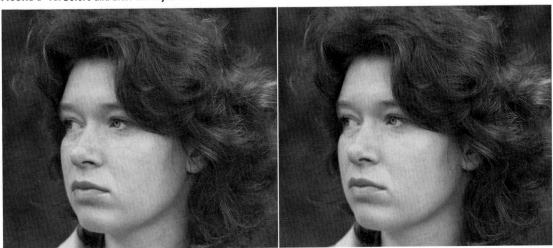

Looking for neutral grays

In an RGB file, color is created by an imbalance in the three channels. When a pixel's red component is substantially greater than the green and blue components, for example, the pixel's color will tend to fall into the red hue. Conversely, when the three numbers are close in value, the pixel becomes neutral in color. Whenever the three components are the same, the pixel will have no color and can be only a neutral gray. For example, 20/20/20 would produce a dark gray, and 210/210/210 would produce a light gray.

Sampling an image for neutral grays can lead to many insights for improving color. If you sample areas that *should* be neutral—like shadows in hair—and they show a substantial dominance in one color, that's a good hint that you should reduce that color in the shadows.

On the other hand, if an area that should have vibrant color is grayish and neutral, that tells you that the color balance in that area is too close between the three and one or two need to be more dominant.

Using the Vibrance Adjustment

The Vibrance adjustment is a very useful method for quickly making colors in an image more vibrant. **Vibrance** refers to the intensity of a color. The measure of a pixel's vibrance is called **saturation**. High saturation produces a vibrant color, like the red of a tomato. Reduced saturation produces a dull, more neutral color, like the dull red of a radish. A pixel with no saturation is a neutral gray. The Vibrance adjustment provides two settings: Vibrancy and Saturation. The Saturation setting is more of a blunt instrument; it simply increases or decreases the saturation value of all the pixels selected. The Vibrancy setting uses a more complex method for improving the image. It increases the saturation of pixels that need it without affecting pixels that are already saturated. Jon is pleased with the adjustments you made to the image with the Color Balance adjustment but asks that you improve the overall vibrancy of the color in the image.

STEPS

1. **Verify that the Color Balance 1 adjustment layer is targeted on the Layers panel, click the Create new fill or adjustment layer button ⬛, then click Vibrance**
   The Adjustments panel opens with settings for the Vibrance adjustment.

2. **Drag the Saturation slider all the way to the left**
   The image is completely desaturated and resembles a black-and-white image. Even though the image appears black-and-white, the file is still an RGB file, and all pixels still have an RGB component. In this case, all RGB values are all equal for all pixels.

3. **Drag the Saturation slider all the way to the right, then compare your result to Figure E-19**
   The image is oversaturated.

4. **Click the Reset to adjustment defaults button ↻, then drag the Vibrance slider all the way to the right**

5. **Hide and show the Vibrance 1 adjustment layer on the Layers panel to see a before and after view of the image**
   Even though the move is extreme, the result is very acceptable. The color is vibrant but not oversaturated.

6. **Click the Reset to adjustment defaults button ↻, then drag the Saturation slider to +37**

7. **Hide and show the Vibrance 1 adjustment layer on the Layers panel to see a before and after view of the image**

8. **Compare your result to Figure E-20**

9. **Save your work, then close Color Balance.psd**

FIGURE E-19: Oversaturating the image

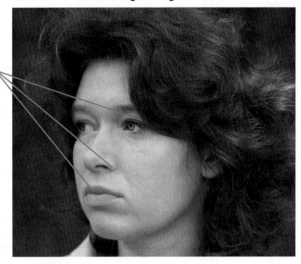

Note oversaturated "hot spots"

FIGURE E-20: Before and after the adjustment

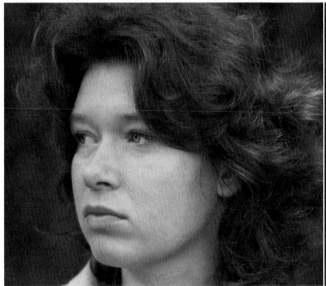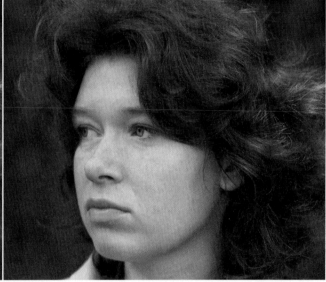

Doing a "super-undo" with the History panel

The History panel, shown in Figure E-21, offers lots of great features; one of them is the ability to quickly revert a file to its state when you first opened it, then to undo the revert to bring it back to its current state. As you work, the History panel records your moves and lists the last 20 of them, called **states**, in the panel. The last state in the list represents the last change you made to the file. You can click a state in the list to go back to that point of your work, and then continue working from that state. At the top of the panel is a thumbnail that represents the file the way that it looked when it was first opened. If you click the thumbnail you will undo all states in the panel. All of the states in the History panel are grayed out. Click any state to continue working from that particular state. For example, if you want to continue working with the file the way it was before you clicked the thumbnail image, click the last state before you continue working. If you undo all states and continue working by accident, you can click File on the Application bar, then click Revert. This will take you back to the status of the file when you last saved it. You may lose some of your work, but at least not *all* of your work.

FIGURE E-21

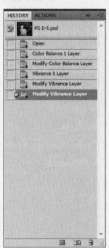

Practice

▼ CONCEPTS REVIEW

FIGURE E-22

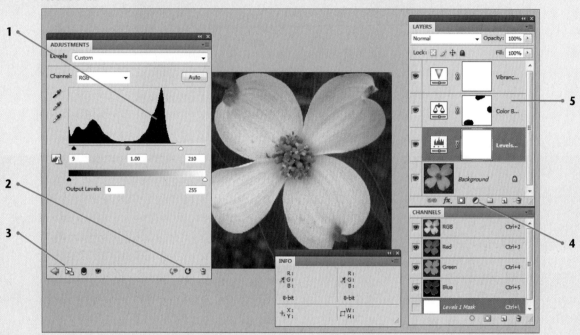

1. Which item is used to create a new adjustment layer?
2. Which item points to an adjustment layer?
3. Which item is used to reset an adjustment to its default settings?
4. Which item is used to expand the view of the Adjustments panel?
5. Which item points to a histogram?

Match each term with the statement that best describes it.

6. **Grayscale mode**
7. **RGB mode**
8. **Shadow point**
9. **Cyan**
10. **Magenta**
11. **Yellow**
12. **Continuous tone**
13. **Vibrance**

a. Darkest pixels in an image
b. "minus blue"
c. Intensity of a pixel's color
d. "minus green"
e. 256 shades of gray available per pixel
f. "minus red"
g. 256 shades available per pixel per channel
h. Smooth transition from shadows to highlights

Select the best answer from the list of choices.

14. **Which of the following is not an adjustment you can make in Photoshop?**
    a. Levels
    b. Bevel and Emboss
    c. Color Balance
    d. Vibrance

15. **Which of the following is not true of an RGB file?**
    a. It has three color channels.
    b. It is larger in file size than a grayscale version of the same file.
    c. Each pixel can be one of 256 shades of gray.
    d. The image can appear to be black-and-white.

16. **Which of the following is not true about a Levels adjustment?**
    a. A histogram is involved.
    b. You can use Levels to adjust a color or a black-and-white image.
    c. You can click a button so that the Levels adjustment will affect only shadows, midtones, or highlights.
    d. You can brighten the midpoint.

17. **Which of the following is not true about the Color Balance adjustment?**
    a. You can move a slider between Magenta and Cyan.
    b. You can move a slider between Blue and Yellow.
    c. You can move a slider between Cyan and Red.
    d. You can move a slider between Green and Magenta.

18. **Which of the following is not involved in assessing the appearance of an image?**
    a. Contrast
    b. Color balance
    c. Shadows
    d. Grayscale

▼ SKILLS REVIEW

1. **Understand grayscale.**
   a. Open PS E-6.psd, verify the Background layer is targeted, then save the file as **Grayscale Skills**.
   b. Click the Background layer, click Image on the Application bar, point to Mode, then note that Grayscale is checked.
   c. Open the Info panel, click the Info panel list arrow, click Panel Options, then verify that First Color Readout and Second Color Readout are both set to RGB Color.
   d. Click the Eyedropper tool and position it over different areas of the image, noting the readouts on the Info panel.
   e. Position the Eyedropper tool at the very bottom of the gradient on the right, then move slowly to the top of the gradient, sampling as you go.
   f. Sample areas in the background to see grayscale information for the darker areas of the image.
   g. Sample areas in the flower at the center to find mid-range areas of the image.
   h. Sample the petals and try to find the lightest pixels in the image.

2. **Investigate a grayscale image.**
   a. On the Layers panel, make the Chart layer visible.
   b. Look at the image flower and the background and try to see it not as a picture but as a range of tones from shadows to midtones to highlights.
   c. Using the chart as a guide, sample different areas of the image to identify shadows, highlights, and midtones.
   d. Move the Info panel to the upper-left corner, click Image on the Application bar, point to Adjustments, click Posterize, then drag the Levels slider to 3.
   e. Position the cursor over the image and note the before/after readouts on the Info panel.
   f. In the Posterize dialog box, change the Levels value to 16.

    g. Change the Levels value to 200.

    h. Click Cancel, then hide the Chart layer.

    i. Save your work, then close Grayscale Skills.psd.

3. Use the Brightness/Contrast adjustment.

    a. Open PS E-7.psd, then save it as **Brightness Contrast Skills**.

    b. Sample the highlight areas in the river and where sunshine strikes the rocks to get a general range of the values of the highlights in the image.

    c. Sample the dark areas of the rocks to get a general range of the shadows in the image.

    d. Click the Create new fill or adjustment layer button on the Layers panel, then click Brightness/Contrast.

    e. Drag the Brightness slider and sample the image until the lightest pixels in the water fall into the 220–235 range.

    f. Drag the Contrast slider to 90.

    g. Reduce the Brightness to 56.

    h. Close the Adjustments panel.

    i. Hide and show the Brightness/Contrast 1 adjustment layer and compare your before and after appearance to Figure E-23.

    j. Save your work, then close Brightness Contrast Skills.psd.

4. Adjust highlight and shadow points with levels.

    a. Open PS E-8.psd, then save it as **Levels Skills**.

    b. Take a moment to make a visual analysis of the image and its tonal range.

    c. Sample the image to find the darkest and lightest pixels in the image.

    d. Click the Create new fill or adjustment layer button on the Layers panel, then click Levels.

    e. Drag the black triangle toward the right to the beginning of the histogram, and drag the white triangle toward the left to the end of the histogram.

    f. Sample the image, trying to find shadow pixels that have a value of 10 or lower and highlight pixels that have a value of 240 or higher.

    g. Adjust the black and white triangles as necessary to produce the best shadow and highlight points.

    h. Hide and show the Levels adjustment layer on the Layers panel to see the before and after view of the image.

    i. Save your work.

5. Adjust the midpoint with levels.

    a. Take a moment to note the overall "feel" of the image, then relate that impression to the histogram in the Adjustments panel.

    b. Click the Create new fill or adjustment layer button on the Layers panel, then click Levels to add a second Levels adjustment layer.

    c. Drag the gray midpoint triangle left until the text box reads 1.30.

    d. Evaluate the appearance of the adjusted image.

    e. Drag the gray midpoint triangle right until the text box reads .79.

    f. Hide and show the new Levels adjustment layer to see the change.
(*Hint*: Be sure the Levels adjustment layer is showing when you're done.)

    g. Set the Foreground color to black, click the Brush tool, then on the Options bar, set the Master Diameter to 175 and the Hardness to 0%.

    h. Click the Opacity list arrow on the Options bar, then set the opacity to 30%.

    i. Target the layer mask on the Levels adjustment layer, then paint to lighten the center of the flower slightly.

    j. Compare your result to Figure E-24, save your work, then close Levels Skills.psd.

FIGURE E-23

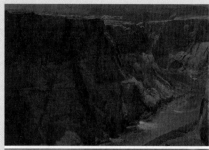

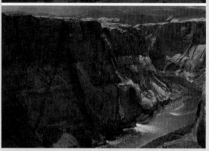

FIGURE E-24

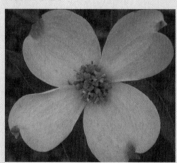

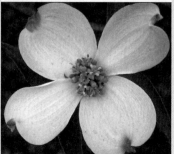

6. Investigate an RGB image.

   a. Open PS E-9.psd, then save it as **Color Balance Skills**.
(*Hint*: The file has been saved in RGB Color mode.)

   b. Click Edit (Win) or Photoshop (Mac) on the Application bar, point to Preferences, click Interface, click the Show Channels in Color check box, if necessary, then click OK.

   c. Verify that the two readouts in the Info panel are set to RGB Color, click the Eyedropper tool, then position it over different areas of the image.

   d. Click Window on the Application bar, click Channels, then click the channel thumbnail on the Red channel.

   e. Click the Green channel thumbnail to see the Green channel, click the Blue channel thumbnail to see the Blue channel, then click the RGB channel thumbnail to see the color image.

   f. Select the right half of the canvas, fill the selection with white, deselect, then position the Eyedropper tool to sample the white pixels.

   g. Click the Red channel thumbnail, fill the channel with black, then click the RGB channel thumbnail to see the composite image.

   h. Undo the fill to restore the Red channel, fill the Green channel with black, then click the RGB channel thumbnail.

   i. Undo the fill to restore the Green channel, fill the Blue channel with black, then click the RGB channel thumbnail.

   j. Click File on the Application bar, then click Revert.

7. Use the Color Balance adjustment.

   a. Take a moment to look at the image and assess your feelings about what it looks like and how you might think it could be better.
(*Hint*: Elephants are usually gray, not brown.)

   b. Click the Eyedropper tool, sample different areas of the image, and note the RGB readouts in the Info panel.
(*Hint*: Red dominates almost every pixel in the image.)

   c. Sample the whites in the tusk.

   d. Click the Create new fill or adjustment layer button on the Layers panel, then click Color Balance.

   e. Take some time to experiment with the sliders, noting the effect on the image, then click the Reset to adjustment defaults button on the panel.

   f. Verify that the Midtones option button is selected, then drag the Red slider to -34.

   g. Drag the Green slider to -6, then drag the Blue slider to +20.

   h. Click the Highlights option button, drag the Red slider to -25, then drag the Green slider to -12.

   i. Close the Adjustments panel, hide and show the Color Balance adjustment layer to see the before and after view of the image, then save your work.

8. Use the Vibrance adjustment.

   a. Verify that the Color Balance adjustment layer is targeted on the Layers panel, click the Create new fill or adjustment layer button, then click Vibrance.

   b. Drag the Saturation slider all the way to the left.

   c. Drag the Saturation slider all the way to the right.

   d. Click the Reset to adjustment defaults button, then drag the Vibrance slider to +40.

   e. Hide and show the Vibrance adjustment layer on the Layers panel to see a before and after view of the image.

   f. Drag the Saturation slider gradually to +10.

   g. Hide and show the Vibrance adjustment layer on the Layers panel to see a before and after view of the image.

   h. Compare your result to Figure E-25.
(*Hint*: The figure shows the image before and after all adjustments.)

   i. Save your work, then close Color Balance Skill.psd.

FIGURE E-25

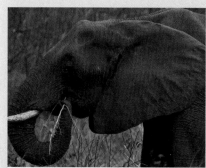

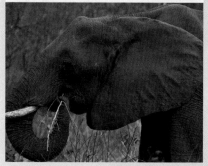

▼ INDEPENDENT CHALLENGE 1

You're designing a brochure of photos from your hometown and want to adjust an image to make it look its best.

FIGURE E-26

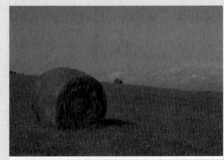

a. Open PS E-10.psd, then save it as **Hay Bale**.

b. Create a Brightness/Contrast adjustment layer.

c. Drag the Brightness slider to +35, then sample the brightest cloud in the sky.

d. Drag the Contrast slider to +60.

e. Sample the bright cloud again and verify that its values are somewhere between 200–225.

(*Hint*: Because the cloud is very distant, you shouldn't make it too bright.)

f. Sample the shadows in the hay bale and on the ground to be sure they haven't become too black.

g. Create a Vibrance adjustment layer.

h. Drag the Vibrance slider all the way to the right.

i. Drag the Vibrance slider to +85, then compare your result to Figure E-26.

j. Save your work, close Hay Bale.psd.

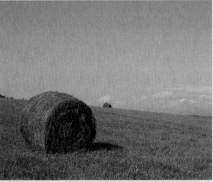

▼ INDEPENDENT CHALLENGE 2

You work for a boating magazine and are working on a photo you're going to use in a layout. The creative director tells you that the foreground of the image is great but that she'd like you to give the sky and the mountains in the distance "more weight for detail."

a. Open PS E-11.psd, then save it as **Sailboat**.

b. Create a Levels adjustment layer.

c. Drag the midpoint triangle right to .63.

d. Click the Brush tool.

e. Use various brush sizes and hardness values to mask the adjustment so that it affects only the sky and the mountain in the distance.

f. Save your work, compare your screen to Figure E-27, then close Sailboat.psd.

FIGURE E-27

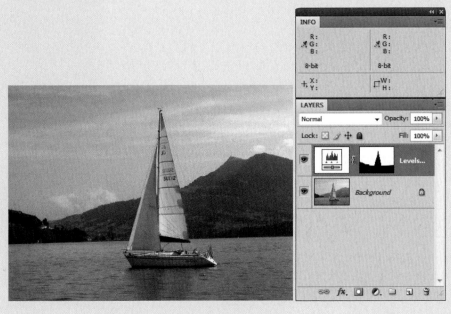

Improving Images with Adjustment Layers

▼ INDEPENDENT CHALLENGE 3

You're a designer for a greeting card company. You download an image from an online stock photography Web site and decide to improve it with some adjustments.

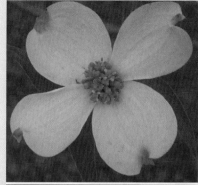

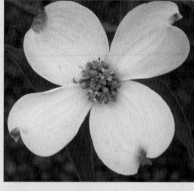

a. Open PS E-12.psd, then save it as **Color Flowers**.
b. Create a Levels adjustment layer.
c. Drag the black slider toward the right to where the histogram starts, then drag the white triangle toward the left to where the histogram ends.
d. Create a Brightness/Contrast adjustment layer, then drag the Contrast slider to +35.
e. Create a Color Balance adjustment layer.
f. Drag the Red slider to +6, drag the Green slider to -12, then drag the Blue slider to -26.
g. Click the Levels adjustment layer, then drag the midpoint triangle left until the text box reads 1.15.
h. Drag the black triangle right until the text box reads 40.
i. Target the Color Balance adjustment layer on the Layers panel, then create a Vibrance adjustment layer.
j. Drag the Saturation slider to +30.
k. Compare your results to Figure E-28.

Advanced Challenge Exercise

- Click the Levels adjustment layer.
- Slowly drag the white triangle left to see the white petals begin to lose detail and "blow out."
- Keep dragging left until the petals are entirely white with no detail.
- Drag the white triangle right and sample with the Info panel to find the point where the pixels in the petals are their brightest but not at 255.

l. Save your work, then close the Color Flowers.psd.

▼ REAL WORLD INDEPENDENT CHALLENGE

You're a talented amateur photographer. You use great equipment and your photos download from your camera looking really good. You just returned from your trip west and are using Photoshop to tweak your photos to go from looking good to looking great.

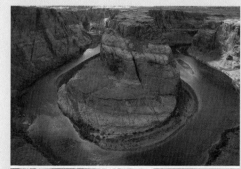

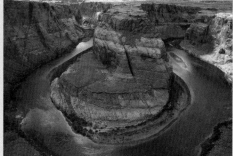

a. Open PS E-13.psd, then save it as **Canyon**.
b. Create a Levels adjustment layer.
c. Drag the black triangle right to 12, then drag the white triangle left to 212.
d. Drag the midpoint slider right to .90.
e. Create a Color Balance adjustment layer.
f. Drag the Red slider to +5, then drag the Blue slider to -10.
g. Create a Vibrance adjustment layer.
h. Drag the Vibrance slider to +60.

Advanced Challenge Exercise

- Open the History panel.
- Click the PS E-13 thumbnail at the top of the panel to see the image in its original state.
- Click the Modify Levels Layer state on the History panel.

i. Compare your results to Figure E-29, then close Canyon.psd.

▼ VISUAL WORKSHOP

Open PS E-14.psd, then save it as **Visual Solution**. Apply adjustments to the image so that the canvas resembles Figure E-30.

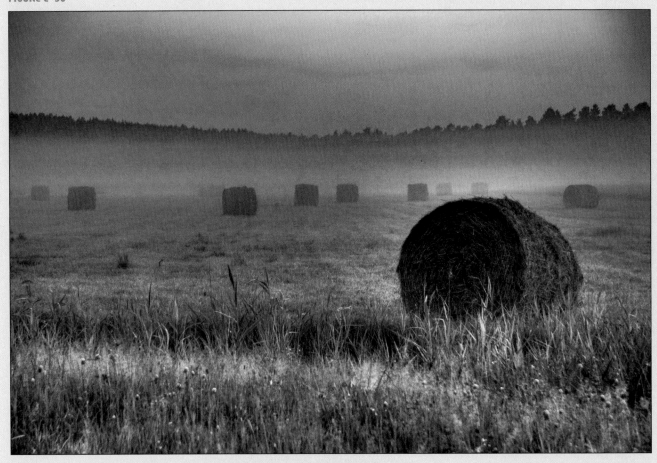

UNIT
F

Photoshop CS4

Working with Brushes and Color Effects

Manipulating color in Photoshop tends to take on two different roles: improving realistic color to make a better image or creating special effects with color. In Unit E, you used adjustment layers to improve color in color images. In this unit, you will use a variety of techniques to create color effects. These techniques include adjustment layers, layer masks, and color adjustment utilities.

Because many color effects involve using layer masks with adjustments, working effectively with the Brush tool and the Brushes panel becomes an important set of skills. You use brushes for both practical and artistic painting effects. Of all the Photoshop panels, the Brushes panel is arguably the most multi-faceted and complex. In many ways, you never stop learning about brushes and using them effectively. Jon assigns you many different projects, all which need improvements in color.

OBJECTIVES

Create custom brushes

Paint with automatic brush strokes

Paint a complex mask

Understand the color picker

Modify color with the Hue/Saturation adjustment

Use the Replace Color dialog box

Use the Black & White adjustment

"Colorize" a Black & White adjustment

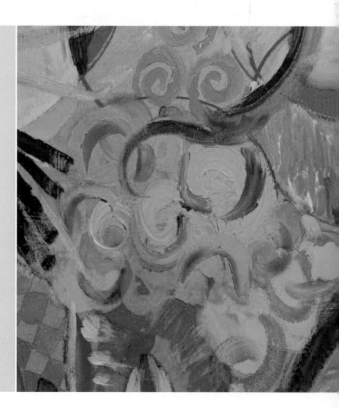

Creating Custom Brushes

Photoshop comes with hundreds of brushes on the Brushes panel, but many designers like to create their own set of brushes with specific characteristics. Photoshop allows you to create and save your own custom brushes. The two most basic characteristics of a brush are the diameter—the size of the brush—and the hardness—how hard or soft the edge of the brush is. ▰▰▱▱▱ Jon asks you to create two medium-sized brushes—one hard-edged, one soft—to use for future projects.

STEPS

1. Open PS F-1.psd, then save it as Connect the Dots

2. Click the Brush tool 🖌, click the Brushes panel list arrow, then verify that Expanded View at the top of the menu is checked

3. Click the Brushes panel list arrow again, click Reset brushes, then click OK in the dialog box that follows

   The brushes on the Brushes panel are reset to the default collection of brushes.

4. If necessary, scroll to the top of the Brushes panel, then click the brush named Hard Round 19 pixels

   As shown in Figure F-1, this brush has the Shape Dynamics and Smoothing options applied to it. You can read more about the Shape Dynamics option in the Clues to Use below named *Turn off Shape Dynamics*. The Smoothing option enables mouse path smoothing.

5. Click the Shape Dynamics check box to remove the check mark, then click Brush Tip Shape

6. Drag the Diameter slider on the Brushes panel to 31 px

7. Click the Brush Preset picker list arrow on the Options bar, drag the Hardness slider to 0%, click the Brushes panel list arrow, then click New Brush Preset

   The Brush Name dialog box opens.

8. Type Soft Round 31 in the Name text box, then click OK

   The new brush is added to the Brushes panel and is automatically selected.

9. Drag the Hardness slider to 100%, click the Brushes panel list arrow, click New Brush Preset, type Hard Round 31 in the Name text box, then click OK

Turning off Shape Dynamics

The Shape Dynamics option, when activated, offers you greater control for painting, such as using a brush that fades or a brush that responds to the pressure you apply when painting. Shape Dynamics are essentially programmed for users using a pressure-sensitive stylus pen instead of a mouse. For this entire chapter, be sure that the Shape Dynamics option is not checked when you select a brush. This is not as simple as it sounds, because many brushes on the Brushes panel have been designed with Shape Dynamics as their default setting, and therefore Shape Dynamics will be activated automatically if you click that brush.

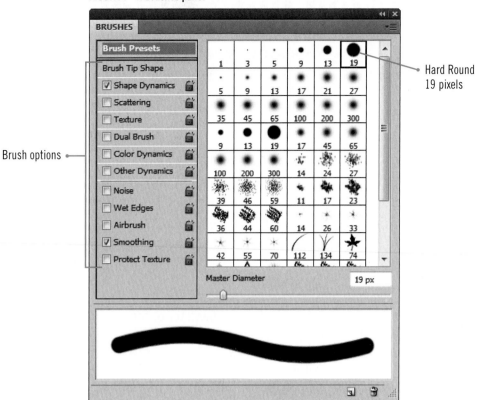

Hard Round
19 pixels

Brush options

Setting preferences for brushes

The paintbrush icon for the Brush tool does not change when you change the size of the brush you are using. However, you can change the preference settings for painting cursors in the Cursors section of the Preferences dialog box, as shown in Figure F-2. Notice that the Normal Brush Tip is the default option. To change this option, click Edit (Win) or Photoshop (Mac) on the Application bar, point to Preferences, click Cursors, then choose a new option, such as Full Size Brush Tip. The Full Size Brush Tip setting displays the Brush tool icon as a circle representing the size and shape of the Brush tool.

FIGURE F-2: Preferences for painting cursors

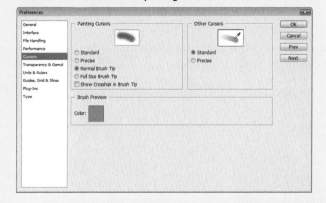

Painting with Automatic Brush Strokes

One of the fastest and most effective ways of working with the Brush tool—especially when painting masks—is to use the automatic brush technique. Rather than click and drag, simply click the Brush tool, press and hold [Shift], then click in a different location. The Brush tool automatically paints a connecting brush stroke between the two points. Using automatic brush strokes is like a digital game of connect-the-dots. It's a great way to cover a lot of ground quickly with the Brush tool. Jon tells you to expect a job coming in that will require painting lots of complex masks. To prepare, he asks that you practice painting with the automatic brush strokes technique.

STEPS

1. **Verify that the Hard Round 31 brush is selected on the Brushes panel and that the Foreground color is set to black**

2. **Press 〖] 〗 seven times to increase the diameter of the brush to 80 pixels**
   Pressing the right-bracket key increases the diameter of the brush; pressing the left-bracket key decreases the diameter. Pressing the bracket keys does not affect the hardness of the brush, only its diameter. The new brush diameter is displayed on the Brushes panel and on the Options bar.

3. **Target the Hard brush layer on the Layers panel, then click point #1 on the canvas**

QUICK TIP

If you get an odd or incorrect result, chances are it's because the Shape Dynamics option is activated for the brush you are using.

4. **Press and hold [Shift], click point #2, then compare your canvas to Figure F-3**
   As shown in the figure, the Brush tool paints automatically between the first and second points.

5. **Using the same method, click each point to point #6, then target the Soft Brush layer on the Layers panel**

6. **Click the Soft Round 31 brush on the Brushes panel, then change the Foreground color to white**

7. **Click where point #1 would be if it were visible, press and hold [Shift], then click point #2**

8. **Using the same method, click each point to point #6, then compare your canvas to Figure F-4**
   The Brush tool paints with a soft-edged stroke.

9. **Save your work, then close Connect the Dots.psd**

Painting with a soft-edged brush

Brush settings allow you to specify the edge of a brush in terms of hardness: 100% is the hardest-edged brush and 0% is the softest-edged brush. You can think of a soft brush as having a feathered edge, and a brush with 0% hardness as having the most feathered edge. It's important to note that the size of the feathered edge increases and decreases proportionally with the size of the brush. In other words, if you're using a soft brush with a diameter of 100 pixels, the feathered edge on that brush will be much wider than the feathered edge on a brush with a diameter of 10 pixels. Note too that a soft brush will affect pixels outside of the circle that represents the Brush tool. In other words, if you're painting with a big brush having a soft edge, expect that pixels will be affected outside of the brush icon you're painting with.

FIGURE F-3: Connecting point #1 with point #2

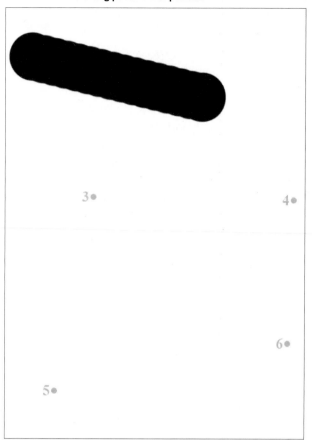

FIGURE F-4: Painting a soft-edged stroke

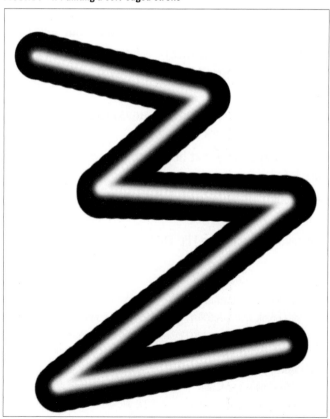

Painting a Complex Mask

Painting masks is something you'll do over and over and over again in Photoshop. It's just an essential behavior when using the program. Especially when making color adjustments, you'll find that you'll want to mask some of the adjustment to manipulate how it affects the artwork. Because masking is so essential, it's important that you develop skills for using the Brush tool effectively. This means using the best diameter and edge hardness for a given goal. The decisions you make—especially for the edge hardness—will have a direct effect on the success of the mask. Jon tells you about a new beachwear client who has asked that a photo of sandals be altered in color for a catalog. Jon tells you that he's already added an adjustment to change the color and asks that you mask the adjustment to complete the effect.

STEPS

1. **Open PS F-2.psd, save it as Flip Flops, then hide and show the adjustment layer to see the effect of the color adjustment**

   The goal is to mask the adjustment so that it affects the sandals only.

2. **Zoom in on the sandals to 400% to get a sense of the hardness of the edge pixels where the sandals meet the stone background**

   The image is very well lit and in focus, and the edge where the sandals meet the background is crisp. The texture of the actual object—rubber sandals—calls for a fairly hard mask.

3. **Zoom out to 300%, click the Brush tool ✎, if necessary, press and hold [Spacebar] to access the Hand tool, then position the image so that the toe of the left sandal is centered on your screen**

4. **Click the Hard Round 31 brush on the Brushes panel, reduce the Diameter to 18 px, then set the Hardness to 80%**

QUICK TIP
Continue viewing the canvas at 300% while working; use the [Spacebar] to access the Hand tool to scroll as you paint. Reduce and enlarge the diameter of the brush as you see fit.

5. **Click the adjustment layer mask thumbnail on the Hue/Saturation 1 layer, verify that the Foreground color is set to black, then using the automatic brush strokes technique, paint the edges of both sandals in the layer mask so that your canvas resembles Figure F-5**

6. **Press [Alt](Win) or [option](Mac), click the layer mask to view it, click the Magic Wand tool ✦, set the Tolerance to 8, then verify that the Contiguous check box is checked on the Options bar**

7. **Click the white background on the canvas to select it, click Select on the Application bar, point to Modify, then click Expand**

8. **Type 8 in the Expand By text box, click OK, zoom out to 100%, then compare your mask to Figure F-6**

9. **Fill the selection with black, click the adjustment layer thumbnail, then compare your canvas to Figure F-7**

10. **Save your work, then close Flip Flops.psd**

Determining the real edge

When painting a mask, your choice for the hardness of the brush will have a big impact. You wouldn't mask a rabbit with a 100% hard brush, and you wouldn't mask a rowboat with a brush set to 0% hardness. Within those extremes, though, the choice of hardness can become very subjective. In this lesson, you masked an image of rubber flip-flop sandals. We used this image specifically because they are a fairly common item; without having them in front of you, you know pretty much what they look and feel like.

When choosing a Hardness setting for the brush to mask an item, your choice is based on the actual item itself. You know that sandals have a defined edge, but the material itself is malleable. The real item impacts your choice of hardness for the brush to mask the image of the item. In Lesson 3, we chose a hardness setting of 80% to mask the sandals. After some experimentation I discovered that 80% allowed for the best amount of softness for the mask edge to help the transition between the item and the background.

FIGURE F-5: Masking the edges of the sandals

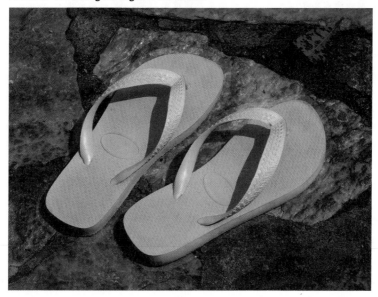

FIGURE F-6: Making a selection in the mask

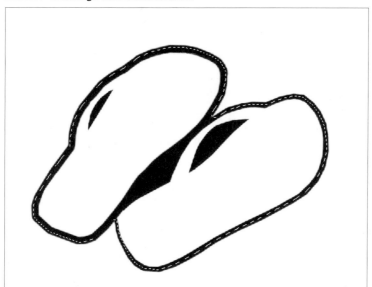

FIGURE F-7: Finished artwork

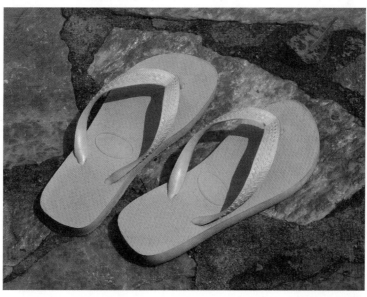

Working with Brushes and Color Effects

Understanding the Color Picker

The Color Picker is one of the essential dialog boxes in Photoshop. It allows you to choose any color available as a foreground or background color. The Color Picker is designed in terms of HSB, and an understanding of HSB is great clarification for how the Color Picker works. Like RGB, HSB is a color model, and every pixel in Photoshop can be identified by its HSB values. **Hue** represents the name of the color: red, orange, and blue are all hues. In the Color Picker, Photoshop offers 360 hues to work with. **Saturation** refers to the intensity of the color: how close it is to a pure hue. **Brightness** affects a hue in terms of how light or dark the color is. If the Brightness setting is set to 0%, it's as though you were looking at a color in a completely dark room: all you would see is black. ▆▆▆ Jon asks you to experiment with the Color Picker to get a better understanding of HSB and how the Color Picker dialog box is designed.

STEPS

1. **Open PS F-3.psd, save it as HSB, then set your Foreground color to black**

QUICK TIP
The Hue slider is the set of triangles pointing to the rainbow bar in the dialog box. Dragging one triangle moves both of them.

2. **Click the Foreground color button on the Tools panel to open the Color Picker, verify that the H (Hue) button is activated, then drag the Hue slider up and down, noting the changes in the H (Hue) text box**

   The H (Hue) value changes as you drag the slider. The H value is specified in degrees because the slider represents a standard color wheel of 360 degrees. There are 360 hues available in Photoshop.

3. **Drag the slider until the H value reads 85°**

4. **Click and drag in the large color box to the left of the Hue slider, and note the changes to the new box as you drag**

   As shown in Figure F-8, the new box represents the new foreground color. The current box represents the current foreground color. As you drag in the color box, the new box color continually changes. Notice that the Hue value remains at 85°. The new color represents hue 85 with varying percentages of saturation and brightness.

5. **Drag the circle in the color box all the way to the upper-right corner**

   In the upper-right corner, the S and B values are 100%. This color is the "pure" hue 85—the brightest and most saturated.

6. **Drag down along the right edge of the color box**

   As you drag down, the brightness is reduced and the color is darkened. 0% brightness is equal to black.

7. **Click the upper-left corner, then drag down along the left edge of the color box**

   Wherever you click along the left edge, you will see a shade of gray. At the left edge, there is 0 saturation, and 0 saturation equals zero color, or white. The left edge changes from white to black as the brightness decreases.

8. **Click near the center of the color box, then drag the circle right and left, noting the changes in the S (Saturation) text box and the new box**

   As you drag right, the saturation increases. As the saturation increases, the intensity of the color increases.

9. **Click near the center, then drag slowly toward the upper-right corner**

   As shown in Figure F-9, as you drag up and right, both the saturation and the brightness increase, and the color is brightened and intensified dramatically.

10. **Click Cancel to close the Color Picker dialog box**

FIGURE F-8: Changing the hue in the Color Picker

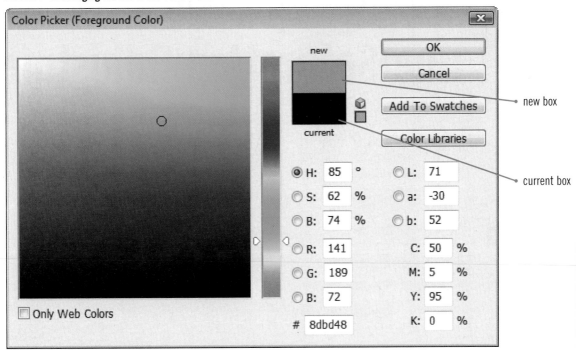

FIGURE F-9: Changing the saturation and brightness in the Color Picker

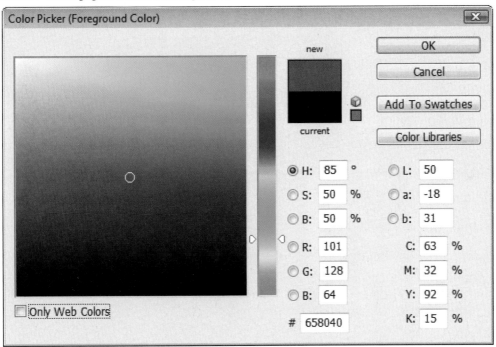

RGB and HSB working hand in hand

In Unit E we discussed RGB and working in the RGB Color mode. Note that in the Color Picker you can specify color as RGB and HSB. RGB and HSB are both color models that Photoshop uses to describe the color of a pixel. They are independent of one another, but they don't conflict. It's like reading the same novel in English and in Italian—same story, just a different language. The best approach to the two color models is to keep them separate in your mind. When you are evaluating an image in terms of color balance, you're looking at the image in terms of RGB. Is it too red? Is the green too heavy in the highlights? At other times, you'll be evaluating images in terms of brightness/contrast, or you'll want to make the color of an image more intense, as with the Vibrance adjustment. In that case, you're looking at the image in terms of HSB. Become comfortable with both, because each offers a powerful and effective way to assess a color image.

Modifying Color with the Hue/Saturation Adjustment

Hue/Saturation is one of the most powerful adjustments in Photoshop, one that you'll use often for both practical color improvements and to create special effects. The adjustment is composed of three values. The Hue slider changes only the Hue value of all selected pixels. The Saturation slider changes only the saturation, intensifying or muting the color of selected pixels. The Lightness slider increases or decreases the brightness of selected pixels. Be sure to read the Clues to Use called *Lightness Versus Brightness* at the end of this lesson to learn more important information about the Lightness value in the Hue/Saturation adjustment. Jon gives you an image of an automobile and asks that you change its color to a bright yellow.

STEPS

1. **On the Info panel, click the eyedropper icon on the first readout, then click HSB Color to change the display to HSB**

2. **Click the adjustment layer on the Layers panel to show the Hue/Saturation adjustment**
   The layer was prepared with a mask for this lesson, but none of the HSB settings have been changed. In other words, it's not presently having any effect on the image.

3. **Drag the Hue slider on the Adjustments panel right to +30, then position the mouse pointer over the canvas to see the before and after values on the Info panel**
   As shown in Figure F-10, the Hue value for all pixels affected by the adjustment is increased. If a pixel's hue was 100, it is now 130. If it was 50, it is now 80.

4. **Drag the Hue slider left to –40**

5. **Drag the Saturation slider right to +20**

6. **Hide and show the Hue/Saturation adjustment layer, then compare your result to Figure F-11**

7. **Save your work, then close HSB.psd**

FIGURE F-10: Changing the hue

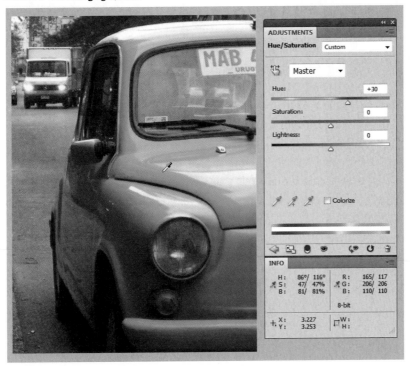

FIGURE F-11: Before and after the Hue/Saturation adjustment

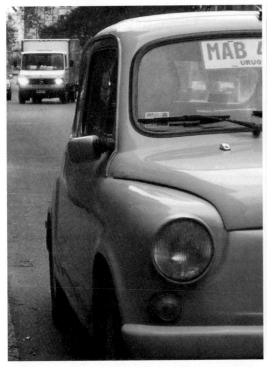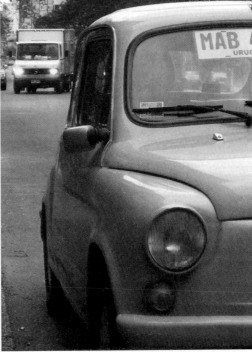

Lightness Versus Brightness

In the Color Picker and on the Info panel, Hue/Saturation is specified in HSB: Hue, Saturation, and Brightness. But in the Hue/Saturation adjustment, the sliders are HSL: Hue, Saturation, and Lightness. So what is going on here? Here's the deal: Photoshop doesn't want you to confuse "Lightness" in the Hue/Saturation adjustment with "Brightness" in the Brightness/Contrast adjustment. The Lightness slider in the Hue/Saturation adjustment has its uses, but it's not to brighten or darken an image the way you do with the Brightness/Contrast adjustment. Just experiment with the Lightness slider and you'll see right away that the result is not what you're expecting. In fact, it is usually detrimental to the image. Use the Brightness/Contrast adjustment to brighten or darken an image as opposed to the Lightness slider in the Hue/Saturation adjustment.

Using the Replace Color Dialog Box

It will often be the case that you'll want to modify the color in areas that are difficult to select with the selection tools or even with a layer mask. In these cases, the Replace Color dialog box can be very useful. The Replace Color dialog box offers tools that allow you to target various areas of an image based strictly on similarity in color. When you target an area, the dialog box shows you a black-and-white mask, with the white areas representing the pixels that will be affected by any changes you make. You can drag the Fuzziness slider to increase the targeted area, or you can use the Add to sample tool to click a specific area to add that area to the target. Once you have targeted an area of the image, you can change the Hue and Saturation values to modify the color only in those areas. Whenever you want to modify Hue/Saturation in non-specific areas of an image, think of using the Replace Color feature. Jon gives you an image that will be used on a Web site. He asks you to change the color of the door, but "don't spend too much time on it." You decide that Replace Color is the best utility to quickly modify the specific area.

STEPS

1. Open PS F-4.psd, then save it as Replace Color

2. Duplicate the Background layer, rename the duplicate Replace Color, then zoom in on the image so that the door fills your screen

3. Click Image on the Application bar, point to Adjustments, then click Replace Color

4. Drag the Fuzziness slider to 36, click the Eyedropper tool ⌖ in the Replace Color dialog box, then click a light green area on the door, as shown in Figure F-12

   Fuzziness controls which pixels will be affected by any changes you make in the Replace Color dialog box. The greater the fuzziness value, the more pixels will be included in the sample you select. A mask is generated based on tolerance from the point you sampled with the Eyedropper tool. The white areas of the mask represent the areas of the image that will be affected by any adjustments you make.

5. Drag the Fuzziness slider to 70

   The white areas of the mask are increased.

6. Drag the Hue slider to +175

7. Click the Add to Sample tool ⌖, click a dark green area of the image, as shown in Figure F-13, then click any remaining greenish pixels, if necessary

   The targeted area expands to the shadow areas.

8. Click OK, then hide and show the Replace Color layer

   The change was successful on the door, but it has also affected areas in the girl's clothes and boots. Because Replace Color is not an adjustment layer like, it affects the layer directly.

9. Add a layer mask and quickly mask any unwanted results of using Replace Color

10. Save your work, then close Replace Color.psd

> **QUICK TIP**
> The Replace Color move missed a green reflected highlight in the girl's hair. You could correct this with a Color Balance adjustment.

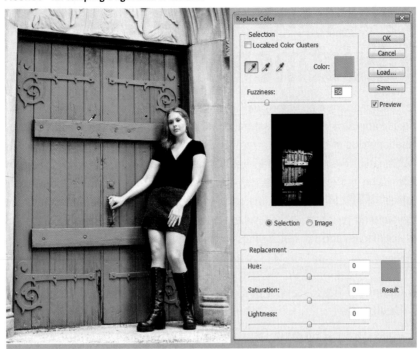

FIGURE F-12: Sampling a light area of the door

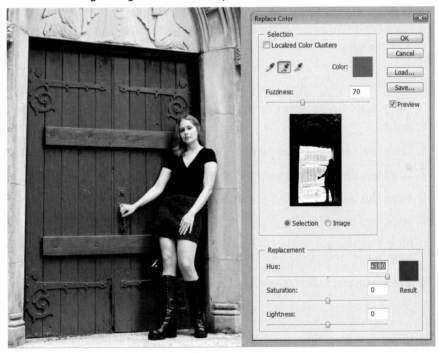

FIGURE F-13: Adding a dark green area to the sample

Replace Color is not an adjustment layer

The Replace Color feature is not an adjustment layer. When you make an adjustment—like Levels, for example—the adjustment appears as a layer on the Layers panel. You can hide it or show it, and you can use its default layer mask to mask the adjustment. You can readjust the adjustment at any time, and you can even delete it. You can't do any of that with Replace Color. When you alter artwork on a layer with Replace Color, after you click OK, that alteration is applied directly to the layer. That's it—other than using the Undo command, the alteration is permanent. That's why, whenever you use Replace Color, it's a smart idea to duplicate the layer you want to modify and apply Replace Color to the duplicate artwork, as we did in this lesson. That way, you preserve the original artwork, and you can use a layer mask on the duplicate art to control how the Replace Color alteration affects the original.

Using the Black & White Adjustment

The fastest, and most common, way to make a color image appear as a black-and-white image is to desaturate it completely with a Hue/Saturation adjustment. When you do so, the adjustment simply reduces the saturation value of every pixel to zero, and you're left with the results. A better method is to use the Black & White adjustment, which offers you brightness controls for converting the color original to black-and-white. Using these controls, you can create a stunning, eye-catching, black-and-white version of a color original. Jon e-mails you a color image that he tells you must be used as a black and white. He tells you to do your best to "keep all the colors distinct" in the black-and-white version. You decide to take two approaches and see which offers the best result.

STEPS

1. **Open PS F-5.psd, save it as Color Fan, duplicate the Background layer, then rename it Desaturate**

2. **Press [Ctrl][U] (Win) or ⌘[U] (Mac) to open the Hue/Saturation dialog box, drag the Saturation slider all the way left to –100, then click OK**

   This Hue/Saturation adjustment is made directly to the layer, unlike using a Hue/Saturation adjustment layer.

3. **Hide the Desaturate layer, then target the Background layer**

4. **Click the Create new fill or adjustment layer button** ⬤ **on the Layers panel, then click Black & White**

   The image becomes black-and-white, and the Adjustments panel shows settings for the Black & White adjustment.

5. **Drag sliders in different directions on the Adjustments panel to experiment with various results**

6. **Click the Reset to adjustment defaults button** ⟳ **on the Adjustments panel**

7. **Drag the Blues slider to –10, then drag the Yellows slider to 80**

8. **Drag the Reds slider to 54, then drag the Greens slider to 20**

9. **Hide and show the Desaturate layer to compare the quality of the two different results**

   As shown in Figure F-14, the Black & White adjustment is clearly the better result of the two, with obviously better contrast and much clearer distinctions between various colors.

10. **Save your work, then close Color Fan.psd**

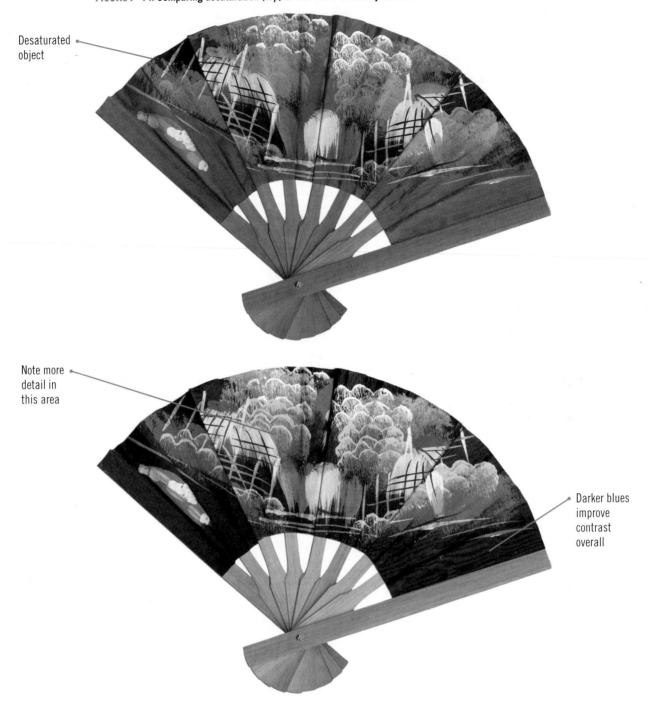

Desaturated
object

Note more
detail in
this area

Darker blues
improve
contrast
overall

Converting to Grayscale mode

Another way to create black and white from color is to convert the file from RGB Color mode to Grayscale mode. When you do, Photoshop discards all color data from the file, reducing the file from three color channels to a single grayscale channel. This is an effective method, but it is a bit of overkill for the simple task of creating a black-and-white image. For one thing, you've completely lost all color data for the file, so any other components you create, like type, will by definition be limited to shades of gray. Also, as with dragging the Saturation slider to 0, converting to grayscale produces a take-it-or-leave-it result; you can't control how the resulting image appears. Of the many options for producing black and white from color, the Black & White adjustment is by far the best method for producing the best result.

"Colorizing" a Black & White Adjustment

There are many techniques for adding color to a black-and-white image to create a "colorized" effect. One of the simplest is to use the layer mask on a Black & White adjustment layer to gradually introduce color to a specific area of an image. Jon e-mails you a color image with a Black & White adjustment layer. He asks that you create a "colorized" effect by gradually fading in color to one area of the image.

STEPS

QUICK TIP

Be sure the Black & White adjustment layer is showing when you are done.

1. Open PS F-6.psd, then save it as Colorize

2. Hide and show the Black & White adjustment layer

3. Target the layer mask, click Edit on the Application bar, then click Fill

4. Enter the settings shown in Figure F-15, then click OK

   A small amount of color shows in the image.

5. Click the Brush tool ✐, set the Diameter to 1800, set the Hardness to 0%, then set the Opacity to 20%

6. Position the brush at the center of the image, then click two times

7. Press ⎣ [⎦ three times to reduce the brush size to 1500, then click the image twice

8. Press ⎣ [⎦ three times, then click the image twice

9. Repeat Step 8, then compare your result to Figure F-16

10. Save your work, then close Colorize.psd

FIGURE F-15: Fill dialog box

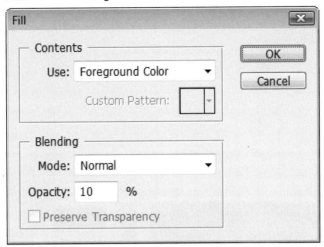

FIGURE F-16: Colorize effect

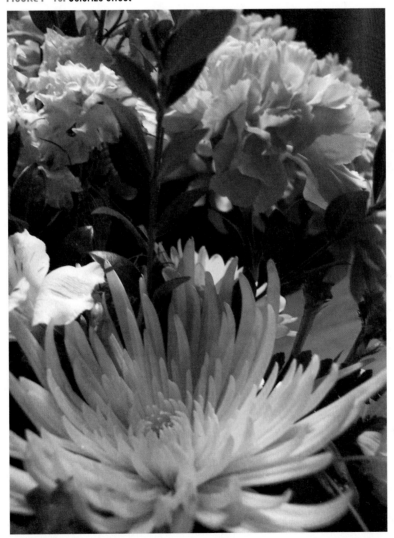

Creating a radial gradient—by hand

The brush technique you used in this lesson is an alternative to using a radial gradient. The result is similar; in this case, a radial gradient with a black center that gradates out to a very light gray. You can think of the brush technique you used as a radial gradient done by hand. It's not nearly as smooth and perfect as a radial gradient, but sometimes it's exactly that hand-drawn imperfection that you want. Consider redoing the exercise with a radial gradient in the layer mask to compare and contrast the results.

Practice

FIGURE F-17

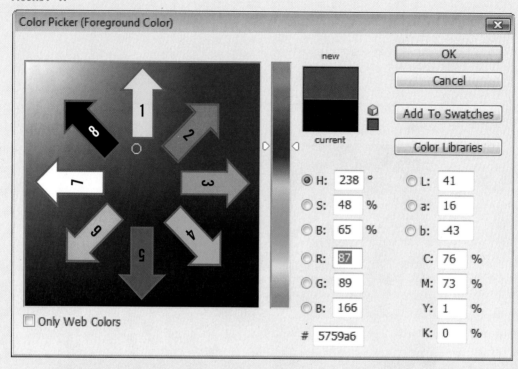

1. Which arrow decreases both brightness and saturation?
2. Which arrow increases just brightness?
3. Which arrow increases brightness and decreases saturation?
4. Which arrow increases just saturation?
5. Which arrow decreases just saturation?
6. Which arrow decreases brightness and increases saturation?
7. Which arrow decreases just brightness?
8. Which arrow increases both brightness and saturation?

Match each term with the statement that best describes it.

9. **Hue**	**a.** Defines a brush's size
10. **Saturation**	**b.** Modifies color based on sampling
11. **Replace Color**	**c.** Photoshop panel
12. **Brushes**	**d.** Photoshop adjustment
13. **Black & White**	**e.** Defines a brush's edge
14. **[Shift]**	**f.** Intensity of a color
15. **Hardness**	**g.** Name of a color
16. **Diameter**	**h.** Used when creating automatic brush strokes

Select the best answer from the list of choices.

17. Which of the following is not a Photoshop color adjustment?

a. Hue/Saturation

b. Black & White adjustment

c. Replace Color

d. Color Balance

18. Which of the following cannot be used to make a color file appear as a black and white?

a. Black & White adjustment

b. Hue/Saturation adjustment

c. Convert to Grayscale

d. Vibrancy adjustment

19. Which key is involved in making automatic brush strokes?

a. Alt/option

b. Shift

c. Ctrl/⌘

d. Spacebar

20. Which of the following is not an option for defining a brush?

a. Length

b. Diameter

c. Hardness

d. Shape Dynamics

21. Which of the following is a component of the Replace Color dialog box?

a. Brightness/Contrast

b. Levels

c. Color Balance

d. Hue/Saturation

▼ SKILLS REVIEW

1. Create custom brushes.

a. Open PS F-7.psd, then save it as **Dots**.

b. Click the Brushes panel list arrow, then verify that Expanded View at the top of the menu is checked. (*Hint*: If Expanded View is not checked, click it to activate it.)

c. Click the Brushes panel list arrow again, click Reset brushes, then click OK in the dialog box that follows. (*Hint*: If a dialog box appears asking if you want to save the current set of brushes, click Yes or No, depending on your wishes.)

d. Scroll to the top of the Brushes panel, then click the brush named Hard Round 19 pixels.

e. Remove the check mark in the Shape Dynamics check box, then click Brush Tip Shape.

f. Drag the Diameter slider in the Brushes panel to 37, drag the Hardness slider to 0%, click the Brushes panel list arrow, then click New Brush Preset.

g. Type **Soft Round 37** in the Name text box, then click OK.

h. Drag the Hardness slider to 100%, click the Brushes panel list arrow, click the New Brush Preset command, type **Hard Round 37** in the Name text box, then click OK.

2. Paint with automatic brush strokes.

a. Verify that the Hard Round 37 brush is selected on the Brushes panel and that the Foreground color is set to black.

b. Press 7 multiple times to enlarge the diameter of the brush to 80 pixels.

c. Target the Hard brush layer, then click point #1 on the canvas.

d. Press and hold [Shift], then click point #2.

e. Using the same method, click each point through point #6, then target the Soft Brush layer on the Layers panel.

f. Click the Soft Round 37 brush on the Brushes panel, then change the Foreground color to white.

g. Click where point #1 would be if it were visible, press and hold [Shift] then click point #2.

h. Using the same method, click each point through point #6.

i. Save your work, then close Dots.psd.

3. Paint a complex mask.

a. Open PS F-8.psd, save it as **Heels**, then hide and show the adjustment layer to see the effect of the color adjustment.

b. Zoom in to 400% to get a sense of the hardness of the edge pixels where the shoe meets the satin background.

c. Zoom out to 300%, click the Brush tool, click the Hard Round 37 brush on the Brushes panel, set the Hardness to 55%, then verify that the Foreground color is set to black.

d. Using the automatic brush strokes technique, paint in the layer mask completely around the entire edge of the shoe. (*Hint*: Reduce and enlarge the diameter of the brush as you see fit.)

e. Paint to mask the satin background within the ankle strap.

f. Press [Alt](Win) or [option](Mac), click the layer mask to view it, click the Magic Wand tool, set the Tolerance to 8, then verify that the Contiguous check box is checked.

g. Click the white background to select it, click Select on the Application bar, point to Modify, then click Expand.

h. Type **8** in the Expand By text box, click OK, then fill the selection with black.

i. Click the adjustment layer thumbnail to view the artwork.

j. Click to activate the layer mask, then mask the metal buckle and the white interior of the shoe from the adjustment.

k. Save your work, and keep the file open.

4. Understand the Color Picker.

a. Click the Foreground color button on the Tools panel to open the Color Picker, verify that the H button is activated, then drag the Hue slider up and down, noting the changes to the H value.

b. Drag the slider until the H value reads 185.

c. Click and drag in the large color box to the left of the hue slider, and note the changes to the new box as you drag.

d. Continue clicking and dragging and note the changes to the H, S, and B text boxes.

e. Drag the circle all the way to the upper-right corner of the color box.

f. Drag down along the right edge of the color box.

g. Click the upper-left corner, then drag down along the left edge of the color box.

h. Click near the center of the color box, then drag the circle right and left, noting the changes to the S text box and the new box.

i. Click near the center, then drag slowly toward the upper-right corner.

j. Click Cancel to close the Color Picker dialog box.

5. Modify color with the Hue/Saturation adjustment.

a. On the Info panel, click the eyedropper icon on the first readout, then click HSB Color to change the display to HSB.

b. Click the adjustment layer on the Layers panel to show the Hue/Saturation adjustment layer.

c. Drag the Hue slider right to +69, then sample the canvas to see the before and after values on the Info panel.

d. Drag the Hue slider left to –54.

e. Drag the Saturation slider right to +30.

f. Drag the Saturation slider left to –100.

g. Hide and show the Hue/Saturation adjustment layer.

h. Save your work, compare your screen to Figure F-18, then close Heels.psd.

FIGURE F-18

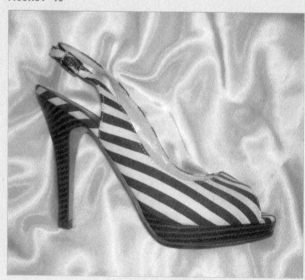

▼ SKILLS REVIEW (CONTINUED)

6. **Use the Replace Color dialog box.**
   a. Open PS F-9.psd, then save it as **Replace Color Skills.**
   b. Duplicate the Background layer, rename the duplicate **Replace Color**, click Image on the Application bar, point to Adjustments, then click Replace Color.
   c. Drag the Fuzziness slider to 36, click the Eyedropper tool, then click a light green area on the sandal.
   d. Drag the Fuzziness slider to 70.
   e. Drag the Hue slider left to –139.
   f. Click the Add to Sample tool, then click in the dark green shadow area created by the sandal strap.
   g. Use the Add to Sample tool to click a remaining green pixel in the sandal.
   h. Click OK, then hide and show the Replace Color layer.
   i. Add a layer mask and quickly mask any part of the Replace Color that may have affected the background.
   j. Save your work, then close Replace Color.psd.

7. **Use the Black & White adjustment.**
   a. Open PS F-10.psd, save it as **B&W Skills**, duplicate the Background layer, then rename it **Desaturate.**
   b. Press [Ctrl][U] (Win) or ⌘[U] (Mac) to open the Hue/Saturation dialog box, drag the Saturation slider all the way left to –100, then click OK.
   c. Hide the Desaturate layer, then target the Background layer.
   d. Click the Create new fill or adjustment layer button on the Layers panel, then click Black & White.
   e. Drag sliders in different directions to experiment with various results.
   f. Click the Reset to adjustment defaults button on the Adjustments panel.
   g. Drag the Blues slider to –14, then drag the Cyans slider to 20.
   h. Drag the Reds slider to 50, then drag the Yellows slider to 85.
   i. Hide and show the Desaturate layer to compare the quality of the two different results.
   j. Save your work.

8. **"Colorize" a Black & White adjustment.**
   a. Verify that the Desaturate layer is hidden.
   b. Target the layer mask on the B&W adjustment layer, click Edit on the Application bar, then click Fill.
   c. Click the Use list arrow, click Foreground Color, change the Opacity to 10%, then click OK.
   d. Click the Brush tool, set the Diameter to 1500, set the Hardness to 0%, then set the Opacity to 20%.
   e. Position the brush at the center of the girl's face, then click two times.
   f. Press [ ] three times to reduce the brush size to 1200, then click the image twice.
   g. Press [ ] three times, then click the image twice.
   h. Repeat Step g, then compare your result to Figure F-19.
   i. Save your work, then close B&W Skills.psd.

FIGURE F-19

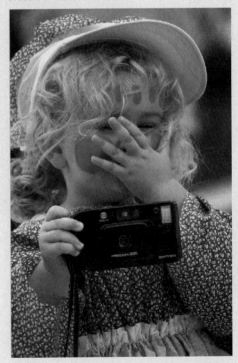

▼ INDEPENDENT CHALLENGE 1

You need an image of a stop sign for a Web site, so you snap a picture with your digital camera, copy it into Photoshop, then use a layer mask to isolate the sign from the background.

a. Open PS F-11.psd, then save it as **Stop Sign**.

b. Duplicate the Background layer, name the new layer **Stop Sign**, then fill the Background layer with black.

c. Add a layer mask to the Sign layer, then click the Brush tool.

d. Choose a brush size of 27 px, then set the Hardness to what you think is best to outline an image of a stop sign.

e. Use the automatic brushes technique to mask the outline of the sign quickly.

f. Switch to view the layer mask itself.

g. Select the white background of the layer mask – *outside* of the strokes you painted, with the Magic Wand tool.

h. Expand the selection by 6 pixels so that the selection of the white background overlaps slightly the black strokes you painted.

i. Fill the selection with black.

j. Deselect the mask, click the Sign layer thumbnail, then compare your result to Figure F-20.

k. Save your work, then close Sign.psd.

FIGURE F-20

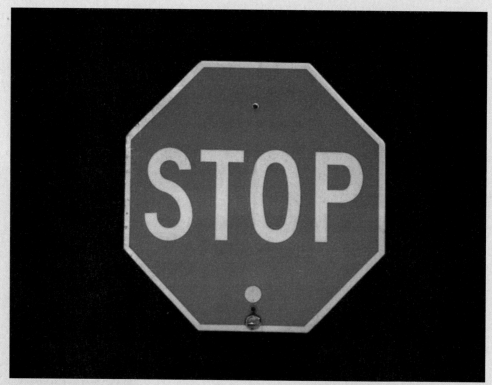

▼ INDEPENDENT CHALLENGE 2

You're designing a catalogue for a children's' clothing company. Your client e-mails you a photo to use but tells you that they would prefer to show the dress in green rather than blue. You realize that trying to change the color with a layer mask would not be the best method, so you decide to use the Replace Color dialog box.

a. Open PS F-12.psd, then save it as **Green Dress**.

b. Duplicate the Background layer, rename the duplicate **Green Dress**, click Image on the Application bar, point to Adjustments, then click Replace Color.

c. Drag the Fuzziness slider to 36, click the Eyedropper tool, then click a light blue area on the left sleeve of the dress.

d. Click the Add to Sample tool, then click in a darker blue area inside the same sleeve.

e. Drag the Fuzziness slider to 70.

f. Drag the Hue slider left to –55.

g. With the Add to Sample tool, click in the dark blue shadow area underneath the camera.

h. Use the Add to Sample tool to click any noticeable blue area (if necessary).

i. Click OK, then hide and show the Green Dress layer.

j. Add a layer mask and quickly mask any part of the Green Dress layer that may have affected the background, especially above the hat. (*Hint:* In this case, it would be a smart idea to mask the face and hair whether or not you see any changes—just to be sure.)

k. Save your work, compare your screen to Figure F-21, then close Green Dress.psd.

FIGURE F-21

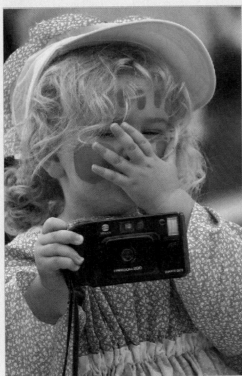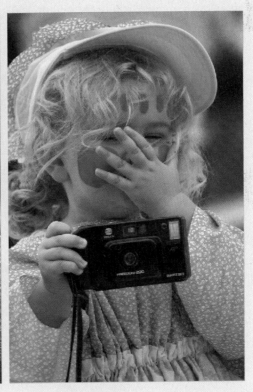

▼ INDEPENDENT CHALLENGE 3

You design a monthly newsletter, and you've run into a tricky problem. The newsletter is printed in black and white, but your client has given you a *very* colorful image to include in this month's edition. You decide to use a few different methods to create black and white from color so you'll have options for picking the best result.

a. Open PS F-13.psd, save it as **Newsletter**, duplicate the Background layer, then rename it **Desaturate**.

b. Open the Hue/Saturation dialog box, then drag the Saturation slider all the way left to –100.

c. Hide the Desaturate layer, then target the Background layer.

d. Create a new Black & White adjustment layer.

e. Drag sliders in different directions to experiment with various results. (*Hint*: An interesting situation with this image is that the actual colors are not really important once adjusted. It doesn't really matter, for example, if the original yellows get darker than the original reds. Now that this is a black-and-white image, all that matters is that the result is a black and white with many grays—a full range of grays.)

f. Click the Reset to adjustment defaults button.

g. Drag the Yellows slider to 28, drag the Reds slider to 28, then drag the Greens slider to 46.

h. Drag the Cyans slider to 43, drag the Blues slider to 101, then drag the Magentas slider to 77.

i. Hide and show the Desaturate layer to compare the quality of the two different results, then verify that the Desaturate layer is turned off.

Advanced Challenge Exercise

- Target the Background layer.
- Click Image on the Application bar, point to Mode, then click Grayscale.
- Click Yes in the warning box about the adjustment layer being discarded, then click Discard when you are asked to confirm the conversion.
- Compare the Grayscale conversion on the Background layer to the artwork on the Desaturate layer.

j. Compare your results to Figure F-22, save your work, then close Newsletter.psd.

FIGURE F-22

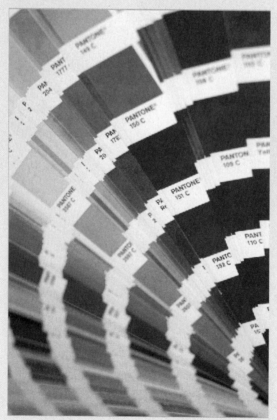

▼ REAL WORLD INDEPENDENT CHALLENGE

You're a talented amateur photographer. You use great equipment and your photos download from your camera looking really good. You just returned from your trip out west and are using Photoshop to tweak your photos to go from looking good to looking great.

    a. Open PS F-14.psd, then save it as **Pylon**.

    b. Duplicate the Background layer, name the new layer **Pylon**, then fill the Background layer with white.

    c. Add a layer mask to the Pylon layer, then click the Brush tool.

    d. Set the Hardness to what you think is best to outline an image of a pylon.

    e. Use your best brush techniques to mask the background—without a shadow—completely.

    f. Duplicate the Pylon layer, then name then new layer Pylon Shadow.

    g. Drag the Pylon Shadow down below the Pylon layer.

    h. Hide the Pylon layer.

    i. Fill the layer mask on the Pylon Shadow layer with white.

    j. Using a large soft brush, mask everything except the base of the pylon and the shadow beneath the base.

    k. Show the Pylon layer.

Advanced Challenge Exercise

    ■ Click the Foreground Color button on the Tools panel.

    ■ Drag the Hue Slider up approximately half way until you see green in the Color box.

    ■ Click and drag in the large color box, then note the HSB values and the RGB values.

    ■ Click Cancel to close the Color Picker dialog box.

    l. Save your work, compare your screen to Figure F-23, then close Pylon.psd.

FIGURE F-23

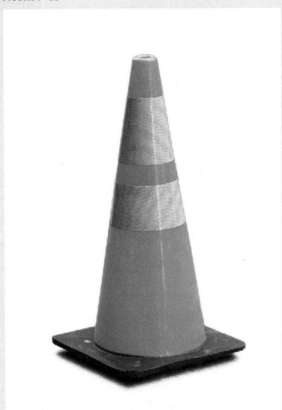

Open PS F-15.psd, then save it as **Snow Cones**. Duplicate the original cone and its shadow to produce two more cones. Position the two new cones on either side of the original cone, then reduce their sizes so that they appear to be behind the center cone. Apply adjustment layers to change the colors of the cones so that your result resembles Figure F-24.

FIGURE F-24

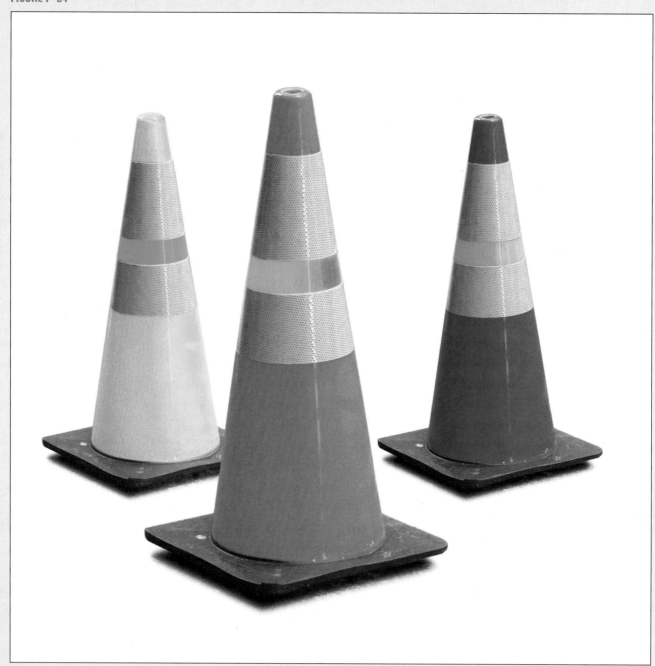

Creating Special Effects

When you study Photoshop, you learn one thing at a time. When you practice Photoshop, you practice one thing at a time. But when you work in Photoshop—really work on a full-scale project—you must use *many* skills in tandem to achieve your goal. This chapter—Creating Special Effects—will be a good opportunity for you to make a shift in consciousness and really start looking at Photoshop in "the big picture." You can learn exactly what all the tools and commands and panels in Photoshop do, but it's up to you and your own artistic sense to decide *when* to use them, and to what effect. Photoshop does not make art, any more than a paintbrush or a palette knife makes art. Photoshop is a collection of tools, commands, and layers that are simply there for you—the artist—to create your creation. Photoshop doesn't make art. You do. Jon tells you about a new client that is well known for their cutting-edge graphics. To prepare you for working with them, he asks you to test out various special effects using blending modes, filters, and transformations.

OBJECTIVES

Use the Color blending mode

Use the Multiply blending mode

Add noise with the Overlay blending mode

Sharpen with the High Pass filter

Apply the Lens Flare filter with Screen mode

Apply the Motion Blur filter

Apply non-destructive filters

Distort images

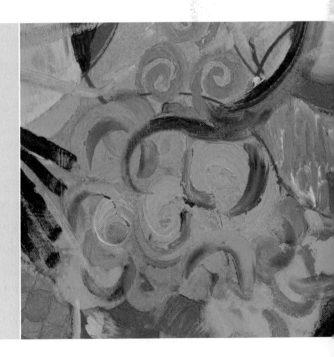

Using the Color Blending Mode

Blending modes are mathematical algorithms that define how pixels affect pixels beneath them to create a specific effect. You can apply blending modes throughout many Photoshop features—like layer styles—but they are most prominent on the Layers panel and for options with specific tools, like the Brush tool. The best way to think of blending modes is with three colors: The **base color** is the color of the original pixel; the **blend color** is the color being applied; and the **result color** is the color produced by blending the first two colors with the blending mode. The Color blending mode is very useful for colorizing monochromatic images. It applies the hue of the blend pixel to the base pixel and automatically affects the saturation of the base pixel so that the base pixel beneath it takes on the color of the blend pixel. ▞▞▞▞ A new client at MegaPixel offers a service of colorizing old photos. They deliver you an image and ask you to colorize it for them to use on their Web site. Jon tells you to do the work using the Color blending mode.

STEPS

1. **Start Photoshop, open PS G-1.psd, save it as Colorize with Color Mode, click the Create new fill or adjustment layer button 🞂 on the Layers panel, then click Solid Color**
   The Pick a solid color dialog box opens. Note it is the same dialog box as the Color Picker.

2. **Change the color to 134R/154G/174B, click OK, click the blending mode list arrow on the Layers panel, click Color, then compare your Layers panel and image to Figure G-1**
   The hues of all the base pixels take on the hue of the blend layer. The saturation of the base pixels is automatically adjusted. The brightness values of the base pixels are not affected.

3. **Using the Brush tool 🖌, mask the entire woman so that the change in color affects only the background area of the image**

4. **Create a new layer above the Color Fill 1 layer, name the layer Sweater, then set the blending mode to Color**

5. **Set the foreground color to 196R/223G/155B, click the Brush tool 🖌, then paint the sweater green**
   Because the blending mode of the layer is set to Color, any color you paint on the layer will be transparent and will affect the color of the artwork on layers beneath.

6. **Create a new Hue/Saturation adjustment layer, then set the blending mode for the layer to Color**

7. **Click the Colorize check box on the Adjustments panel, set the Hue to 35, then set the Saturation to 30**
   The adjustment affects the entire image. The Colorize option is necessary to apply color to a black-and-white image. See the Clues to Use on the next page to learn more about the Colorize option.

8. **Name the layer Face, then use a layer mask so that the Hue/Saturation adjustment affects the face and the lips, but not the eyes, as shown in Figure G-2**

9. **Use the same method you used in Steps 6 through 8—with different values for Hue and Saturation—to finish colorizing the image**
   Figure G-3 shows one potential result.

10. **Save your work, then close the file**

FIGURE G-1: Solid color blended over the image

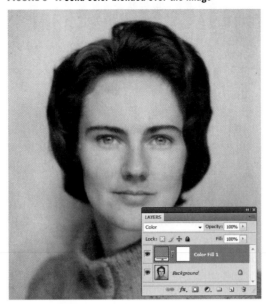

FIGURE G-2: Painting in a layer set to Color mode

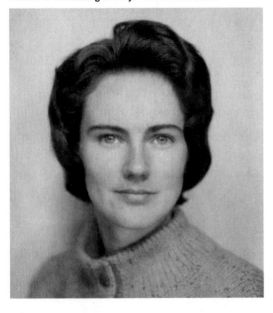

FIGURE G-3: Colorized image

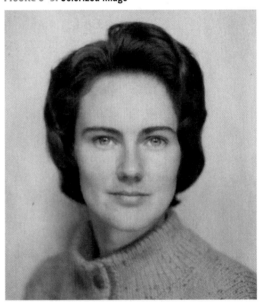

Using the Colorize option in the Hue/Saturation Adjustments panel

The Colorize option in the Hue/Saturation Adjustments panel is necessary to colorize a black–and-white image. Normally, moving the Hue and Saturation sliders in the Hue/Saturation Adjustments panel modifies the existing hue and saturation values of selected pixels. In a black-and-white image, however, all of the pixels have a saturation value of 0. Therefore, any adjustments you make in the Hue/Saturation adjustment to black-and-white base art will have no effect: you can't modify color where there is no color in the first place. The Colorize option overrides the 0% saturation of the base art and allows you to apply Hue/Saturation color adjustments to the base pixels. Remember, whenever you want to use the Hue/Saturation dialog box to apply color to black-and-white art, you must activate the Colorize option.

Brightness and the Color blending mode

It's important to understand the Color blending mode does not in any way affect the brightness value of base pixels; it affects only hue and saturation. This is a critical component of what makes the Color blending mode so effective. Because brightness is not affected, the integrity of the tonal grayscale range from black to white is maintained. Thus, the image changes color, but it continues to appear realistic.

Using the Multiply Blending Mode

Imagine you had a black–and-white printed image, and you placed a sheet of ruby red transparent film over that image. If you can imagine what the image would look like through the red film, that's a great analogy for the Multiply blending mode. Multiply is perhaps the most common blending mode. It makes the blend pixels transparent, and any base art will be seen *through* that color. That's why Multiply mode is always used when creating shadows and drop shadows: shadows in nature are always transparent. Two important things to remember about Multiply mode: When you multiply black, the result is always black. When you multiply white, white always becomes invisible. Jon mentions a project you worked on a long time ago. The client has asked that the art be more "eye-catching." Jon suggests you use Multiply blending effects for the layered artwork.

STEPS

1. Open PS G-2.psd, then save it as Final Roman Holiday

2. Show the Understand Multiply layer, then study it a bit

3. Set the Understand Multiply layer blending mode to Multiply, then hide and show the Understand Multiply layer to see its effect

   As shown in Figure G-4, everything becomes transparent, but the black area behind the letter M still appears black because the result of multiplying any color with black is black. The white M becomes completely invisible because white always becomes 100% transparent when multiplied. The black-to-white gradient on the left transitions from black on the top to completely transparent on the bottom.

4. Hide the Understand Multiply layer, target the Roses Shadow layer, then set its blending mode to Multiply

   The artwork on this layer is a simple gray fill with a feathered edge. When multiplied, it becomes transparent and looks like a realistic shadow.

5. Change the blending mode of the Couple Shadow layer to Multiply

   When working with black or very dark colors, the Multiply blending mode effect is not so noticeable. Nevertheless, you should always set the blending mode of any artwork that is functioning as a shadow to Multiply.

6. Set the blending mode of the Colosseum and Bottom Coin layers to Multiply

   The images themselves become transparent, creating the effect of seeing the passport background through the images.

7. Target the hidden Understand Multiply layer, click the Create new fill or adjustment layer button ⬤ on the Layers panel, then click Solid Color

   The Color Picker opens.

8. Set the color to 255R/225G/0B, then click OK

9. Change the blending mode to Multiply

10. Reduce the Opacity to 60%, compare your result to Figure G-5, then save your work

FIGURE G-4: Understanding the Multiply blending mode

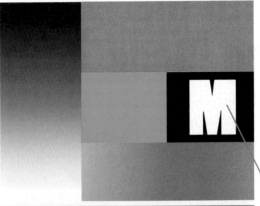

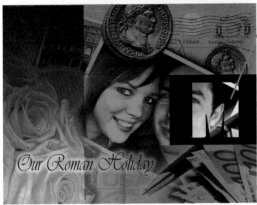

White becomes
completely
transparent

FIGURE G-5: Multiplying a solid color

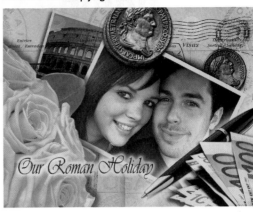

Grouping blending modes on the Layers panel

On the Layers panel, note how the blending modes have been grouped into six sections. This grouping is intentional and specific. Though each blending mode is programmed to produce a different effect, the effects themselves fall into similar behaviors. The blending modes are grouped based on those similarities.

Moving from the top of the menu down:

• The blending modes in the second section all darken the base art when applied. White pixels become transparent with these blending modes.

• Blending modes in the third section all lighten the base art when applied. Black pixels become transparent with these blending modes.

• The blending modes in the fourth section all increase contrast in the base art when applied. Gray pixels become transparent with these blending modes.

As you work through this book, refer back to this bulleted list. Once you get a sense of the similarity of blending modes, it opens the door to experimenting with different but similar blending modes to find the best effect.

Working with the Color Burn and Linear Burn blending modes

Color Burn and Linear Burn are two effective blending modes that are similar to the Multiply blending mode but produce effects that are subtly different. Both use an algorithm that is far more complex than Multiply, but you can think of Color Burn as a multiply blending mode with increased contrast. Often, if you use the Multiply blending mode on a lighter color over dark shadows, the shadows brighten slightly and become weak. Color Burn can be a smart

alternative, because it increases contrast. Linear Burn creates a multiply effect by decreasing brightness. Of the three, it's probably the least used, but in the right circumstance, it can be the best choice. Bottom line: when you apply a multiply effect with a solid color, take a moment to experiment with Color Burn and Linear Burn. You might like the results even more.

Adding Noise with the Overlay Blending Mode

Noise is a term used to describe a blanket of high-contrast pixels that produce a grainy effect over an image. Sometimes, noise is a problem. You've probably seen noise as what you'd call "grain" in low-quality images online or especially in photos you download from a cell phone. On the other hand, adding noise to an image is a technique that designers often use to "finish" a design. A layer of noise over an image can add a heightened sense of sharpness and focus to an image. Noise is especially effective with multiple images used in a montage. Often, in a montage of images from different sources, the challenge is to make the final montage appear to be one piece of artwork, not a composition of different pictures. A layer of noise adds a consistent texture across the artwork and can be very effective in achieving this goal. Jon tells you that, at MegaPixel, it is standard procedure to add noise to any artwork that involves a montage to help unify the artwork as one complete piece and to add a sense of artificial sharpness or "crunchiness" to the montage. He tells you that MegaPixel always adds noise using a technique with the Overlay blending mode, which he wants you to try.

→ unifies artwork.

STEPS

1. **Hide the Color Fill 1 layer, show the Understand Overlay layer, rename it** Noise, **then set its blending mode to** Overlay

    As shown in Figure G-6, the Overlay blending mode uses the blend colors to increase the contrast of the base art. Darker blend colors will have a different effect than lighter blend colors. The figure shows the black blend color drastically darkens the shadow point of the base art, while the white blend color dramatically brightens the highlight point of the base art. Note an important fact: The gray middle blend color becomes transparent in Overlay mode.

2. **Change the blending mode to Normal, click** Edit **on the Application bar, then click** Fill

3. **Click the** Use list arrow, **click** 50% Gray, **then click** OK

    The layer is filled with gray. Note that it is solid gray. The term 50% Gray refers to its color—exactly between black and white—not its opacity.

4. **Click** Filter **on the Application bar, point to** Noise, **then click** Add Noise

5. **Enter the settings shown in the Add Noise dialog box shown in Figure G-7, then click** OK

6. **Change the blending mode to** Overlay, **zoom in on the image if necessary so that you are viewing it at 100%, then compare your result to Figure G-8**

    Since this artwork is a montage of various images, the noise effect creates a consistent texture across the image, adding a sense that it is one unified image. It also adds a sense of sharpness or "crunchiness" to the artwork.

7. **Reduce the Opacity to** 50%

8. **Save your work**

FIGURE G-6: Understanding the Overlay blending mode

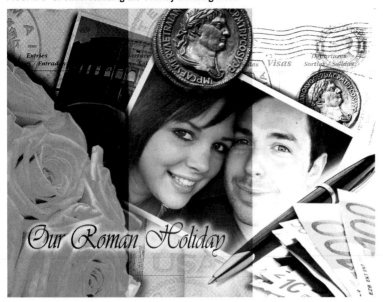

Shadows darkened dramatically

No change

Highlights brightened dramatically

FIGURE G-7: Add Noise dialog box

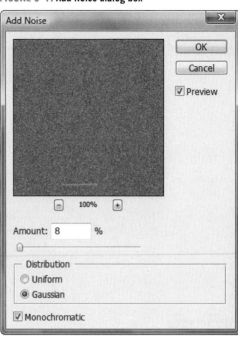

FIGURE G-8: Viewing results of the Noise filter

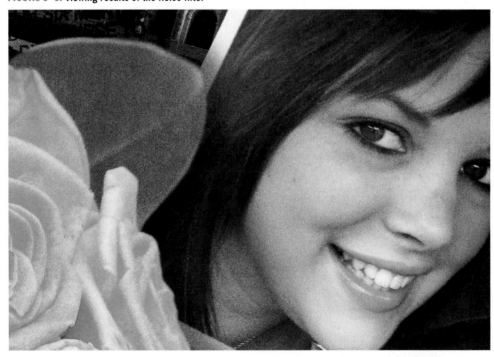

Understanding the Noise Overlay technique

The technique you used in this lesson for adding noise started by filling a layer with gray pixels. This was necessary because you cannot add noise to an empty layer; Photoshop creates noise from existing pixels. Thus, we added the gray fill to add noise then set the blending mode to Overlay, knowing that gray becomes transparent with the Overlay blending mode. The result is that we're left with only the noise being visible.

There is another technique for adding noise, one worth examining for its built-in flaw. Create a single copy/merged layer of the entire image at the top of the layer stack. Then, add noise to that layer. The built-in flaw is that it's not editable. With the Noise Overlay technique, you can continue to edit the artwork, move layers, add adjustments, etc. The noise is on its own layer, independent of the artwork. With the copy/merged technique, if you edit the image, you need to recreate the noise layer to reflect the changes.

Sharpening with the High Pass Filter

Sharpness is more a Photoshop term than it is a real-world photography term. In order to understand sharpness, you first need to understand edges. **Edges** are any areas in an image where highly contrasting pixels meet. For example, if you had an image of a yellow leaf on dark blue velvet, the point where the bright yellow pixels at the very edge of the leaf meet the dark pixels of the blue background would be defined as an edge. High Pass is a filter that is very effective at finding and isolating edges. It finds edges using a mathematical algorithm to identify where in the image pixels of high contrast abut. It then fills the layer with solid gray everywhere except in the edge areas. Essentially, High Pass isolates edge areas. Edges are mostly involved in blurring and sharpening an image. When you blur edges, Photoshop reduces the contrast where edge pixels meet. When you sharpen an image, Photoshop finds edge areas and increases the contrast. The result is a sense of heightened focus to the image. Jon likes the noise you've added to the montage and asks you to finish the piece by "sharpening" it. He tells you that MegaPixel always sharpens using a technique that combines the High Pass filter with the Overlay blending mode.

STEPS

1. **Target then hide the Noise layer**

   Whenever you sharpen a file—using any method—turn off any noise layers; you seldom want to sharpen noise.

2. **Select all, click Edit on the Application bar, click Copy Merged, click Edit on the Application bar, then click Paste**

   A merged copy of all the layers is pasted onto one layer.

3. **Name the new layer High Pass**

4. **Click Filter on the Application bar, point to Other, then click High Pass**

   The image is filled with gray. Edge pixels—places where highly contrasting pixels meet—are visible through the gray.

5. **Enter the settings shown in Figure G-9, then click OK**

6. **Set the blending mode to Overlay, then zoom in so that you are viewing the image at 100%**

   With the High Pass filter, most of the image is filled with gray. Only edge pixels are visible. With the Overlay blending mode applied, the edge pixels are overlayed over the layered image. Thus, contrast is increased in edge areas, creating the effect of sharpness and focus.

7. **Hide and show the High Pass layer**

   Many areas are improved. Some areas—like the sharp highlight on the man's tooth and the glints in the eyes—are too sharp.

8. **Reduce the opacity on the layer to 70%, add a layer mask, then mask any areas that are too sharp**

9. **Show the Noise layer, then compare your artwork to Figure G-10**

10. **Save your work, then close Final Roman Holiday.psd**

FIGURE G-9: Applying the High Pass filter

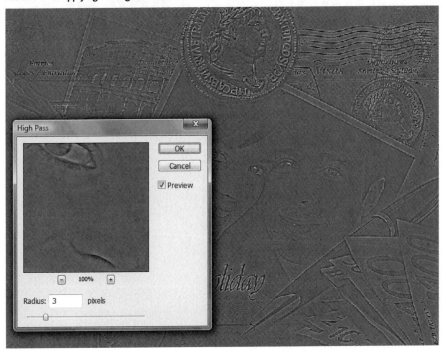

FIGURE G-10: Viewing the sharpened file

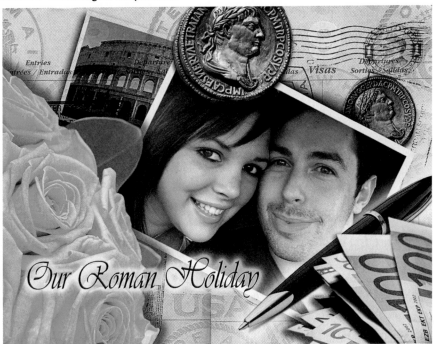

Understanding how the Overlay/High Pass technique works

Whenever you use the Overlay blending mode, it increases contrast in the base art. When you duplicate an image and overlay it over itself, it dramatically increases contrast overall and especially at the edges. The Overlay/High Pass technique essentially does just that—overlays an image on top of itself—but only at the edges. The filter works by filling the layer with 50% gray, which will become transparent when overlayed. The only areas that aren't filled with gray are edge areas. The more you increase the Radius value, the greater the area of the image that Photoshop will define as an edge area. When you apply the Overlay mode to the filtered artwork, most of the filtered artwork becomes transparent, because it's been filled with gray. The edge areas—which aren't filled with gray—remain visible to be overlayed, thus increasing the contrast dramatically.

Applying the Lens Flare Filter with Screen Mode

A lens flare is a bright spot often captured in the glass of a camera lens, especially when the camera is pointed at a bright light source. You have probably noticed lens flares in photos of the sun or photos of a bright sunny day. Photoshop offers the Lens Flare filter, which is very useful for adding glints or bright spots to artwork, especially artwork that involves metallic textures, like swords or chrome. The Lens Flare filter can't be created in an empty layer; it needs to be applied to already existing pixels. However, you often will want just the lens flare itself as part of your artwork, so a good technique to use is to fill a layer with black, apply the Lens Flare filter, then use the Screen blending mode to make the black areas transparent, leaving just the flare. 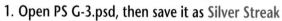 Jon tells you that the client has approved one of your typography compositions and has asked that you "liven it up" a bit for their Web site. He suggests that you start by adding a lens flare.

STEPS

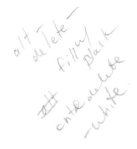

1. **Open PS G-3.psd, then save it as Silver Streak**

   The file has been saved in RGB Color mode. The Lens Flare filter is available in RGB Color mode but not in CMYK Color mode.

2. **Create a new layer at the top of the Layers panel, fill it with black, then name the new layer Lens Flare**

3. **Click Filter on the Application bar, point to Render, then click Lens Flare**

4. **Click each option button in the Lens Type section of the Lens Flare dialog box to sample them, click the 50-300mm Zoom option button, drag the Brightness slider to 110, then click OK**

5. **Click Image on the Application bar, point to Adjustments, then click Desaturate**

   The goal is to have the flare reflect the silver metallic texture of the letters.

   > **QUICK TIP**
   > The Screen blending mode functions as the exact opposite of the Multiply blending mode

6. **Change the blending mode of the Lens Flare layer to Screen**

   In Screen blending mode, white pixels show and black pixels become invisible. Thus, the black background of the layer becomes 100% transparent, allowing you to see only the lens flare effect on the layer and the type artwork on the layers beneath.

7. **Move the center of the white flare over the letter S, so that your screen resembles Figure G-11, click Edit on the Application bar, point to Transform, click Scale, then scale the lens flare 80% so that your screen resembles Figure G-12**

   When you scale the lens flare, the rectangular edge of the flare artwork becomes visible, which is an obvious problem. However, we want only the flare to be visible, not the midtones, so we can remove the midtones from the equation.

8. **Press and hold [Alt] (Win) or [option] (Mac), click the Create new fill or adjustment layer button ⊘ on the Layers panel, then click Levels**

9. **Click the Use Previous Layer to Create Clipping Mask check box in the New Layer dialog box, click OK, then drag the black triangle immediately below the histogram in the Adjustments panel to the right until the text box reads 45**

   The midtones disappear.

10. **Compare your result to Figure G-13, then save your work**

FIGURE G-11: Positioning the screened lens flare

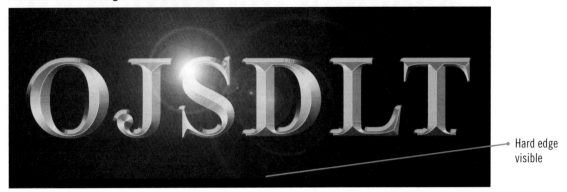

Hard edge visible

FIGURE G-12: Scaling down the size of the flare

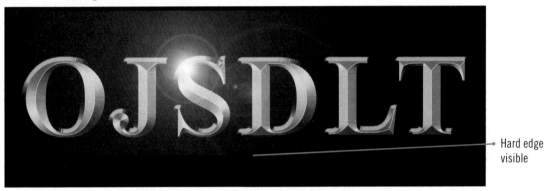

Hard edge visible

FIGURE G-13: The final effect

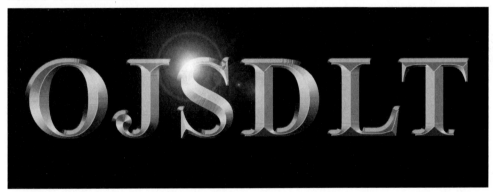

Screen blending mode vs. Multiply blending mode

Make it a point to remember that the Screen blending mode functions as the exact opposite of the Multiply blending mode. In the Screen blending mode, white pixels remain white and black pixels become invisible. However, Screen mode is similar to Multiply mode in that if you screen a color, the color becomes transparent. In Screen mode, though, a screened color always brightens the base color.

Because it makes black pixels invisible, Screen mode is very useful for superimposing bright pixels over an image: for example, smoke.

Smoke is a great design element, but how do you capture a photograph in a way that you can access just the smoke? Screen mode makes this possible. Photograph the smoke against a black background. When you bring the file into Photoshop, use the Levels adjustment to brighten the smoke and darken the black background so that it is actually black. Then, when you apply the Screen blending mode, the black pixels disappear and voila: you've got smoke—and just smoke—to work with.

Applying the Motion Blur Filter

Photoshop offers a number of blur filters. The Motion Blur filter dialog box allows you to specify a distance and an angle for blurring pixels. The result is a blur that can be used to create the appearance of motion. Think of watching a race car flying by you in real life. If you had a photo of that car, you could use the Motion Blur filter to create the effect of the car moving so fast, there's a blur of colors trailing it. The Motion Blur filter can also be used very effectively on text and headlines to create a sense of movement and action. ██████ Jon likes the lens flare you applied to the headline and tells you to finish the piece by applying a motion blur to the text. He tells you to "make it visually not too simplistic." With that in mind, you decide to use multiple blurs in conjunction with each other to create the effect.

STEPS

1. Duplicate both the Inner Bevel and Outer Bevel layers, select both duplicate layers, click the Layers panel list arrow, then click Merge Layers

2. Name the merged layer Motion Blur, then drag it down below the Outer Bevel layer

3. Duplicate the Motion Blur layer, then rename the new layer Motion Blur Top

4. With the Motion Blur Top layer still targeted, click Filter on the Application bar, point to Blur, then click Motion Blur

   The Motion Blur dialog box opens.

5. Set the Angle to 0, set the Distance to 50, then click OK

   Your screen should resemble Figure G-14.

6. Target the Motion Blur layer, open the Motion Blur dialog box, verify that the Angle is set to 0, set the Distance to 100 pixels, then click OK

7. Reduce the Opacity of the Motion Blur layer to 70%

8. Set the blending mode on the Motion Blur Top layer to Screen

9. Compare your result to Figure G-15, save your work, then close Silver Streak.psd

FIGURE G-14: Viewing the first motion blur applied

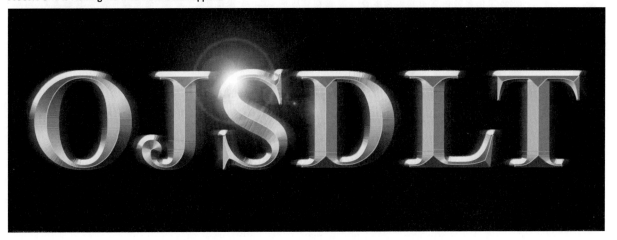

FIGURE G-15: Viewing the final effect with two motion blurs applied

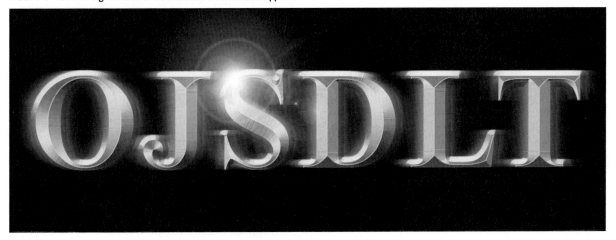

Applying Non-Destructive Filters

Throughout this book, you've learned about "non-destructive" editing, even though you might not have referred to it as such. When you apply a Levels adjustment layer, for example, that's a non-destructive edit. It's called "non-destructive" because the adjustment is not applied directly to the artwork. Instead, the adjustment exists on a separate layer that can be shown, hidden, edited, or even deleted. In any case, the original artwork is not permanently altered. A layer style is another example of a non-destructive edit; it doesn't permanently alter the artwork to achieve the effect. Photoshop also offers you the ability to create non-destructive filter layers, allowing you to create filters on a layer that can be shown, hidden, edited, or deleted. These so-called "smart filters" even come with a layer mask and can be altered with an opacity adjustment or with a blending mode. Non-destructive filters are great because they allow you to experiment with different filters without permanently altering the original artwork. Jon has a client that asked that you apply some filters to an image to make it more interesting. However, the client wants to be able to manipulate the filters you apply to customize the effect. Jon tells you to use smart filters.

STEPS

QUICK TIP
If a dialog box appears, click Don't show again, then click OK.

1. **Open PS G-4.psd, save it as Non-Destructive Filters, then target the Plaza layer**

2. **Click Filter on the Application bar, then click Convert for Smart Filters**

   The artwork on the layer is converted to a smart object, signified by the Smart Object thumbnail icon. Smart objects preserve artwork's original characteristics while allowing you to perform non-destructive editing to the layer.

3. **Click Filter on the Application bar, point to Texture, then click Grain**

4. **Click the Grain Type list arrow, click Speckle, then set both the Intensity and the Contrast settings to 25**

5. **Click OK, then compare your Layers panel to Figure G-16**

   The Grain filter is applied as a layer beneath the Plaza layer. It has a default white layer mask, and it is visible.

6. **Click the Toggle all smart filter visibilities button 👁 to hide the filter, then click again to show the filter**

7. **Double-click the ⬓ button on the Grain layer on the Layers panel**

   The Blending Options (Grain) dialog box opens.

8. **Drag the Opacity slider to 80%, then click OK**

9. **Double-click the word Grain on the Grain layer to open the Grain dialog box, increase both the Intensity and the Contrast settings to 35, then click OK**

10. **Compare your artwork to Figure G-17, save your work, then close Non-Destructive Filters.psd**

FIGURE G-16: The Grain filter as a layer on the Layers panel

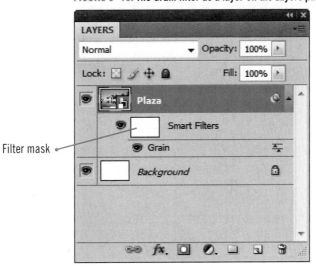

Filter mask

FIGURE G-17: Viewing the filter applied with 80% opacity

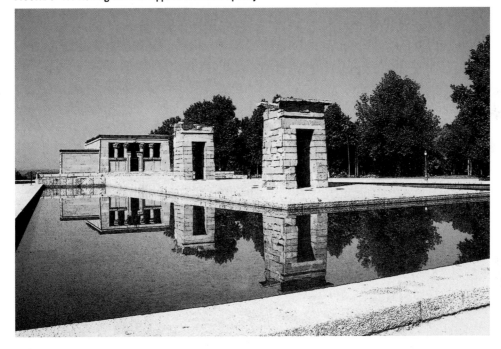

Masking filters

One of the extra great benefits of working with non-destructive filters, as we did in this lesson, is that they are created with a mask—call it a **filter mask**—which functions and which you can use exactly like a layer mask. That means that you can subtly mask or show non-destructive filters using the filter mask in conjunction with the Brush tool, a gradient, etc. One catch, though: if you apply multiple filters, there's still just one mask available, and that mask will hide or show all of the applied filters. You can't mask just one of many filters applied to the same artwork.

Removing smart filters

Because they are non-destructive by definition, smart filters can be removed from layered artwork at any time. You can simply hide the filter or, if you want to remove it permanently, drag it to the Delete layer button on the Layers panel. All smart filters will be deleted from a layer if you convert the layer from a smart object back to a normal layer. To do so, target the smart object layer, click Layer on the Application bar, point to Smart Objects, then click Rasterize. The layer returns to its original state, and all smart filters are deleted.

Distorting Images

Earlier in this book, you learned about transforming images; specifically, you learned how to scale and rotate images and how to flip them horizontally or vertically. Often, you'll want to distort images, sometimes for an artistic effect and sometimes for a practical effect, like creating a sense of three-dimensional artwork. In Photoshop, the Distort command is another type of transformation, just like scaling or rotating. The methodology is similar, but the results can be very dramatic and eye-catching. ████████ MegaPixel has been working with a Hollywood movie studio on an outdoor campaign for a theatrical release. The client likes your design of a billboard, and Jon asks you to "put it in an environment" to give the client a sense of how it will appear on a billboard in the real world.

STEPS

1. **Open PS G-5.psd, save it as Distort, then hide and show the Billboard layer**
   The billboard was duplicated and exists alone on the Billboard layer against a transparent background.

2. **Open Charlie Billboard.psd, select all, click Edit on the Application bar, click Copy, then close the file**

3. **Target the Billboard layer, paste, then name the new layer Charlie**

4. **Press [Alt] (Win) or [option] (Mac), then click between the Charlie layer and the Billboard layer to clip the Charlie layer into the Billboard layer**

5. **Click Edit on the Application bar, point to Transform, then click Distort**
   The Distort command allows you to move all the handles on the transform bounding box independently, thus distorting the artwork.

QUICK TIP

You may have to zoom out to view all four handles.

6. **Move the four handles of the bounding box to the four corners of the Billboard artwork, as shown in Figure G-18**

7. **Press [Enter] (Win) or [return] (Mac) to execute the transformation**

8. **Compare your artwork to Figure G-19**

9. **Save your work, then close Distort.psd**

FIGURE G-18: Distorting the artwork by moving the handles

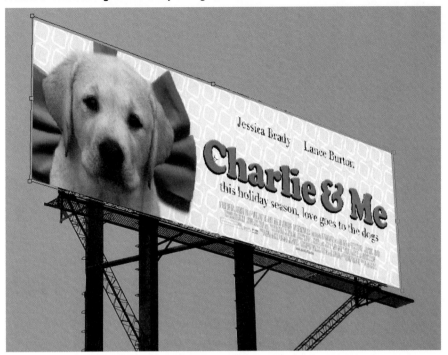

FIGURE G-19: Viewing the final distorted artwork

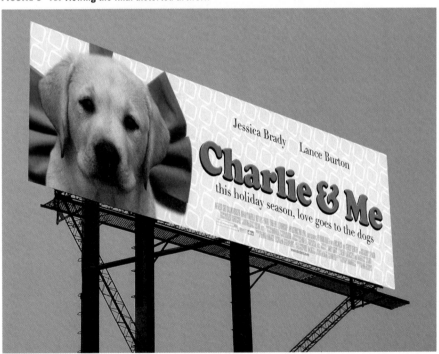

Understanding the Skew and Perspective transformations

In addition to the Distort transformation, you can transform with the Skew, Perspective, and Warp commands. Skew will transform the art as though it were positioned on an angle. With the Skew transformation, the opposite sides of the bounding box always remain parallel. The Perspective command transforms art with a forced perspective toward an unspecified vanishing point. With the Perspective command, one set of opposite sides of the bounding box remains parallel, while the other set is pulled apart to create a perspective effect. You can look at the Distort command as being the extreme version of the transformations: only with Distort can you move the four handles of the bounding box independently of one another.

Practice

▼ CONCEPTS REVIEW

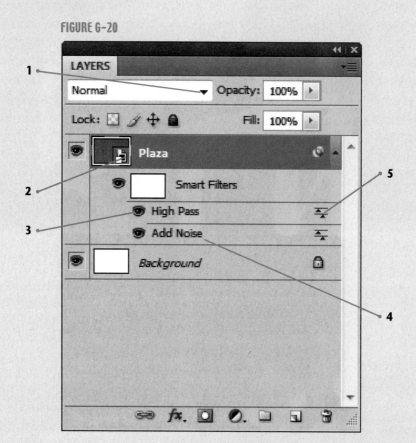

1. Which item indicates that a filter is visible?
2. Which item points to a filter?
3. Which item points to a smart object?
4. Which item opens a filter's dialog box?
5. Which item points to the blending mode list arrow?

Match each term with the statement that best describes it.

6. **Color blending mode**
7. **Black**
8. **White**
9. **Gray**
10. **Multiply blending mode**
11. **Screen blending mode**
12. **High Pass**
13. **Render**

a. Always invisible in Screen mode
b. Filter that can be used to sharpen an image
c. Always lightens base art
d. Modifies both hue and saturation of base color
e. Always invisible in Overlay mode
f. Category of a collection of filters
g. Always darkens base art
h. Always invisible in Multiply mode

Select the best answer from the list of choices.

14. **Which of the following is not a Photoshop blending mode?**
    a. Color Burn
    b. Hue
    c. High Pass
    d. Linear Light

15. **When working with colors and blending modes, what is the color of the original pixel called?**
    a. result color
    b. base color
    c. blend color
    d. hue color

16. **The Distort command is an example of what type of Photoshop operation?**
    a. Transformation
    b. Saturation
    c. Calibration
    d. Resolution

17. **Which of the following is not true of Multiply mode?**
    a. A multiplied color is transparent.
    b. Multiplying always darkens the base art (except if the base pixel is already black).
    c. 50% gray pixels become invisible when multiplied.
    d. When multiplied, anything black remains black.

18. **The Colorize option is in which Adjustments dialog box?**
    a. Levels
    b. Brightness/Contrast
    c. Color Balance
    d. Hue/Saturation

▼ SKILLS REVIEW

1. **Use the Color blending mode.**
    a. Open PS G-6.psd, save it as **Colorize Skills**, click the Create new adjustment or fill layer button on the Layers panel, then click Solid Color.
    b. Change the color to 195R/207G/221B, click OK, click the blending mode list arrow, then click Color.
    c. Mask the Color Fill 1 layer so that it affects only the background area of the image. (*Hint*: Because the background is mostly white and white can't be colorized with Color mode, painting the background will affect only the top right corner of the image.)
    d. Create a new layer above the Color Fill 1 layer, name the layer **Shirt**, then set the blending mode to Color.
    e. Set the foreground color to 172R/211G/115B, click the Brush tool, then paint the shirt green.
    f. Create a new Hue/Saturation adjustment layer, then set the blending mode for the layer to Color.
    g. Click the Colorize check box, set the Hue to 28, then set the Saturation to 43.
    h. Name the layer **Face**, then use a layer mask so that the Hue/Saturation adjustment affects the face, neck and the lips, but not the eyes.
    i. Use the same method you used in Steps f–h—with different values for Hue and Saturation—to finish colorizing the image.
    j. Save your work and keep the file open.

▼ SKILLS REVIEW (CONTINUED)

2. Use the Multiply blending mode.

    a. Click Image on the Application bar, then click Duplicate.

    b. Type **Multiply Skills** in the As dialog box, then click OK.

    c. Click the Shirt layer on the Layers panel, then change the blending mode from Color to Multiply.

    d. Click the Face layer, change its blending mode to Multiply, then reduce its Opacity to 70%.

    e. Click the Color Fill 1 layer, then change its blending mode to Multiply. (*Hint*: The white areas of the background can be colorized with Multiply mode.)

    f. Paint white in the Color Fill 1 layer mask to colorize the entire background and the man's hair.

    g. Position the two open files side by side, then compare your results to Figure G-21.

    h. Save your work, then close both files.

3. Add noise with the Overlay blending mode.

    a. Open PS G-7.psd, then save it as **Shining Future Skills**.

    b. Target the Type layer, create a new layer above it, then name the new layer **Noise.**

    c. Click Edit on the Application bar, then click Fill.

    d. Click the Use list arrow, click 50% Gray, then click OK.

    e. Change the blending mode on the Noise layer to Overlay so that the gray fill becomes transparent.

    f. Click Filter on the Application bar, point to Noise, then click Add Noise.

    g. Set the Amount to 3, set the Distribution to Gaussian, if necessary click the Monochromatic check box to activate it, then click OK.

    h. Zoom in on the image, if necessary, so that you are viewing it at 200%.

    i. Hide and show the Noise layer so that you can see the effect.

    j. Change the blending mode on the three different "moon" layers to Overlay.

    k. Save your work.

FIGURE G–21

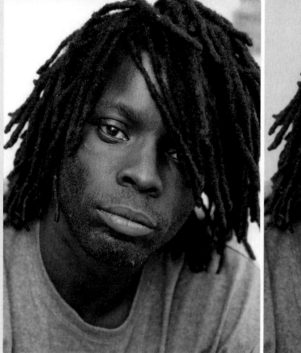 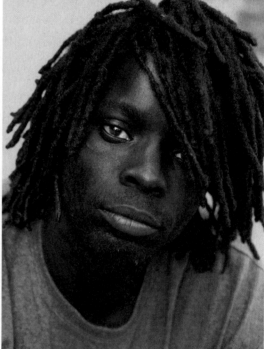

Color mode   Multiply mode

4. **Sharpen with the High Pass filter.**
   a. Target then hide the Noise layer.
   b. Select all, click Edit on the Application bar, click Copy Merged, click Edit again, then click Paste.
   c. Name the new layer **High Pass**.
   d. Click Filter on the Application bar, point to Other, then click High Pass.
   e. Type **2** in the Radius dialog box, then click OK.
   f. Set the blending mode to Overlay, then zoom in so that you are viewing the purple globe at the center of the flower at 200%.
   g. Hide and show the High Pass layer.
   h. Add a layer mask, then mask any areas that are too sharp.
   i. Show the Noise layer.
   j. Save your work.

5. **Apply the Lens Flare filter with Screen mode.**
   a. Create a new layer at the top of the layer stack, fill it with black, then name the new layer **Lens Flare**.
   b. Click Filter on the Application bar, point to Render, then click Lens Flare.
   c. Click each option button in the Lens Type section of the Lens Flare dialog box to sample them, click the 105mm Prime flare option button, drag the Brightness slider to 100, then click OK.
   d. Click Image on the Application bar, point to Adjustments, then click Desaturate.
   e. Change the blending mode on the Lens Flare layer to Screen.
   f. Move the center of the white flare to the 10 o'clock position at the edge of the purple globe.
   g. Add a clipped Levels adjustment layer, then drag the black triangle immediately below the histogram right until the text box reads 30.
   h. Save your work.

6. **Apply the Motion Blur filter.**
   a. Duplicate the Type layer, name the new layer **Type Blur**, drag the new layer beneath the Type layer, then hide the Drop Shadow layer style.
   b. Click Filter on the Application bar, point to Blur, then click Motion Blur.
   c. Set the Angle to 0, set the distance to 166, then click OK.
   d. Show the Drop Shadow layer style.
   e. Save your work.

7. **Apply non-destructive filters.**
   a. Duplicate the Flower layer, name the new layer **Flower Blur**, then drag the new layer beneath the Flower layer.
   b. If it's not already targeted, click the Flower Blur layer, click Filter on the Application bar, then click Convert for Smart Filters.
   c. Click Filter on the Application bar, point to Blur, then click Motion Blur.
   d. Set the Angle to 0, set the Distance to 200, then click OK.
   e. Double-click the ▤ button at the right of the Motion Blur layer on the Layers panel.
   f. Drag the Opacity slider to 90%, then click OK.
   g. Double-click the words Motion Blur on the Motion Blur layer to open the Motion Blur dialog box, reduce the Distance value to 150, then click OK.
   h. Save your work.

8. **Distort images.**
   a. Target the Child layer, create a new layer above it, then name the new layer **Flower shadow**.
   b. Press and hold [Ctrl] (Win) or ⌘ (Mac), then click the Flower layer thumbnail to load it as a selection.
   c. Click Select on the Application bar, point to Modify, click Feather, type **5** in the Feather Radius text box, then click OK.
   d. Verify that the Flower shadow layer is targeted, fill the selection with black, then deselect.
   e. Click Edit on the Application bar, point to Transform, then click Flip Vertical.

f. Move the Flower shadow artwork down so that your screen resembles Figure G-22.

g. Click Edit on the Application bar, point to Transform, then click Distort. (*Hint*: You may need to reduce the view of the canvas substantially to see all four handles of the transform bounding box.)

h. Move the bottom two handles of the bounding box so that your screen resembles Figure G-23.

i. Change the blending mode of the layer to Multiply, then reduce the Opacity to 65%.

j. Duplicate the Background layer, change the blending mode on the duplicate layer to Multiply, then compare your artwork to Figure G-24.

k. Save your work, then close Shining Future Skills.psd.

FIGURE G-22

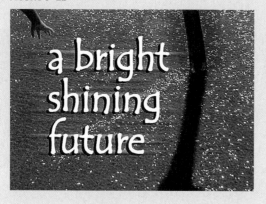

FIGURE G-23

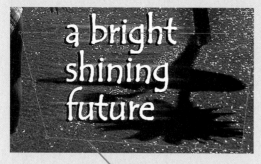

Distort bounding box

FIGURE G-24

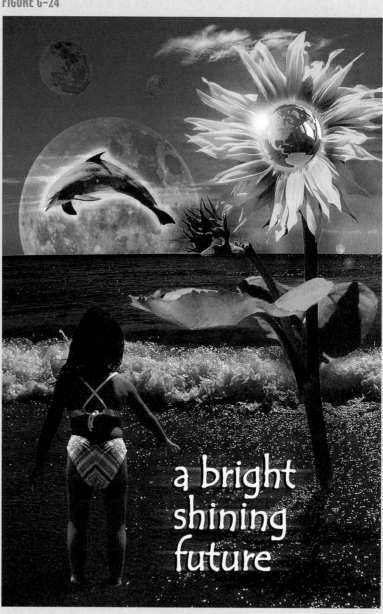

▼ INDEPENDENT CHALLENGE 1

Your creative director comes to you with an image he wants to use for a Web site. She tells you that the image was "damaged." There's a green field over the image—and the image has been flattened. She tells you she needs you to make a "quick fix." You look at the image and decide that, rather than try to mask the damaged area, it'll be fastest and most effective to use Color blending mode to make the fix.

a. Open PS G-8.psd, then save it as **Color Mode Correction**.

b. Create a new layer, name it **Fix**, then set its blending mode to Color.

c. Click the Brush tool, set the Hardness to 0, then set the Diameter to 60.

d. Sample a gray pixel in the jacket's lapel, adjacent to the green mark.

e. Use the Brush tool to paint the green area.

f. Sample a darker gray from the lapel, then repaint the area or parts of the area to see if it improves the correction.

g. Reduce the Opacity of the Brush tool to 50%, then paint over adjacent "non-damaged" areas to help transition from the correction to the original areas.

h. Compare your results to Figure G-25.

i. Save your work, then close Color Mode Correction.psd.

FIGURE G-25

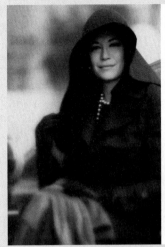
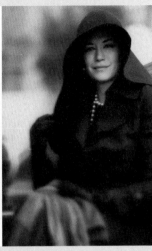

▼ INDEPENDENT CHALLENGE 2

You're designing point-of-purchase displays for a Hollywood movie studio. The client has sent you low-resolution, flattened artwork to use in the layout for the display. You decide to add noise to the artwork and sharpen it for the best display.

a. Open PS G-9.psd, then save it as **Key Art**.

b. Hide and then show the All Type folder on the Layers panel to see how the file is built.

c. Target the Background layer, then create a new layer above it named **Noise**.

d. Fill the Noise layer with 50% Gray.

e. Click Filter on the Application bar, point to Noise, then click Add Noise.

f. Type **4** in the Amount text box, then, if necessary, click the Gaussian option button and the Monochromatic check box.

g. Click OK, then set the blending mode to Overlay.

h. Hide the All Type folder and the Noise layer,

i. Duplicate the Background layer, then rename the new layer **High Pass**.

j. Click Filter on the Application bar, point to Other, then click High Pass.

k. Type **2.0** in the Radius text box, then click OK.

l. Set the blending mode to Overlay.

m. Show all layers, then compare your results to Figure G-26.

n. Save your work, then close Key Art.psd.

FIGURE G-26

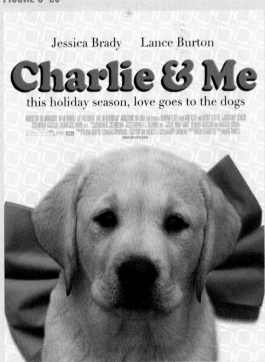

▼ INDEPENDENT CHALLENGE 3

The art director at the point-of-purchase display company you're working for asks you to "skin" the key art into a table display template to give the client a sense of the final piece.

    a. Open PS G-10.psd, then save it **12 Count**.

    b. Open the file named Charlie Key Art.psd, select all, apply the Copy Merged command, then close Charlie Key Art.psd.

    c. Return to the 12 Count.psd file, target the Videos layer, then paste.

    d. Name the new layer **Left Video**, then clip it into the Videos layer.

    e. Click Edit on the Application bar, point to Transform, then click Distort.

    f. Move the four handles of the bounding box so that your screen resembles Figure G-27.

    g. Using the same methods, paste and distort the artwork into the remaining two video covers so that your artwork resembles Figure G-28.

Advanced Challenge Exercise

- Open Backer.psd, Select all, click Edit on the Application bar, then click Copy Merged.
- In the 12 Count file, target the Blue layer, then paste.
- Name the new layer **Backer**, then clip it into the Blue layer.
- Click Edit on the Application bar, point to Transform, then click Perspective.
- Move the handles on the bounding box to position the artwork in perspective.
- Click Enter (Win) or [return] (Mac) to execute the transformation.

    h. Save your work, close all open files, then exit Photoshop.

FIGURE G-27

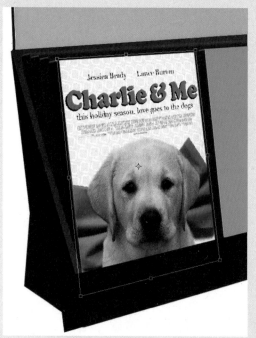

FIGURE G-28

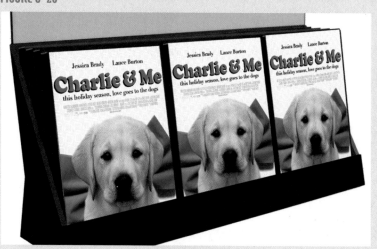

▼ REAL WORLD INDEPENDENT CHALLENGE

Just back from vacation, you snapped a great photo of your daughter jumping off of a dock. You decide that it will make a great postcard and use layer masks to capture the image of your daughter on a separate layer. You then decide to put a motion blur on the image to give it some action and energy.

a. Open PS G-11.psd, then save it as **Diver**.

b. Turn the layers on and off to get an understanding of how the file was built.

c. Verify that all the layers are visible, duplicate the Julie layer, then rename the duplicate **Julie Blur**.

d. Click Filter on the Application bar, point to Blur, then click Motion Blur.

e. Set the Angle to 0, set the Distance to 100, then click OK.

f. Drag the Julie Blur layer down beneath the Julie layer.

g. Add a layer mask to the Julie Blur layer, then mask the blur entirely on the screen-left edge of the Julie artwork, as shown in Figure G-29.

h. Click the Julie layer, click Filter on the Application bar, then click Convert for Smart Filters.

i. Open the Motion Blur dialog box, reduce the Distance value to 16, then click OK.

j. Compare your results to Figure G-30.

Advanced Challenge Exercise

- Click the filter mask to target it.
- Click the Brush tool, set the Diameter to 70, then set the Hardness to 0%.
- Reduce the Opacity of the Brush tool to 20%.
- Gradually mask the blur on the girl's face and other areas that you want to keep in better focus.

k. Save your work, compare your results to Figure G-30, then close Diver.psd.

FIGURE G-29

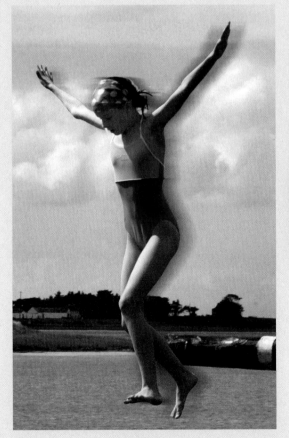

FIGURE G-30

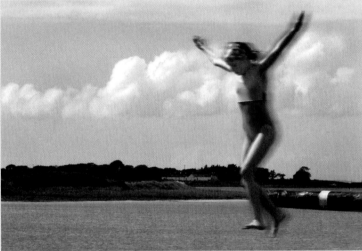

▼ VISUAL WORKSHOP

Open PS G-12.psd, then save it as **Two Motion Blurs**. Create horizontal and vertical motion blurs of the artwork. Reduce the opacity of the blurred letters so that your result resembles Figure G-31.

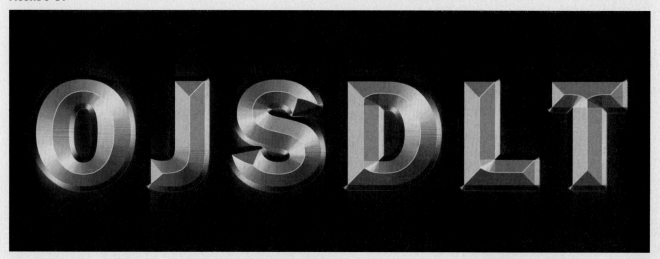

UNIT
H
Photoshop CS4

Improving Productivity

Photoshop is not only about design and photography; in fact, Photoshop plays many roles in a graphics environment, roles that don't necessarily incorporate any kind of design or photography skills. For example, at a Web design and development company, you'd find that a number of job descriptions are dedicated to managing assets, processing images, uploading content, and other types of non-design work. Recognizing this, Adobe has designed Photoshop to be something of a workhorse, with many built-in modules dedicated to making Photoshop very effective as an image processor in a graphics workflow environment. MegaPixel has contracted with a new client to produce a series of international Web sites. Jon tells you to expect to be working with a large number of images, all of which will need to be managed and processed daily to maintain the Web sites. He asks that you explore various options for automating workflow to make the best use of the department's time.

OBJECTIVES

Use the Image Processor

Create and run an action

Batch process an action

Use the History panel

Create a snapshot and use the History Brush tool

Clone with the Clone Stamp tool

Clone with the Healing Brush tool

Experiment with cloning options

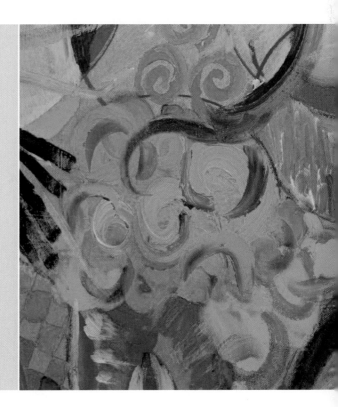

Using the Image Processor

Certain types of workflows call for repetitive tasks. You'll tend to see this especially in a Web environment. For example, it's often the case when maintaining a client's Web site that the client will send folders full of images that need to be converted to the same file format. They might all be .psd files that need to be saved as JPEGs, or as both JPEGs and TIFFs. Photoshop's Image Processor feature is great for quickly converting groups of files to other file formats. Jon gives you a CD with seven .psd files and asks that you make two copies of each, one set saved as JPEGs for the Web site and one set saved as TIFFs for archiving. You decide to use the Image Processor.

STEPS

1. **Open the seven files in the Automation folder located in the folder where your Data Files are stored**

   The files are all .psd (Photoshop) files.

2. **Click File on the Application bar, point to Scripts, then click Image Processor**

3. **In Section 1, click the Use Open Images option button**

4. **In Section 2, click the Save in Same Location option button**

5. **In Section 3, click the Save as JPEG check box, then type 12 in the Quality text box**

6. **In Section 3, click the Save as TIFF check box**

7. **Verify that nothing is checked in Section 4, then compare your Image Processor dialog box to Figure H-1**

8. **Click Run**

   The Image Processor saves the two sets of files. The seven original .psd files remain open after the Image Processor is done.

9. **Navigate to the Automation folder, then open the Automation folder**

   The Automation folder now contains a folder named JPEG and a folder named TIFF. These two folders contain the JPEG and TIFF copies generated by the Image Processor.

10. **Keep all the files open**

FIGURE H-1: Image Processor dialog box

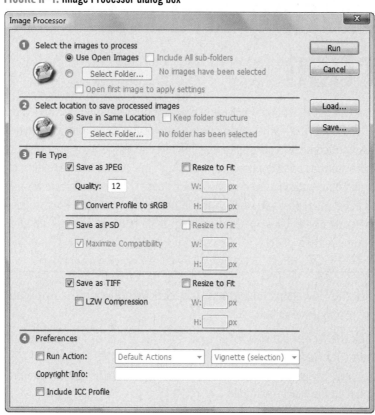

Investigating other options with the Image Processor

Take some time to note some other options available to you in the Image Processor dialog box. Section 1 allows you the option of not having to open the files you want to process; you can simply direct the Image Processor to a folder of files that you want to process. Section 2 allows you to save to a folder other than the one that contains your original files. And don't forget this one: Section 3 will convert CMYK files to RGB files if you are saving them as JPEGs. It's often the case that you will have CMYK print files that someone will want to use on a Web page, which is always an RGB environment. The Image Processor will instantly convert those files for you as it processes.

Creating and Running an Action

Actions are about repetition. Photoshop is also about repetition. If you're a designer, you're going to soon find—if you haven't already—that you do some of the same things over and over and over again. This is where Actions come into play. Since you'll be executing the same operations repeatedly, it's a smart idea to save those steps as an action, thereby avoiding time consuming repetition of efforts. Actions are created, stored, and automatically saved in the Actions panel. Once you create an action, it will be available in the Actions panel for all files you open in the future, even if you quit Photoshop. ████████ Jon asks you to execute the same operation on a series of images. He tells you to work smart and save time by creating an action in the Actions panel.

STEPS

QUICK TIP
Click the Actions panel list arrow, then verify that Button Mode is not checked. If it is checked, select it to remove the check mark.

1. **Click the Flowers.psd document tab, click Window on the Application bar, then click Actions**
   The Actions panel appears.

2. **Click the Actions panel list arrow, click New Action, type Invert in the Name text box, then click Record**
   As shown in Figure H-2, a new action named Invert appears on the Actions panel. The red Begin recording button on the panel is activated.

3. **Click Image on the Application bar, point to Adjustments, then click Invert**
   The file is inverted.

QUICK TIP
Remember to stop recording or Photoshop will record your steps for hours!

4. **Click File on the Application bar, click Save, click File on the Application bar, then click Close**
   As shown in Figure H-3, the three commands that were executed—Invert, Save, and Close—are listed as commands under the Invert action.

5. **Click the Stop playing/recording button ▣ on the Actions panel**
   When you click the Stop playing/recording button, Photoshop stops recording the steps you execute as part of the given action.

QUICK TIP
This is a critical step and easy to miss. When executing an action, you must first click the action's name on the Actions panel.

6. **Click the Marble.psd document tab, then click the word Invert on the Actions panel to highlight it**

7. **Click the Play selection button ▶ on the Actions panel**
   You will see nothing happening except that the Marble.psd image closes. However, the Marble image was inverted, saved, and then closed, because Close was the last command in the Invert action. Note that after you ran the Invert action, Invert is automatically highlighted again in the Actions panel.

8. **Apply the Invert action to the remaining open files**
   When you are done, all the files will be closed.

9. **Open all seven .psd files in the Automation folder**
   All seven images have been inverted.

10. **Close all the files**

FIGURE H-2: New action added to the Actions panel

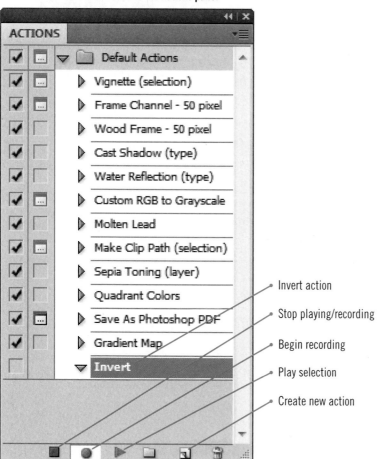

- Invert action
- Stop playing/recording
- Begin recording
- Play selection
- Create new action

FIGURE H-3: Three commands added to the Invert action

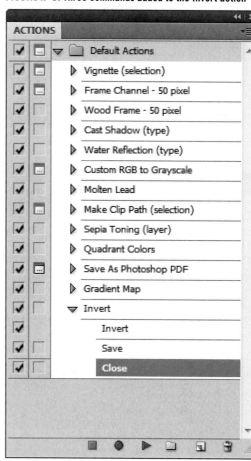

Exporting an action

Let's say you're a freelance designer and you work at a number of different locations for a number of different clients. One of the skills that make a designer valuable is the ability to work fast, and having a smart set of actions to rely upon can be a big plus for getting your work done quickly. If you work on different computers, you can export a set of actions to a portable file that you can copy to a CD or simply email to yourself to have it available wherever you are. To export a set of actions, click the folder on the Actions panel that you want to export, click the Actions panel list arrow, then click Save Actions. The saved file will have an ATN extension. When you're at a different computer and want to access your actions, click the Actions panel list arrow, click Load Actions, then load the .atn file you saved. And voilà—actions to go!

Understanding what it means to invert

In this lesson, you used the Invert command for the first time. What is it? If you apply the Invert command to a black-and-white image, it will make the image look just like an X-ray photograph. Blacks become white, whites become black: that's the key to the Invert command. From a grayscale perspective, it's easy to understand how Photoshop creates the invert effect: it changes a pixel's grayscale value to its opposite on the grayscale. For example, any pixel that has a grayscale value of 0 (black) changes to 255 (white); a grayscale value of 1 becomes 254; a grayscale value of 253 becomes 2; and so on. Invert is seldom used as a visual effect—how many times do you need an X-ray effect in a design?—but the Invert command has a great practical use. When you create an adjustment layer—let's say you use Levels to dramatically brighten an image—a layer mask is automatically created with the adjustment and is automatically targeted. Simply press [Ctrl][I] (Win) or ⌘ [I] (Mac) to invert the mask from white to black. That completely masks the adjustment, and you can use the Brush tool with a white foreground color to gradually "brush the adjustment in" to affect the artwork. Give it a try—it's a great way to work with adjustments.

Batch Processing an Action

Imagine that you had an action that you wanted to apply to a folder of images—an action more complicated than something like converting to a JPEG or TIFF, which you could do with the Image Processor. For example, you want to change the image size of a file to 72 ppi, then convert it to Grayscale. You could create an action with those commands, then batch process an entire folder with that action. Batch process means, rather than opening each image in the folder and executing the action by hand, you can simply tell Photoshop to apply the action to a folder of images. 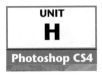 Jon gives you a disk containing seven files and tells you he wants you to invert all the files. You decide to batch process an action to do this quickly.

STEPS

1. Click File on the Application bar, point to Automate, then click Batch

2. In the Play section, click the Action list arrow to see all the actions available, then click Invert

   All of the actions on the Actions panel are listed in the Action list.

3. In the Source section, verify that Folder is chosen, then click the Choose button

4. Navigate to and select the Automation folder, then click OK (Win) or Choose (Mac)

5. Verify that none of the four check boxes in the Source section is checked

   Because of the work we did with the Image Processor in the first lesson of this chapter, the Automation folder contains two subfolders—JPEG and TIFF. We do not want to apply the action to the contents of those folders.

6. In the Destination section, verify that None is chosen

   No destination means that we want to affect the targeted images in the folder and for those images to be saved with the change(s). If we wanted to affect them and save the affected images as *copies*, then we'd need to specify a destination for the copies, which we'd do in the Destination section.

7. In the Errors section, verify that Stop For Errors is chosen, then compare your Batch dialog box to Figure H-4

8. Click OK

   The seven images are opened, affected by the action, then closed.

9. Open all seven .psd files from the Automation folder

   All seven files are inverted again and appear as they did originally.

10. Close all the open files

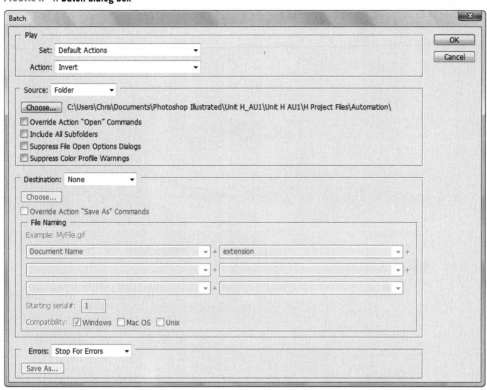

Understanding the difference between batch processing and the Image Processor

You might be wondering what the difference is between batch processing an action and using the Image Processor dialog box. Think of the Image Processor as being about file formats. Its primary function is to convert files from one file format to another. The actions on the Actions panel are more customized. You can save all kinds of Photoshop operations as actions. Batch processing takes it a step further and allows you to apply a single action simultaneously to a bunch of images.

Photoshop CS4

Using the History Panel

The History panel offers lots of great features; one of them is the ability to quickly revert a file to its state when you first opened it, then bring it back to its current state. As you work, the History panel records your moves and lists the last twenty of them, called **states**, in the panel. The last state in the list represents the last change you made to the file. You can click a state in the list to go back to that point of your work, and then continue working from that state. ▓▓▓▓▓ Jon asks you to execute a series of commands then note how they are listed on the History panel.

Note: This lesson and the next must be done in one sitting. If you close the file after this lesson, you will not be able to do the next lesson.

STEPS

1. **Open PS H-1.psd, save it as It's History, click Window on the Application bar, then click History**

2. **Click Image on the Application bar, point to Adjustments, then click Desaturate**
   The Desaturate command is listed as a state on the History panel.

3. **Click Filter on the Application bar, point to Stylize, then click Solarize**
   Solarize is listed on the History panel.

4. **Click Image on the Application bar, point to Image Rotation, then click Flip Canvas Horizontal**
   Your canvas and History panel should resemble Figure H-5.

5. **Click Desaturate on the History panel**
   The file is reverted back to the state it was in after you applied the Desaturate command.

6. **Click Flip Canvas Horizontal on the History panel**
   The file is reverted to the state it was in after you applied the Flip Canvas Horizontal command.

7. **Note the thumbnail at the top of the History panel**
   Whenever you open a file, the History panel creates a thumbnail at the top of the panel representing the status of the file at the time it was opened. In this case, the thumbnail's name is listed as PS H-1.psd because that was the name of the file when it was opened.

8. **Click the PS H-1.psd thumbnail at the top of the History panel**
   The file is returned to its state when you first opened it. This option is always available to you on the History panel, for every file you work with. Note, however, that once you close the file, this option is lost forever.

9. **Click Solarize on the History panel, then save your work**

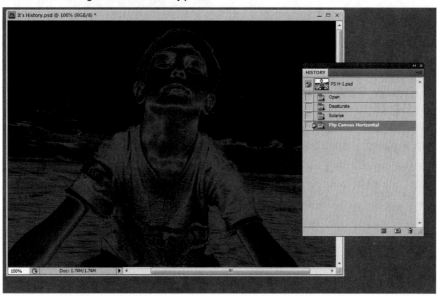

Setting the number of states on the History panel

As you work, the History panel logs each command that is performed as a new state. However, it will log only a specific number of states. That number is determined as a preference. To specify that preference, go to the Performance window of the Preferences dialog box. In the History & Cache section, the History States text box allows you to enter the number of states the History panel will list. Twenty is the default number. The higher the number you enter, the more memory Photoshop will require to keep those states active.

Revert vs. "super" revert

It's important to understand the difference between using the Revert command and reverting a file using the History panel. Let's say you're working on a file for an hour, and over the course of the hour, you save the file three times. The Revert command, on the File menu, will return you to the state of the file *the last time you saved.*

Clicking the default thumbnail at the top of the History panel will take you back to the state of the file *when it was opened.* That's why you can think of it as a "super revert." Remember though, that the default thumbnail is available only as long as you keep the file open. Once you close it, that status is lost.

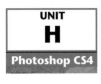
Creating a Snapshot and Using the History Brush Tool

The History panel allows you to create a snapshot of your work at any given state. Creating a snapshot saves the current status of your work as a new thumbnail at the top of the History panel. As long as the file remains open, that status is available for you to return to at any time.

The History Brush tool is a "revert" brush—it paints using any one of the snapshots at the top of the History panel as its source. You use it by clicking the **Sets the source for the history brush** icon beside the thumbnail that you want the History Brush tool to paint from. The History brush tool can function as a practical tool: use it to paint in artwork from a saved state. It can also function artistically. For example, you can set it to a low opacity and gradually "paint in" artwork from a saved state. ░░░░ Jon tells you to create a snapshot of the artwork you are working on, then to use the History Brush tool at different opacities to create a mixed-effect on the artwork.

1. **On the History panel, verify that Solarize is highlighted, then click the Create new snapshot button 📷 on the panel**

   As shown in Figure H-6, a new thumbnail named Snapshot 1 is added to the History panel below the default thumbnail. Snapshot 1 represents the status of the file when you created the snapshot. For as long as the file remains open, you will have access to this thumbnail to revert to that status.

2. **Click Desaturate on the History panel, then note the Sets the source for the history brush icon beside the PS H-1.psd thumbnail on the History panel**

   The icon identifies which thumbnail Photoshop regards as the "active" history status.

3. **Click the History Brush tool 🖌, set the Hardness to 100%, then set the Opacity to 20%**

4. **Paint overlapping strokes over the image of the boy—not the background—so that your canvas resembles Figure H-7**

   The History Brush tool paints using the artwork from the PS H-1.psd status. Essentially, you are painting the file as it was when it was first opened.

5. **Click the gray square to the left of Snapshot 1 on the History panel to change the source for the History Brush tool, as shown in Figure H-8**

   The History Brush tool will use this status of the file when it is used next.

6. **Set the Opacity of the History Brush tool to 50%, then paint overlapping strokes in the background of the image**

   Because the source for the History Brush tool is now Snapshot 1, the History Brush tool uses that artwork as its source.

7. **Save your work, then close It's History.psd**

FIGURE H-6: Viewing the snapshot added to the History panel

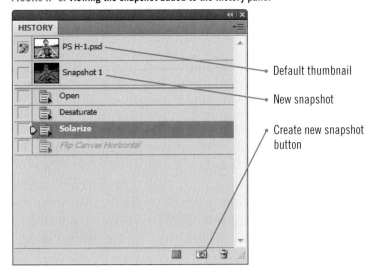

Default thumbnail

New snapshot

Create new snapshot button

FIGURE H-7: Applying the History brush tool to the artwork

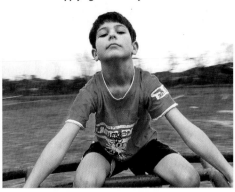

FIGURE H-8: Setting Snapshot 1 as the source for the History Brush tool

Sets the source for the History brush tool

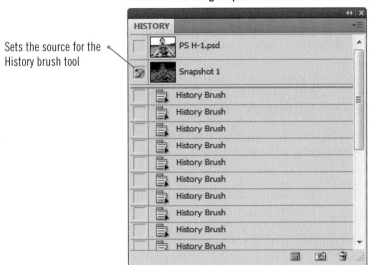

Saving a snapshot automatically

Some of the projects you work on in Photoshop won't last for hours or for days—they'll last for *weeks*. When working on complex projects, you'll find that you hit "landmark" points along the way. For example, you might get to a point where you're happy with the background of an image and start to work on a foreground element. This would be a good time to create a snapshot. That way, you can return to a point when you were happy with the status of the work.

A smart way to work is to have the History panel automatically save a snapshot every time you save. To do so, click the History

panel list arrow, click History Options, then click Automatically Create New Snapshot When Saving. Think of it as an insurance policy: if you mess up some good work you've saved, you can always click the snapshot to return to that state.

Remember though, that the insurance policy does not guard against catastrophe. If you close the file, or if your computer crashes, all the snapshots you create automatically or by hand will be lost.

Using "Fill from History"

Another great way to work with the History panel can be found in the Fill dialog box. Click Edit on the Application bar, then click Fill. Click the Use list arrow, then click History, and the targeted layer on the Layers panel will be filled with the artwork from the targeted

state on the History panel. When you fill using History, the other options in the Fill dialog box remain available to you. So you can fill from History with a specified opacity or blending mode.

Cloning with the Clone Stamp Tool

The Clone Stamp tool is used in cloning. **Cloning** can be defined as copying pixels from one area to another. The Clone Stamp tool is a brush, so when you use it to clone pixels, you get the options of brush size, hardness, and opacity to factor into the clone you create.

Cloning has two parts: the sample and the clone. The **sample** is where you clone from. The clone refers to the copied pixels you create from the sample. Current & Below is one of three sampling options that you can use with the Clone Stamp tool. The Current & Below option means that the Clone Stamp tool will sample artwork from the current layer and all the layers below it. 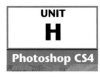 Jon sends you a photo for a client's Web site. He tells you that the client is "allergic to even numbers" and wants to have five geese in the image, not four. Jon asks you to clone one of the geese. He also tells you to create the clone on a separate layer so that it can be moved around if the client wants to make changes.

1. Open PS H-2.psd, save it as Goose Five, create a new layer above the Background layer, then name the new layer Clone

2. Click the Clone Stamp tool ⬚, set the Master Diameter to 150, then set the Hardness to 0%

3. Verify that the Aligned check box on the Options bar is checked

4. On the Options bar, click the Sample list arrow, then click Current & Below
   The Current & Below option is used often because it allows you to create a clone on a layer separate from the artwork you are sampling.

The Sample option is a critical choice when working with the Clone Stamp tool.

5. Press and hold [Alt] (Win) or [option] (Mac), click the beak of the third goose from the left, then release [Alt] (Win) or [option] (Mac)

6. Position the mouse pointer over the upper-left area of the canvas

7. Click and drag to "paint" a clone of the goose in that area
   Your canvas should resemble Figure H-9.

8. Click Edit on the Application bar, point to Transform, click Scale, then reduce the clone to 80% so that it's not an obvious duplicate

9. Add a layer mask to the Clone layer, then mask the darker clouds around the clone so that they blend with the lighter clouds behind them

10. Compare your results to Figure H-10, save your work, then close Goose Five.psd

FIGURE H-9: Viewing the cloned bird

Cloned bird

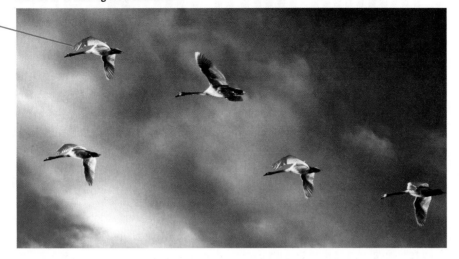

FIGURE H-10: Viewing the finished artwork

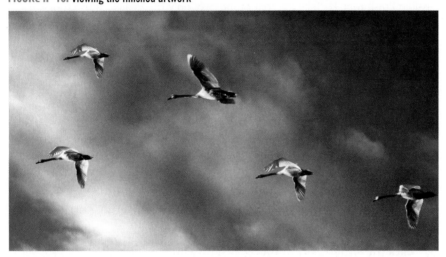

Understanding aligned vs. nonaligned clones

All of the cloning tools—including the Clone Stamp tool—have an Aligned option that is available on the Tools panel when you select the tool. Here's the key to understanding the Aligned option: It's all about what happens after you *stop* cloning. Imagine you start cloning a face in your image, and you stop cloning before you're done. With the Aligned option checked, and without resampling, if you continue cloning, the Clone Stamp tool will pick up where you left off and finish the face. That's an aligned clone.

Using the same example, if you did not activate the Aligned option and stop cloning, then start again, the Clone Stamp tool will automatically start the new clone from the original sample spot.

Cloning on a separate layer

As you've learned throughout this book, the best way to work in Photoshop is "non-destructively." That goes for cloning, too. When you do anything with the Clone Stamp tool, you usually want to work in a way that doesn't permanently affect the original artwork. For example, let's say that you were using the Clone Stamp tool to remove a scar from someone's face. You wouldn't clone out the scar on the original artwork; you'd hide the scar with a clone of clear skin on a separate layer. This way, if the results aren't satisfactory, you haven't irrevocably altered the original artwork.

The Current & Below option is key to this concept, which is why it is the most commonly used option. Regardless of how many layers your artwork contains, when you need to clone, create an empty layer above the artwork for the clone. Then use the Current & Below option. Current & Below allows you to sample all the artwork below the empty layer; then you can clone safely onto the empty layer, protecting the original artwork from the changes.

Cloning with the Healing Brush Tool

Like the Clone Stamp tool, the Healing Brush tool is a cloning tool. But the Healing Brush tool is more complex and plays a different role. As with the Clone Stamp tool, you use the Healing Brush tool to sample from one area and clone to another. However, the Healing Brush tool matches the clone to the texture, lighting, and shading of the area you are cloning to. Practically speaking, the Healing Brush tool is useful for cloning large areas of non-specific data, like the sky or a shirt. If you tried to use the Healing Brush tool to clone an area of a brick wall onto another area, the results wouldn't be satisfying, because the many lines and textures involved would be too specific for the Healing Brush tool to blur and blend together.
Your travel client sends you a disk with an image they want to use on the cover of their summer brochure. They tell you ahead of time that it's damaged, and when you open it, you see the damage right away. Jon tells you this challenge is a good example of the difference between using the Clone Stamp tool and the Healing Brush tool. He tells you that of the two, only the Healing Brush tool will solve the problem.

STEPS

1. Open PS H-3.psd, save it as Sailboat Scratches, create a new layer above the Background layer, then name the new layer Remove Scratches

2. **Analyze the problems with the image**

   The Clone Stamp tool would not be very useful on this image because there's no "clean" place to sample from. Note that the sky at the top of the image is dark blue and gradually fades down to a lighter blue. Unfortunately, all of the dark blue area at the top is marred by the black scratches. This exercise is a great example of how the Healing Brush tool can solve a problem that the Clone Stamp tool can't. The key here is that the Healing brush tool lets you sample the undamaged light blue sky and clone it into the dark blue sky. Incredibly, the tool is sophisticated enough that it adjusts the tone of the light blue sample to match the dark blue sky at the top of the image.

3. Click the Healing Brush tool 🖌️, set the Master Diameter to 150, set the Hardness to 0%, click the Sample list arrow on the Options bar, then click Current & Below

4. Press and hold [Alt] (Win) or [option] (Mac), then click in the light blue sky area beneath the bird

5. Click and drag to "paint" a clone of the clear sky in the upper-left corner

   As shown in Figure H-11, the clear sky is cloned into the upper-left corner, and the color of the clone is automatically modified to match the darker blue area.

6. Using the same method, continue sampling from the clear light blue sky and cloning into the darker damaged sky at the top until the image is repaired

7. Compare your results to Figure H-12, save your work, then close Sailboat Scratches.psd

FIGURE H-11: Viewing the first clone

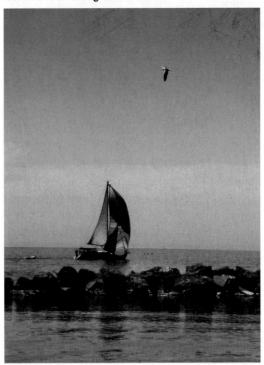

FIGURE H-12: Viewing the finished artwork

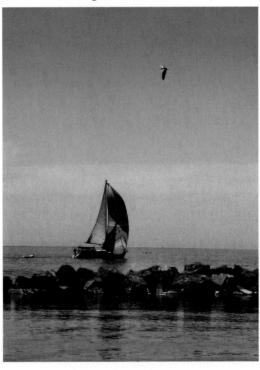

Experimenting with Cloning Options

Both the Clone Stamp tool and the Healing Brush tool share the same sampling options, and it's important to understand the difference between each to work effectively with the cloning tools. First, note the options for these tools fall under the title of "Sample". That's key to what these options do: they control how the cloning tool samples the artwork. The three sampling options are:

Current Layer: The tool samples artwork only on the targeted layer. Artwork or adjustments on layers above or below the targeted layer will not be involved in the sample.

Current & Below: The tool samples the *appearance* of the artwork as a composite of the current layer and all the layers beneath it. Artwork or adjustments on layers *above* the targeted layer are not involved in the sample.

All Layers: The tool samples the appearance of the artwork as the result of all layers in the image.

STEPS

1. **Open PS H-4.psd, save it as Clone Options, then hide and show the Levels adjustment layer**
   The Levels adjustment layer adds much-needed contrast to the image.

2. **Target the Clone layer on the Layers panel**
   The Clone layer is completely empty.

3. **Click the Clone Stamp tool 🖳, click the Sample list arrow on the Options bar, then click Current Layer**

4. **Sample an area from the boy's face and try to clone it in another location**
   Nothing will happen. Because the Clone layer is empty and the brush preference is set to Current Layer, you are sampling from the Clone layer only. There's nothing to sample from, so nothing can be cloned.

5. **Click the Sample list arrow, then choose Current & Below**

6. **Sample the boy's nose, then clone the entire face in the space to the left of the boy**
   As shown in Figure H-13, the boy's face is cloned. Because the brush preference is set to Current & Below, the brush sampled the current layer—Clone layer—*and* all layers below it. In this case, that includes the artwork on the Background layer.

7. **Click the Sample list arrow, then choose All Layers**

8. **Sample the boy's nose, clone the entire face in the space in the upper-right corner of the canvas, then compare your result to Figure H-14**
   The clone is noticeably higher in contrast than the original. Because the brush preference is set to All Layers, the brush sampled all the layers, including the Levels adjustment layer above it. That means that the cloned area reflects the adjustment twice—in the sample and as a result of the Levels adjustment layer above it.

9. **Hide the Levels adjustment layer**
   The second clone still does not match the original. However, the first clone still matches the original, because it was sampled without the Levels adjustment being involved in the sample.

10. **Save your work, then close Clone Options.psd**

FIGURE H-13: Viewing the first clone

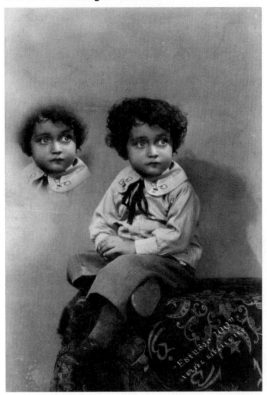

FIGURE H-14: Viewing the second clone

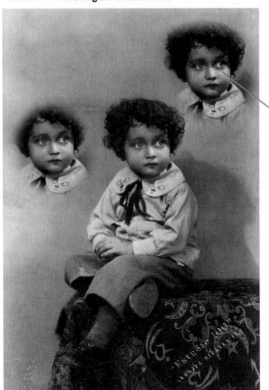

Clone has increased contrast

Practice

▼ CONCEPTS REVIEW

FIGURE H-15

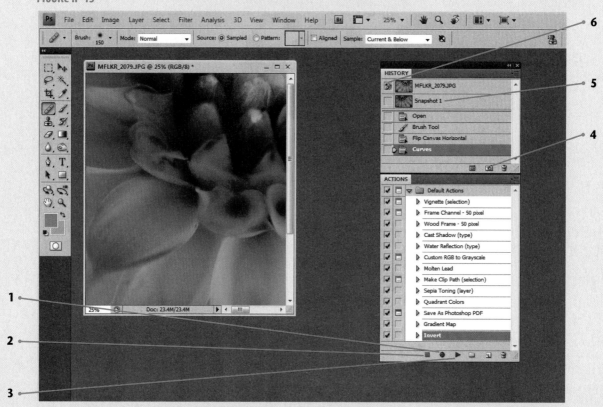

1. Which item points to the Play selection button?
2. Which item creates a snapshot?
3. Which item points to the Stop playing/recording button?
4. Which item points to a snapshot?
5. Which item defines the source for the History Brush tool?
6. Which item points to the Begin recording button?

Match each term with the statement that best describes it.

7. **Healing Brush tool**
8. **History panel**
9. **Action**
10. **Sample**
11. **Snapshot**
12. **Image Processor**
13. **Current & Below**

a. Saves current status
b. Useful for converting file formats of multiple files
c. Sample option for a cloning tool
d. Origin of a clone
e. Can be used to revert to a previous status of a file
f. Cloning tool
g. Recording of a series of steps or commands

Select the best answer from the list of choices.

14. **Which of the following is not a sample option for a cloning tool?**
    a. Current Layer
    b. Current Source
    c. Current & Below
    d. All Layers

15. **Which of the following is not an automated process in Photoshop?**
    a. Using the Image Processor
    b. Batch processing an action
    c. Executing an action
    d. Creating an action

16. **Which of the following does the History panel not do?**
    a. Save a file
    b. Revert a file
    c. Capture a status
    d. Undo a move

17. **Which one of the following actions best describes what the History Brush tool does?**
    a. Clones
    b. Samples
    c. Automates
    d. Reverts

18. **Which of the following best describes the result of using the Clone Stamp tool?**
    a. Paint
    b. Sample
    c. Duplicate
    d. Transform

▼ SKILLS REVIEW

1. **Use the Image Processor.**
   a. Open the seven files in the **Skills Automation** folder located in your Data Files folder. (*Hint*: The files are all .psd files.)
   b. Click File on the Application bar, point to Scripts, then click Image Processor.
   c. In Section 1, click the Use Open Images option button.
   d. In Section 2, click the Save in Same Location option button.
   e. In Section 3, click the Save as JPEG check box, then type **12** in the Quality text box.
   f. In Section 3, check the Save as TIFF check box.
   g. Verify that nothing is checked in Section 4.
   h. Click Run.
   i. Navigate to the Skills Automation folder, then open the Skills Automation folder.
   j. Return to Photoshop.
   k. Keep all the files open.

2. Create and run an action.

a. Click the Girl.psd document tab, click Window on the Application bar, then click Actions to open the Actions panel, if necessary.

b. Click the Actions panel list arrow, click New Action, type **Invert Background** in the Name text box, then click Record.

c. Click Image on the Application bar, point to Adjustments, then click Invert.

d. Click File on the Application bar, click Save, click File on the Application bar, then click Close.

e. Click the Stop playing/recording button on the Actions panel.

f. Click the Petals.psd document tab, then click the words **Invert Background** on the Actions panel to highlight it.

g. Click the Play selection button on the Actions panel.

h. Apply the Invert Background action to the remaining open files.

i. Open all seven .psd files in the Skills Automation folder.

j. Close all the files.

3. Batch process an action.

a. Click File on the Application bar, point to Automate, then click Batch.

b. In the Play section, click the Action list arrow to see all the actions available, then click Invert Background.

c. In the Source section, verify that Folder is chosen, then click the Choose button.

d. Navigate to and select the Skills Automation folder, then click OK (Win) or Choose (Mac).

e. Verify that none of the four check boxes in the Source section is checked.

f. In the Destination section, verify that None is chosen.

g. In the Errors section, verify that Stop For Errors is chosen.

h. Click OK.

i. Open all seven .psd files from the Skills Automation folder. (*Hint*: All seven files are inverted again and appear as they did originally.)

j. Close all the open files.

4. Use the History panel.

Note: Sections 4 and 5 must be done in one sitting. If you close the file after Section 4, you will not be able to do Section 5.

a. Open PS H-5, save it as **History Skills**, then verify that the History panel is open.

b. Press [Ctrl][L] (Win) or ⌘ [L] (Mac) to open the Levels dialog box.

c. Drag the black triangle immediately below the histogram right until the shadow text box reads 29, then click OK. (*Hint*: You've modified the layer directly, not with a Levels adjustment layer.)

d. Enter [Ctrl][U] (Win) or ⌘ [U] (Mac) to open the Hue/Saturation dialog box.

e. Click to activate the Colorize option, drag the Saturation slider all the way left to 0%, then click OK.

f. Click Filter on the Application bar, point to Stylize, then click Solarize.

g. Click the Levels state on the History panel.

h. Click the Hue/Saturation state on the History panel.

i. Click the PS H-5.psd thumbnail at the top of the History panel.

j. Click the Levels state on the History panel.

k. Save the file.

5. Create a snapshot and use the History Brush tool.

a. On the History panel, verify that Levels is highlighted.

b. Click the Create new snapshot button on the panel.

c. Click Solarize on the History panel.

d. Click the gray square to the left of Snapshot 1 to set the source for the History Brush tool.

e. Click the History Brush tool, set the Hardness to 0%, then set the Opacity to 100%.

f. Paint just the boy so that your canvas resembles Figure H-16.

g. Save your work, then close History Skills.psd.

FIGURE H-16

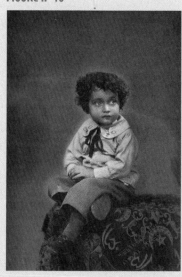

▼ SKILLS REVIEW (CONTINUED)

6. **Clone with the Clone Stamp tool.**
   a. Open PS H-6.psd, then save it as **Skills Clone**.
   b. Create a new layer above the Background layer, then name the new layer **Clone**.
   c. Click the Clone Stamp tool, set the Master Diameter to 70, then set the Hardness to 0%. (*Hint*: Verify that the Aligned check box on the Options bar is checked.)
   d. On the Options bar, click the Sample list arrow, then click Current & Below.
   e. Zoom in on the flying bird and its shadow immediately above the swimming duck.
   f. Press and hold [Alt] (Win) or [option] (Mac), click approximately ½ inch directly to the left of the bird, then release [Alt] (Win) or [option] (Mac).
   g. Click and drag to remove the bird and its shadow.
   h. Using the same method, remove the two birds to the left so that the only birds remaining in the image are the duck and the two birds flying in the reflection of the tree.
   i. Save your work.

7. **Clone with the Healing Brush tool.**
   a. Click the Healing Brush tool, set the Master Diameter to 70, set the Hardness to 0%, then verify that Current & Below is selected on the Options bar for the Clone layer.
   b. Press and hold [Alt] (Win) or [option] (Mac), then click in the reflection of the tree in the water approximately ½ inch to the left of the leftmost bird.
   c. Click and drag to remove the far left bird and its shadow.
   d. Using the same method, remove the remaining flying bird and its shadow.
   e. Compare your results to Figure H-17, save your work, then close Skills Clone.psd.

FIGURE H-17

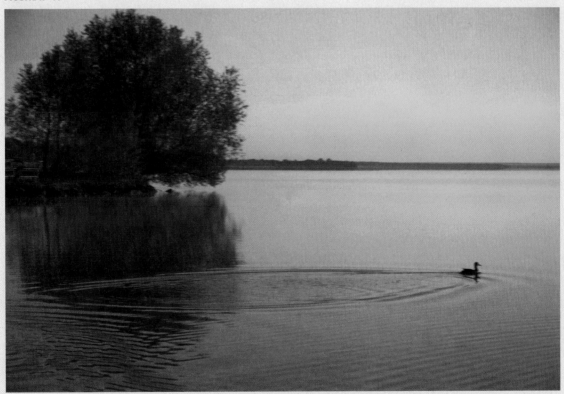

8. Experiment with cloning options.

a. Open PS H-7.psd, save it as **Blue Birds**, then hide and show the Hue/Saturation 1 adjustment layer.

b. Target the Clone layer on the Layers panel. (*Hint*: The Clone layer is completely empty.)

c. Click the Clone Stamp tool, then choose a large soft brush.

d. Click the Sample list arrow on the Options bar, then click Current Layer.

e. Sample the beak of the third bird from the left, and try to clone it to another location. (*Hint*: Nothing will happen.)

f. Click the Sample list arrow, then choose Current & Below.

g. Paint in the upper-left corner of the canvas to clone the bird.

h. Click the Sample list arrow, then choose All Layers.

i. Sample the beak of the same bird, then clone the entire bird in the space in the upper-right corner of the canvas.

j. Compare your result to Figure H-18.

k. Save your work, then close Blue Birds.psd.

FIGURE H-18

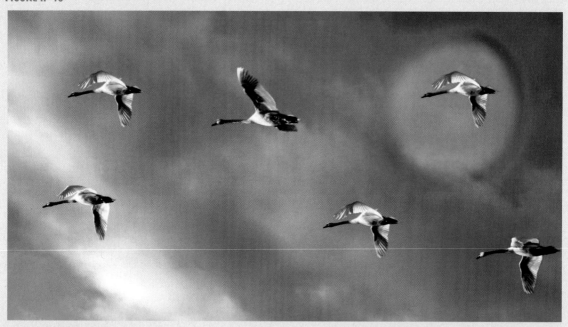

▼ INDEPENDENT CHALLENGE 1

You have some downtime at work. Your creative director suggests that you use the time to create an action for the noise technique that you use repeatedly when finishing layered artwork.

    a. Open PS H-8.psd, then save it as **Noise Action**.

    b. Click the Actions panel list arrow, click New Action, type **Noise 2 Pixels** in the Name text box, then click Record.

    c. Click the Create a new layer button on the Layers panel, then name the new layer **Noise 2.0**.

    d. Click Edit on the Application bar, click Fill, click the Use list arrow, click 50% Gray, then click OK.

    e. Click Filter on the Application bar, point to Noise, then click Add Noise.

    f. Type **2** in the Amount text box, then verify that both the Gaussian option button and the Monochromatic check box are activated.

    g. Click OK.

    h. Change the blending mode on the Noise 2.0 layer to Overlay.

    i. Click the Stop playing/recording button on the Actions panel.

    j. Your Actions panel should resemble Figure H-19.

    k. Save your work, then close Noise Action.psd.

FIGURE H-19

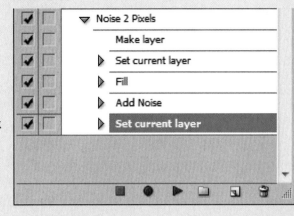

▼ INDEPENDENT CHALLENGE 2

Your creative director gives you a folder of seven images. He asks that you apply noise to all seven images. To get the work done quickly, you decide to batch process an action.

(*Note*: You must first have completed Independent Challenge 1 to have this action listed on your Actions panel.)

    a. Click File on the Application bar, point to Automate, then click Batch.

    b. In the Play section, click the Action list arrow to see all the actions available, then click Noise 2 Pixels.

    c. In the Source section, verify that Folder is chosen, then click the Choose button.

    d. Navigate to the location where you store your Data Files, select the folder named Noise Files, then click OK (Win) or Choose (Mac).

    e. Verify that none of the four check boxes in the Source section is checked.

    f. Click the Destination list arrow, then click Folder.

    g. Click the Choose button under the Destination section, navigate to the location where you store your Data Files, then click OK (Win) or Choose (Mac).

    h. In the Errors section, verify that Stop For Errors is chosen.

    i. Click OK. (*Hint*: Photoshop will run the Noise action on the seven files. If you are prompted, click OK to verify saving options.)

    j. Open the Family.psd file, then compare your Layers panel to Figure H-20.

    k. Close all open files.

FIGURE H-20

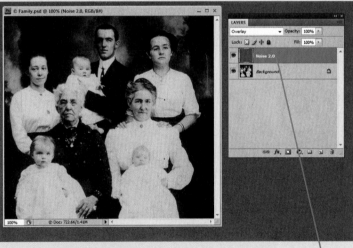

Noise layer

▼ INDEPENDENT CHALLENGE 3

Your client has sent you a close-up image of a flower and asks that you create "an interesting special effect" that involves some amount of a blur and desaturation. Your creative director suggests that you work from saved history in the History panel to create the effect.

    a. Open PS H-9.psd, then save it as **Flowering**.

    b. Click Image on the Application bar, point to Adjustments, then click Posterize.

    c. Type **4** in the Levels text box, then click OK.

    d. Click Filter on the Application bar, point to Blur, then click Gaussian Blur.

    e. Type **24** in the Radius text box, then click OK.

    f. Click Image on the Application bar, point to Adjustments, then click Desaturate.

    g. Click Posterize on the History panel.

    h. Click Gaussian Blur on the History panel.

    i. Click Desaturate on the History panel.

Advanced Challenge Exercise

- Click Edit on the Application bar, then click Fill.
- Click the Use list arrow, then click History.
- Click the Mode list arrow, then click Overlay.
- Type **50** in the Opacity text box.
- Click OK.
- Click the PS H-9.psd thumbnail on the History panel to see the original image.
- Click the Desaturate command on the History panel.

    j. Verify you can see the entire image in the window.

    k. Click the History Brush tool on the Tools panel.

    l. On the Options bar, set the Master Diameter to 800 px, set the Mode to Overlay, set the Opacity to 50%, then verify that the Flow is set to 100%.

    m. In one move, paint the entire canvas with the History Brush tool.

    n. Compare your results to Figure H-21.

    o. Save your work, then close the file.

FIGURE H-21

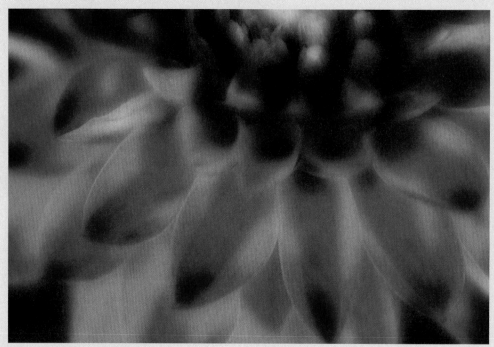

▼ REAL WORLD INDEPENDENT CHALLENGE

Just back from vacation, you snapped some great photos that you want to upload to a stock photography Web site. You go through your photos and circle areas that you want to retouch. You decide on an image of a sailboat to work on. You open it to retouch it and improve its color balance.

- **a.** Open PS H-10.psd, then save it as **Sailboat Cleanup**.
- **b.** Hide the Fixes layer.
- **c.** Create a new layer named **Clone** above the Background layer.
- **d.** Click the Clone Stamp tool, then clone out the bird in the sky.
- **e.** Sample the horizon, then clone out the faint boat on the horizon.
- **f.** Clone out the birds to the right of the boat.
- **g.** Clone out the dinghy to the left of the boat.
- **h.** Compare your results to Figure H-22.

Advanced Challenge Exercise

- ■ Click the Create a new fill or adjustment layer on the Layers panel, then click Levels.
- ■ Drag the gray midtone slider to the right until the text box reads .60.
- ■ Enter [Ctrl][I] (Win) or ⌘ [I] (Mac) to fill the layer mask with black.
- ■ Click the Brush tool, then set the Opacity to 40%.
- ■ Gradually "brush in" the Levels adjustment.

- **i.** Save your work, then close the file.

FIGURE H-22

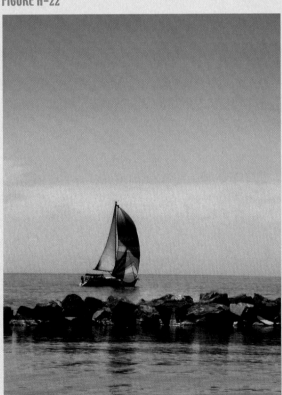

Open PS H-11.psd, then save it as **Dog Balloon**. Compare using the Clone Stamp tool and the Healing Brush tool for cloning out the wires. Use a separate layer for the cloning so that your result resembles Figure H-23. (*Hint*: Use the automatic brush strokes technique with the Clone Stamp tool and Healing Brush tool when cloning out the long straight wires.)

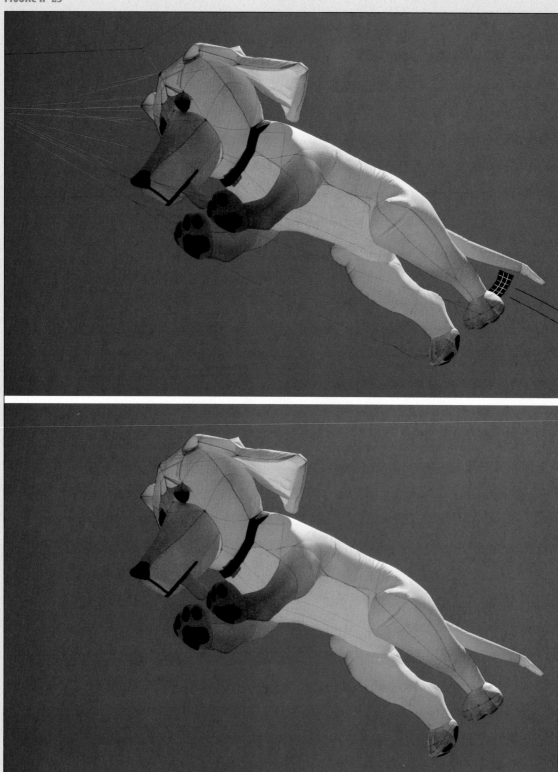

Glossary

Actions Created, stored, and automatically saved in the Actions panel, actions execute specific procedures automatically.

adjustments Operations you do that affect the appearance of an image, such as manipulating brightness and contrast.

adjustment layers Adjustments you make that exist as layers on the Layers panel.

aliased edge A hard selection edge in which the "stair-stepped" pixels are obvious and the edge is noticeably blunt.

alpha channels Saved selections stored in the Channels panel.

anti-aliased edge A crisp but smooth selection edge.

Bitmap graphic A graphic composed of pixels. All Photoshop images are bitmap graphics.

black point The darkest pixel in an image.

blending modes Mathematical algorithms that define how pixels affect pixels beneath them to create a specific effect.

brightness Defined by a pixel's grayscale value: the higher the number, the brighter the pixel.

Canvas The bed of pixels that make up an image.

clipping Term that refers to using artwork on one layer to mask the artwork on a layer above it.

cloning Copying pixels from one area to another.

CMYK Cyan, magenta, yellow and black; a color model in Photoshop; the subtractive primary colors; the four process colors central to conventional offset printing.

color model Defines the colors we see and work with in digital images. RGB (red, green, blue), CMYK (cyan, magenta, yellow, black), and HSB (hue, saturation, brightness) are all color models, and each uses a different method for describing color.

color profile A group of preset settings for controlling how color will appear on your monitor and in a printed document.

color stops Specified colors that make up a gradient.

contiguous Term referring to pixels that border other pixels.

continuous tone A smooth transition from shadows to midtones to highlights.

contrast Represented by the relationship between highlights and shadows.

cropping A basic task in which you define an area of an image that you want to keep and then discard the remainder of the image.

Digital image Image that you get from a digital camera, from scanning a photograph or a slide, or that you create from scratch in Adobe Photoshop.

drop shadow Commonly used effect and/or layer style where artwork appears to cast a shadow.

Feathered edge A soft selection edge created by blending selected pixels and the background image.

flipping Transformation that creates a mirror image of the artwork, vertically or horizontally.

Gloss contours A set of 12 preset adjustments that affect the brightness and contrast of a layer style to create dramatic lighting effects.

gradient Blend between two or more colors.

grayscale image A digital image in which each pixel can be one—and only one—of 256 shades of gray.

Highlights The lightest areas of an image, represented by pixels whose value falls in the upper third of the grayscale range.

"high-res" A shortened form of "high-resolution".

histogram A graph in the Levels and Curves Adjustments panel representing the distribution of pixels in the image across the grayscale.

HSB Hue, saturation and brightness; a color model in Photoshop.

hue The name of a color: red, orange, and blue are all hues.

Image size Refers to the physical dimensions (width/height) of the Photoshop file.

interpolation Process that occurs when an image is enlarged in which new pixels are created based on existing pixels.

Layer mask Used to define which areas of artwork on a single layer are visible, not visible, or partly visible..

linear gradient Blend that progresses straight from one color to another in a linear fashion.

Marquee zoom Dragging the Zoom tool on the image to magnify a specific area.

midtones Pixels whose color falls into the middle range of the grayscale.

montage Multiple art components overlapping to create a single composition.

Noise A blanket of high-contrast pixels that produce a grainy effect over an image.

Opacity Refers to how opaque pixels on a layer are. A layer with 0% opacity is completely transparent and not visible.

Pixel Smallest component of a bitmap graphic; derived from the words picture and element.

posterize A special effect that is created by reducing the number of colors available for the image.

Radial gradient Blend that radiates outward from one color to another, like a series of concentric circles.

rasterize Term that means "convert to pixels" type elements, for example, can be rasterized.

resampling Changing the total pixel count of an image when resizing an image.

resolution The number of pixels per inch (ppi) in a bitmap graphic.

revert A Photoshop command that reverts the file to its status when you last saved.

RGB Red, green, and blue; the most-used color model in Photoshop; the additive primary colors of light; red, green, and blue light can combine to produce all the other colors in the spectrum; colors you see on your monitor are created by mixing varying strengths and combinations of red, green, and blue rotating A transformation that moves an object clockwise or counterclockwise around a given point.

Saturation The intensity of a color: how close it is to a pure hue.

scaling A term for resizing artwork.

selection edge The outermost pixels in a selection.

shadows The darkest areas of an image, represented by pixels in the lowest third of the grayscale range.

sharpness An effect created when edge pixels are high in contrast.

smart filters Non-destructive filter layers that can be shown, hidden, edited, or deleted without permanently affecting artwork.

Tolerance A tool and dialog box setting that determines which pixels will be affected based upon their similarity in color.

transform Operations that change the location of pixels; Photoshop transformations include scaling, rotating, skewing, and distorting pixels.

Vibrance Intensity of a color; interchangeable with the term saturation.

vignette A visual effect in which the edge of an image gradually fades away; usually created with a feathered selection.

White point The brightest pixel in the image.

workspace The application interface; includes the Application bar, the Tools panel, the dock of panels on the right of the screen, and the workspace switcher, which allows you to choose from a list of custom workspaces.

Index

alpha channels, working with, 40–41
applying to pixels on layers, 86–87
background. *See* background colors
blend, and result, 164–165
blending gradients, 94–95
changing with Swatches panel, 39
CMYK, 14–15
Color Balance adjustments, 126–127
Color Picker. *See* Color Picker
filling text with, 84–85
foreground. *See* foreground colors
glow, 68–69
in gradients, 96–97
HSB, 144–145
Hue/Saturation adjustments, 146–147
Replace Color dialog box, 148–149
Replace Green feature, 149
RGB color, 124–125
Vibrance adjustment, 128–129
combining layer styles, 92–93
commands
See also specific command
keyboard. *See* quick keys
composite channel, 124
computer monitors, and viewing edges, 43
contiguous pixels, and Magic Wand tool, 36, 37
continuous tones, 116
contours, gloss, 90–91
contrast
and black and white point, 120–121
and brightness adjustments, 118–119
and Color Burn, 167
and gloss contours, 90
converting
color images to black-and-white, 150–153
image files to specific formats, 190–191
type layers to pixels, 87
copying
See also cloning
layers, 62, 149
creating
actions, 192–193
bevel layer style, 92–93
clipping masks, 98–99, 118–119
crop marquees, 18–19
layers, 62
marquees with Zoom tool, 7
new documents, 14–15
new gradients, 96–97
radial gradients by hand, 153
snapshots of your work, 198–199
special effects, 163–179
crop marquees
described, creating, 18–19
moving, 21
Crop tool
options, 20
setting opacity, 19
using, 18–19
cropping
images, 18–19
images to specific sizes, 20–21
crosshair icon, 64–65
cursors, painting, 139
custom workspaces, 4
cutting. *See* cropping
cyan, 124

▶ **D**

deleting
See also removing
layer styles, 92–93
layers, 62
Desaturate layer, 150–151
deselecting selections, 32
diameter, brush settings, 138–139
diamond gradients, 95
digital images
See also images
described, 2
distorting images, 178–179
documents
color model, and modes, 15
creating new, 14–15
saving, 8–9
size, 18
Don't show again check box, 62
draw programs described, 3
Drop Shadow layer style options, 70
drop shadows
and Multiply blending mode, 166
using layer style, 70–71
duplicating. *See* copying

▶ **E**

edges
described, sharpening, 170–171
determining real, 142
feathered, working with, 44–45
refining selection, 46–47
of selections, anti-aliasing, 42–43
editing, 'non-destructive,' 176–177
effects
See also specific effect
creating special, 163–179
with lightness and brightness, 146–147
layer styles. *See* layer styles
showing layer, 68
type bevel and emboss, 88–89
Elliptical Marquee tool, 32, 44
emboss effects on type, 88–89, 92–93
enlarging. *See* scaling
.eps files, 8
exporting actions, 193
Eyedropper tool, 114

▶ **F**

fading type, 102–103
feathered edges
brush option, 140
described, 44
working with, 44–45
file formats
converting files to specific, 190–191
standard Photoshop (table), 8
files
converting to specific formats, 191
file format for Photoshop files (table), 8
file size vs. image size, 11
Fill dialog box
using, 153
using History panel, 199
filling text with colors, 84–85

filter masks, 177
filters
applying non-destructive, 176–177
High Pass, 170–171
Lens Flare, 172–173
masking, 177
Motion Blur, 174–175
Fit on Screen command, View menu, 62
flipping, vs. rotating artwork, 66–67
fonts
See also type
choosing, 84
and rasterizing type, 87
foreground colors
and Brush tool, 72
changing, 39
filling selection with, 84
working with, 40
formatting, typographical, 85
fuzziness, adding to images, 148–149

▶ **G**

.gif files, 8
gloss contours, applying to layer styles, 90–91
glow colors, adding layer style, 68–69
Gradient Editor, using, 96–97
gradient ramp, Gradient Editor dialog box, 96–97
Gradient tool, 94–95, 98–99
gradients
applying, 94–95
clipping into type, 98–99
creating new, 96–97
described, 94
fading type, 102–103
radial, 94–95, 153
stair-stepping, 116–117
working with, 83
Grain filter, 177
grainy effects, 168–169
graphics
See also specific type
standard file formats (table), 8
graphics programs described, 3
grays, neutral, 127
grayscale
Brightness/Contrast adjustment, 118–119
highlights, shadows, midtones, 116–117
images, analyzing, 116–117
midpoint of, 122–123
working with, 114–115
Green channel, RGB colors, 124–125
grouping blending modes on Layers panel, 167

▶ **H**

halos, removing from edges, 46
Hand tool, using, 6–7
hardness
brush settings, 138–139
edges, 142
Healing Brush tool, cloning with, 202–203
Help, getting Photoshop, 5
hiding
filters, 176
layer effects, 68
layers, 86
High Pass filter, sharpening with, 170–171